Advances in Behavioral Economics

Professor Dr. Horst Todt

Friedel Bolle · Michael Carlberg (Eds.)

Advances in Behavioral Economics

Essays in Honor of Horst Todt

With 31 Figures and 11 Tables

Springer-Verlag Berlin Heidelberg GmbH

Series Editors
Werner A. Müller
Martina Bihn

Editors

Professor Dr. Friedel Bolle
Europa-Universität Viadrina
Lehrstuhl für Volkswirtschaftslehre,
insbesondere Wirtschaftstheorie
(Mikroökonomie)
Grosse Scharrnstraße 59
15230 Frankfurt (Oder)
Germany
Email: bolle@euv-frankfurt-o.de

Professor Dr. Michael Carlberg
Universität der Bundeswehr
Institut für Theoretische Volkswirtschaftslehre
Holstenhofweg 85
22043 Hamburg
Germany
Email: carlberg@unibw-hamburg.de

ISSN 1431-1933
ISBN 978-3-7908-1358-6

Cataloging-in-Publication Data applied for
Die Deutsche Bibliothek – CIP-Einheitsaufnahme
Advances in behavioral economics: essays in honor of Horst Todt; with 11 tables / Friedel Bolle; Michael Carlberg. – Heidelberg; New York: Physica-Verl., 2001
(Contributions to economics)
ISBN 978-3-7908-1358-6   ISBN 978-3-642-57571-6 (eBook)
DOI 10.1007/978-3-642-57571-6

Softcover Design: Erich Kirchner, Heidelberg

SPIN 10789363   88/2202-5 4 3 2 1 0 – Printed on acid-free paper

Preface

This volume is dedicated to Horst Todt who celebrated his seventieth anniversary on March 14, 2000.

All the contributors know Horst Todt personally and (with the exception of two younger co-authors) have accompanied his scientific career for several years, some as his assistants, some as his colleagues at the Frankfurt or Hamburg University, some as fellow members in scientific societies. All who know him acknowledge inspiring conversations on a broad field of issues often reaching far beyond the scope of economics. Being friendly and entertaining and without exaggerated personal ambition he often initiated work which others completed. In particular the two editors of this volume experienced and enjoyed the stimulating atmosphere at his Chair of Economics at the Hamburg University. We like to remember these scientifically and personally fruitful years under the tutorship of Horst Todt.

The editors would like to thank the contributors to this volume for their readiness to cooperate and for the promptness of their delivery.

The initial idea for a coherent theme was to pose questions rather than to give answers. A hundred years after David Hilbert (1900, on a conference in Paris) gave his famous catalogue of hundred important unsolved problems in Mathematics, might there be the time to formulate an equivalent catalogue in Economics?

From the very beginning, we were not as ambitions as that. First of all, Economics are quite different from Mathematics though some outsiders to the professions may have the impression of a convergence. While in the case of all the hundred questions Hilbert posed, the underlying field had been developed by definitions and assumptions so that Hilbert could directly pose clear questions, in the cases of Economic problems, the main task is to develop the field. This is not a simple problem. While there is essentially *one* theory of Differential Equations and *one* Number Theory there are many Bargaining Theories and many Theories of International Trade. (The latter is apparent, if you compare the contributions of Hans Wismeth and Klaus Schöler in this volume.) In order to pose a concrete economic question, you first have to create an adequate environment for your question. Of course, you might define *this* as the main part of the problem.

For our second remark, we have to apologize in advance; but we are sure that finally, all our renowned colleagues will agree with us. There is no Hilbert in Economic Science, and there has not been a Newton or a Gauss on whose shoulders a Hilbert could stand.

Thus, a repetition of Hilbert's famous catalogue, this time in economics, is not possible. But it is never worthless to strive for high aims! We think that all the contributions of this volume have gained by the attempt to clarify the underlying assumptions, by the necessity to develop the field in order to arrive at precise questions. As examples for such attempts, you may regard the contributions of Manfred Holler and Arnis Vilks.

We do not try to give an overview of the contributions here. From a thematic point of view the contributions are as heterogeneous as Horst Todt's interests in Economics are. The red threat through all these contributions may be conceptual and admittedly it is more or less visible. You may read the contributions to this volume under such a point of view but - of course - on the other hand every contribution is a self-contented piece of work which should arouse the interest of specialists on the respective topic.

The editors and, as we think, all the contributors would like to thank Horst Todt for the inspiring common discussions we had. We all hope to continue having pleasant and fruitful times together.

Frankfurt (Oder), Hamburg
October 2000

Friedel Bolle
Michael Carlberg

Contents

Part I

On Horst Todt

1 In Honor of Horst Todt

Horst Todt was born on the 14th of March 1930 in Frankfurt am Main. He went to school at Aschaffenburg and afterwards was an apprentice clerk there. From 1951 to 1955 Horst Todt studied economics at the University of Frankfurt. Subsequently, for about a year, he was a British Council Scholar at the University of Birmingham.

From 1958 to 1968 Horst Todt was a research assistant with Professor Heinz Sauermann at the University of Frankfurt. During this time, in 1961, he was married to Waltraut Todt, née Borchers. And in 1965 their daughter Antje was born. In the same year, Horst Todt completed his doctoral dissertation "Über die räumliche Ordnung von Reisezielen" (On the Spatial Order of Tourist Destinations).

Some years later, he won a "Habilitationsstipendium der Deutschen Forschungsgemeinschaft" (which is a grant for a second dissertation, awarded by the German Research Council). In 1970 Horst Todt completed his Habilitationsschrift "Ein Markt mit komplexen Interessenstrukturen – Eine theoretische und experimentelle Untersuchung" (A Market with Complex Interests – Theory and Experiments). The focus of this book is on an oligopoly with six sellers.

For about a quarter century, from 1971 to 1995, Horst Todt was a professor of economics at the University of Hamburg. His lectures and seminars dealt with

- Regional Science
- Urban Economics
- Input-Output Analysis
- The Theory of Games
- Allocation and Competition

His research was mainly devoted to regional science and urban economics. To give some examples:

- Competition by Choice of Location: Two Sellers in a Plane
- The Hierarchical Order of Regions According to Two Principles: The Principle of Minimum Potential and the Principle of Shortest Paths
- Demarcation and Pattern of the Central Business District (CBD) in Hamburg
- Regularities of CBD Land Use in Hamburg
- The Dynamics of the Inner City
- Competition by Choice of Location in a Plane: The Cournot Solution and the Stackelberg Solution

Important tools in his research are the law of gravitation, the potential, and the mapping of potentials. In addition, he was interested in simulation and the General Purpose Systems Simulator. All of this is highly topical today. Think for instance of the New Economic Geography lead by Paul Krugman, and think of the surge in Experimental Economics.

Besides, Horst Todt has been an active member of

- Verein für Socialpolitik (the German Economic Association)
- Ausschuss für Sozialwissenschaft (Social Science Group)
- Ausschuss für Regionalwissenschaft (Regional Science Group)

For some time, he was Vorsitzender des Ausschusses (Chairman of the Group) and Mitglied des Vorstandes (Member of the Board).

All in all, Horst Todt has had some 30 PhD students, including his research assistants. His research seminar was famous for its lively and stimulating discussions. He always has had plenty of time for his students. And what is more, he has taken a personal interest in them. For all of this, his students owe him a debt of gratitude.

Last but not least, for many years, Horst Todt gave lectures in the Law School of Hamburg University. And in 1999 he was appointed to the post of a visiting professor at the University of Tartu in Estonia.

2 Horst Todt in Tartu

Karin Peschel

How can he leave his nice desk in Hamburg in order to go to this scientific desert? This was the main question on people's minds when **Horst Todt** left for Estland in 1994 to work at the newly founded EuroFaculty at the University of Tartu. How can he spend so many months a year away from the magnificent metropolitan city of Hamburg, preferring a small provincial town in which every corner reminds of its sorrowful past? How can **Horst Todt** – jogging and lightly dressed as a sportsman – stand the cool climate when he could be enjoying the sun of the Mediterranean sea? And why does he spend such energy in his "old days" learning such a difficult language as Estonian? Well – do these questions really call for an answer? Certainly not for those who know **Horst Todt** personally, who have met with his courage, his humor and his energy.

The explanation can certainly be found in the many tasks and problems who seem to have only waited for a person with **Horst Todt's** abilities in Tartu, as well as in the enthusiasm he soon met with. Before I would like to support this by testimonials from Tartu, I believe some words about the project EuroFaculty would be appropriate.

The EuroFaculty was founded in 1993 by the newly created COUNCIL OF BALTIC SEA STATES, being an initiative of the two Foreign Ministers Hans-Dietrich Genscher and Uffe Ellemann-Jensen. EuroFaculty centers were installed at the universities in Tartu, Riga and Vilnius. In short: The EuroFaculty is an academic programme to support, develop, and upgrade the faculties and schools at the participating Baltic universities to meet the international level in economics, law and political science. The first aim of the programs at the EuroFaculty was the introduction of basic study programs up to the level of a masters degree - comprising approximately the same requirements at all Baltic universities. Still at the beginning it was not perfectly clear how this goal was to be reached. And unsurprisingly, many unforeseen barriers arose. For instance the cooperation between the staff of the EuroFaculty and the university committees as well as the lecturers at the Baltic universities often showed itself difficult - mutual understanding was often problematic, and that not merely out of language discrepancies. The priorities on both sides were set differently. For many Baltic colleagues at the beginning of the reform process financial problems arose, threating their mere existence. It soon became clear that in order to promoţe a willingness to participate in the re-training programs and bind them to the university, incentives had to be offered to the faculty members, for example in form of financial bonuses. The Western method of teaching and learning (discussion instead of reception) also demanded unforeseen efforts from the students. To make it even more challenging, the present infrastructure (libraries, information technology...) was not up to the demands of modern teaching and researching. In conclusion it can be said that the renewal of the Baltic faculties proved to be a complicated and time-consuming process, whose elements constantly had to be adapted to existing conditions and needed great modification. It certainly won't surprise that the need for funding at the EuroFaculty soon grew bigger than anticipated, while the acquisition of fonds especially through the EU became more and more complicated. From the German side the EuroFaculty is financed by the *Deutscher Akademischer Austauschdienst* (DAAD).

As the programs and the achievements vary in each of the EuroFaculty Centers and from discipline to discipline, I will limit myself to the Economics Department at the Tartu University. It is commonly seen as the most successful case. And that's certainly a lot thanks to **Horst Todt**.

The foundation for the positive development of the EuroFaculty in Tartu was already set before the fall of the Iron Curtain. Already in the eighties did colleagues from Tartu visit the West. For instance Professor Janno Reiljan, who energetically supported the EuroFaculty, spent some time in Kiel. The good relations between the Economics Faculty in Kiel and in Tartu (today the School of Economics and Business Administration) led to many contacts even in the phase where the Western partners were still debating over the foundation of the EuroFaculty as well as its instititutionalization and program. Two weeks before the official opening of the Rectorate at the EuroFaculty, courses were already offered in Riga on micro- and macroeconomics by colleagues from the Kiel University (Professor Herberg and Dr. Klingen) for economists from all three Baltic states. Approximately at the same time a group of professors of the Helsinki University offered courses in law, which were hardly visited though.

At the time the idea dominated that the classes could be held in block seminars from Western colleagues. And it was spoken about sharing the work between Lettland, Lithuania and Estland, offering special courses by special professors at each university, thus demanding traveling from university to university from the students. However, it soon became apparent that the students couldn't be so mobile, mainly because next to courses at the EuroFaculty they were also taking classes at their home universities. It also became evident that the "flying professors" could not satisfyingly fulfill the set requirements. The task of the Euro-Faculty was not seen as merely adding another program of studies to those of the existing Baltic universities. The goal was to restructure the Baltic universities themselves to meet Western standards of education. This could only be achieved if the Western colleagues could acquire enough knowledge about the present situation and could have enough time at their disposal for Baltic colleagues and students next to their teaching commitment. Therefore the "flying professors" from the opening time were replaced by lecturers employed for one year at least.

Naturally at the beginning the language problem was a great barrier to be taken. Surprisingly, the language teaching quickly showed great results.

Apparently Estlanders are unusually gifted for languages. Other problems came from the fact that there was apparently no suitable literature in the home language. The colleagues from Tartu therefore spent a big amount of work transferring teaching material into their language. What also hadn't been thought of at the foundation was that the material infrastructure in all Baltic countries didn't meet the requirements of modern teaching and learning. But even here the situation in Tartu was especially favorable. The Rector of the Tartu University and the government of Estland decided to offer financial resources for the reconstruction of the human sciences building and house the EuroFaculty therein. The German and Finish government financially supported the project. The money was enough for new furniture, the installment of a computer lab, teaching auditoriums and a functioning library. Everything is modest according to Western standards, but represented a huge step forward in 1994.

In spite of the relatively favorable conditions, the years weren't easy for **Horst Todt** and the other members of the EuroFaculty. University teachers are also only humans, even if usually very smart ones. Changes are difficult for them, even if wished for and welcome. And if the material situation is so bad that the work at university is not sufficient to secure the family's living, it takes a lot of strength not to resign but to keep following unknown planets. Naturally not everyone was ready to step into new worlds; others simply couldn't for very objective reasons. It soon became apparent that not all Baltic colleagues were able to change their teaching programs according to what the Western colleagues imagined in such a short time. And the latter in no way always agreed on curricula and detailed teaching contents. The quick education of highly talented young people and the teaching of future university teachers therefore became the main aim. Multiple models such as team teaching were developed (a guest lecturer and home staff). But it has been and still is a problem to find Ph.D. programs abroad for those students who graduated, as the EuroFaculty can't offer one itself. Another point is the difficulty of keeping the highly qualified graduates at the university, as the private market can offer so much more money. And naturally well educated people are also needed in the public service.

Horst Todt was one of the main actors in the creation of the EuroFaculty and its integration into the local economics faculty since 1993. He was actively teaching, for example Micro-economics, Game theory, History of economic thougth, Regional science, Theory of international trade and Welfare economics. He helped to establish new study plans meeting Western standards for the BA as well as for the MA program. And he was always present at the university, thus living the ideal of a university representing a community of teachers and students. "You could talk to him about politics and everything", is reported by students from Estland. "We were enthusiastic about his seminars" says another student voice. "We always had active discussions, there was a happy atmosphere, he was generous, even when we talked nonsense." In my opinion his success is mainly based on his capacity to establish friendly contacts with his colleagues from Estland and the students. He knew how to convince them of his vision of academic life in a quiet way, friendly but with strength.

Following a proposal of the School of Economics and Business Administration, **Horst Todt** now teaches not only at the EuroFaculty, but also as guest professor at the University of Tartu. The high regard he is presented with in Estland can maybe best be shown through a sentence by Urmas Varblane, Vice Director of the EuroFaculty Center Tartu: "Professor **Todt** has served as a really good ambassador for Germany."

Part II

Scientific Contributions

3 How Do Decisions Emerge?
Generating Ultimatum Proposals

Werner Güth*

Abstract. The basic idea of decision emergence is to generate the preferred decision alternative instead of assuming exogeneously given preferences like in neo-classical economics and game theory. For ultimatum proposals one can rely on experimental observations when speculating how choices emerge. Our approach distinguishes primary and secondary concerns of ultimatum proposers and illustrates how qualitative learning can (re)shape preferences over choices.

3.1 Introduction

In game theory and, more generally, in neo-classical economics one usually assumes exogenously given preferences determining the decision behavior of the various parties. Although it is possible to derive preferences endogenously (see, for instance, Güth and Kliemt (1994), who rely on the indirect evolutionary approach), this determines only rather special preferences or choices, e.g. the evolutionarily stable ones.

Usually preferences and the choices, which they induce, are not exogenously given, but have to be generated by a dynamic reasoning process. Güth (1995, forthcoming) describes in general terms how choices of boundedly rational decision makers may emerge. Basic ideas are a behavioral repertoire, based on former experiences, and its recommendations for qualitatively and even quantitatively similar situations and a hierarchy of decision routines according to which one first applies simple rules and moves on with more sophisticated ones only if the former yield unacceptable results.

The weakness of such a general approach is that it rests on many hypotheses of which only few can be supported by the available empirical, mostly experimental evidence. To avoid this we concentrate here on a particular choice problem, namely the proposal making in **ultimatum bargaining**. Here a positive monetary amount c, the "pie", has to be allocated among the parties X and Y in the following way: The proposer X first selects a proposal (x, y) with $x + y = c$ and $0 \leq y \leq c$ which the responder can accept or reject. If Y accepts, X receives x and Y the residual amount $y = c - x$, otherwise both parties get nothing.

* I thank Friedel Bolle, Katrin Borcherding, Steffen Huck, Reinhard Selten, and Eric Van Damme for helpful comments. Support from the Deutsche Forschungsgemeinschaft (SFB 373, Quantifikation und Simulation ökonomischer Prozesse) is gratefully acknowledged.

The challenge of the task is due to the dramatic discrepancy between the behavior (x close to c, acceptance of all positive offers y), predicted by game theory (either by the subgame perfect equilibrium or by once repeated elimination of dominated or inferior strategies), and the usual experimental results (many 50 : 50-proposals, an average demand x of 60 % (of c), and frequent rejections of low offers y). Although explaining responder behavior ("why do they reject unfair, but still substantial offers y, e.g. $y = \$ 40$?") seems to be crucial, we focus on generating proposals. The main reason is that we do not want to avoid how other's choices are anticipated. In light of the available experimental evidence we will try to outline the likely considerations of proposers by which they generate their offers.

Unlike in neoclassical repairs, Güth (1995), we do not stick to (commonly known) rationality, but concentrate on the considerations of boundedly rational decision makers who may not specify complete plans and expectations. The frequent criticism that we do not offer a generally applicable behavioral algorithm presupposes implicitly that game theory provides such predictions. But to apply game theory one needs to know the payoffs, including material and immaterial concerns, the expectations about others' concerns, beliefs etc. Finding out these aspects is as difficult as filling out the gaps of our behavioral model how ultimatum proposals emerge.

Whereas in other choice problems it may already need quite an effort to know all the available choices, this is quite obvious in a typical ultimatum bargaining experiment where the proposer X can choose between all offers y with $0 \leq y \leq c$ to responder Y. Of course, a proposer will usually restrict his attention to a few such offers y, e.g. to the equal split $y = c/2$, $y = c/3$ and a very small value y.

In spite of the rich experimental evidence our study does not mainly test hypotheses, but tries to discuss the crucial aspects of ultimatum proposals in an illustrative (partly graphical) way. We first explore the reasoning process by which an inexperienced proposer X will derive his offer y where we distinguish primary (Section 3.2) and secondary (Section 3.3) concerns. Afterwards (Section 3.4) it will be discussed how qualitative learning (see, for instance, Selten and Buchta (1998)) due to repeated play can shape proposals.

Our conclusions discuss the general problem of decision emergence in the light of our results which cover only a very specific choice problem, but are based on empirical observations and therefore less speculative. It will take a long time and require many scholars before having more general and empirically validated results. For this long journey we recommend to rely - as in our study - on empirical (field or experimental) observations when trying to develop theories how decisions emerge.

3.2 Primary Concerns of Inexperienced Proposers

It may appear contradictary that one assumes **basic desires**, e.g. for scarce resources like money, when explaining how preferences for certain choices are generated. Other studies, most likely evolutionary ones (see, for instance, Güth and Kliemt (1994)) might try to justify basic desires or primary concerns. Here it is simply assumed for the case at hand that proposers primarily care for their monetary gains.

Fig. 3.1. The sequential decision process of ultimatum bargaining

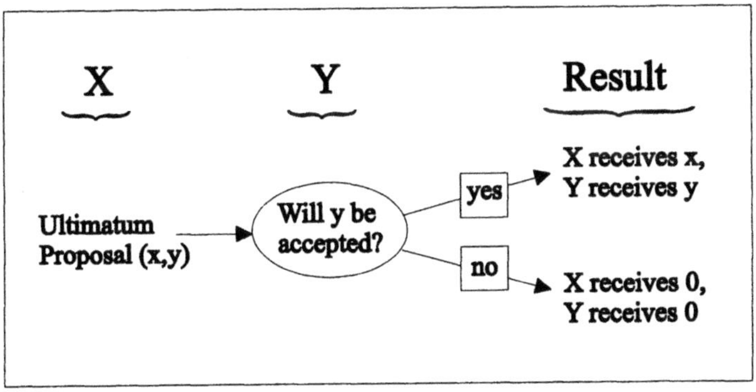

Consider an individual who is the proposer X in an ultimatum game and who envisages such an experiment for the first time. Although most persons will have experienced ultimatum proposals before, they hardly seem to be able to translate their previous experiences to the abstract ultimatum game. Since the monetary gain of proposer X depends on both (as illustrated by figure 3.1), the demand and the acceptance decision, an inexperienced proposer X has two major **primary concerns**, namely his demand $x = c - y$ and the "certainty" that his demand will be accepted.

Being aware of these two primary concerns the immediate task is to find out whether they are **complimentary or conflicting**. Such an investigation requires a cognitive model how responder Y will react to the offers y under consideration. When generating a preference for one offer y, an inexperienced proposer X therefore has to imagine how a typical responder Y will decide between accepting or rejecting it.

This does not mean that proposer X himself would react in such a way. The data of the so-called consistency tests where the same participant plays two ultimatum games in different roles, Güth et al. (1982), clearly indicate that some participants do not expect others to behave as they do. More specifically, 5 of 37 participants were **inconsistent** in the sense that their demand x and their **acceptance threshold** $\underline{y}$ - in the sense that only offers

$y \geq \underline{y}$ would be accepted - add up to more than to c and 17 in the sense of $x + \underline{y} < c$.

An obvious idea to predict response behavior in ultimatum games is to assume that most responders view the situation as basically symmetric since both parties (X and Y) are needed for an agreement. The **basic symmetry** is, for instance, reflected by the **characteristic function** v of the ultimatum game with $v(\{X\}) = v(\{Y\}) = 0$ and $v(\{X, Y\}) = c$. This implies a natural **aspiration level** $y = c/2$ of proposer Y. In terms of the two primary concerns this means that the equal split offer $y = c/2$ will be surely accepted (what is always true in normal ultimatum games, but not necessarily in ultimatum subgames, see Güth and Tietz (1990), table 3.1).

Fig. 3.2. How X expects Y to react

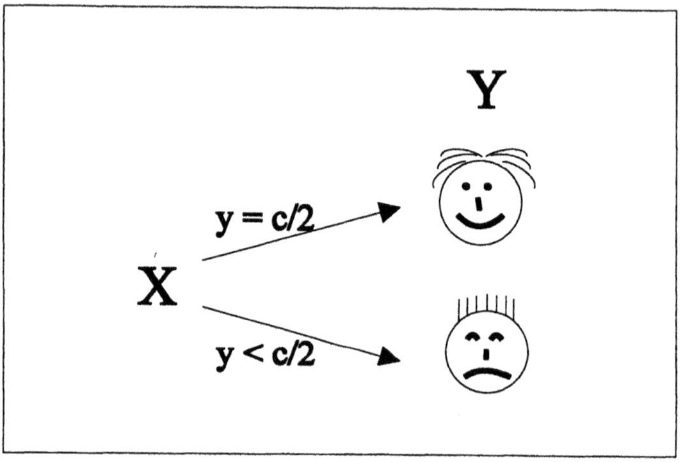

If responders expect $y = c/2$, all less favourable offers y with $y < c/2$ could trigger unfriendly emotions of responders and therefore be rejected (see the graphical illustration by figure 3.2). The likely result of imagining response behaviour is therefore:

Prediction: All offers $y < c/2$ will be less certainly accepted than the equal split $y = c/2$ which will be surely accepted.

For the two primary concerns of inexperienced proposers this, of course, means that these concerns are partly conflicting. The prediction seems to explain why many inexperienced decision makers shy away from any risk of rejection by offering the equal split (in the study of Güth and Huck (1997), for instance, 16 of 22 proposers X allocating a cake of DM 16,- suggested an equal split by offering $y =$ DM 8,-). Apparently these proposers resolved the conflict between the two primary concerns by giving **priority** to the "certainty of having one's offer accepted". In view of the psychological theory of **cognitive dissonance**, Festinger (1957), this can be explained as a reevaluation of primary concerns ("it is much more important to guarantee acceptance than trying to achieve more") or as a reinterpretation of facts ("in spite of its sequential decision process the game is basically symmetric").

Of course, not all inexperienced proposers X avoid the "less certain" offers $y < c/2$. A more ambitious proposer X probably imagines that a responder Y will grudgingly accept an offer $y < c/2$ provided that the cost of choosing conflict are prohibitively high. An idea for imagining Y's response behaviour for offers $y < c/2$ could be to predict Y's acceptance threshold $\underline{y}$ with $0 < \underline{y} < c/2$ in the sense that X expects only offers $y \geq \underline{y}$ to be accepted.

An acceptance threshold is a rather extreme form of imagining response behaviour. A more realistic picture how proposers imagine response behaviour is graphically illustrated in figure 3.3. Here the range of offers $0 \leq y < c/2$ is partitioned into three subregions, namely a subinterval $0 \leq y \leq s$ of offers y with $s > 0$ which one views as highly risky. In the subregion $t \leq y \leq c/2$ of offers y with $c/2 > t > s$ proposer X views Y's cost of conflict as prohibitively high, i.e. for X a rejection of such offers y is rather unlikely.

Fig. 3.3. Imagined responses to "low" offers $y < c/2$

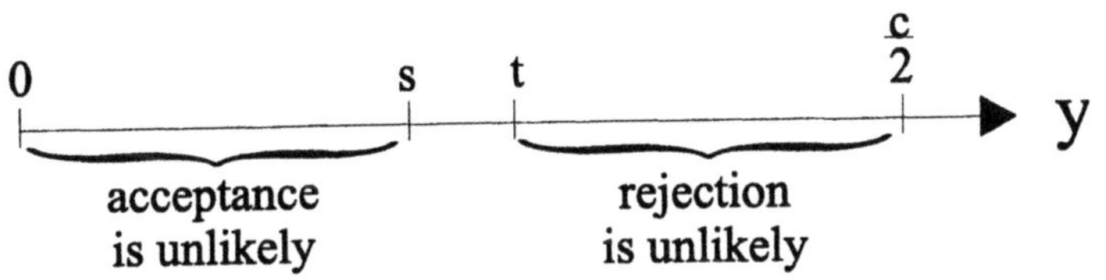

To have an easy notation we refer to t as an **acceptance border** and to s as a **rejection border**. Whereas an acceptance threshold $\underline{y}$ assumes that these borders coincide, our hypothesis is that s is usually smaller than t and that proposers X do not dare to offer amounts y lower than t. The range of offers y with $s < y < t$ could be viewed as a **transition range** from unlikely acceptance to unlikely rejection. In our view, proposers do not form any definite expectations concerning offers y with $s < y < t$ which they expect neither to be likely accepted nor to be likely rejected.

It seems natural that the acceptance border t increases less than proportionally with the "pie" c (experimental studies claiming "high stakes" are, for instance, Cameron (1995), Hoffman, McCabe, and Smith (1996), Slonim and Roth (1998)) and with Y's entitlement in the sense of Y's legitimate claims to participate in "eating the pie c". **Entitlement** is most convincingly introduced in reward and labour allocation experiments, Shapiro (1975), provided that both, the work effort and the reward, are sufficiently high. Another way to provide entitlement is to auction experimental positions, e.g. the positions of X and Y in an ultimatum game (Güth and Tietz (1986), for an ambiguous, but nevertheless effective alternative see Hoffmann and Spitzer (1985)).

Hypothesis: The acceptance border t with $0 < t < c/2$ increases with the pie size c less than proportionally and also with the entitlement of responder Y.

That the acceptance border t should increase less than proportionally with the pie size c follows immediately from the idea that t represents the minimal cost preventing conflict. If c becomes very large, these costs should increase less than proportionally since the rejection becomes more and more costly. More specifically, t should depend on c in a way intermediate to a constant and to t being proportional to c (see the bold curve in figure 3.4 where the concavity of $t = t(c)$ is natural, but not well supported, see Güth and Tietz (1990)).

Fig. 3.4. An illustration of how the acceptance border t should depend on the cake size c

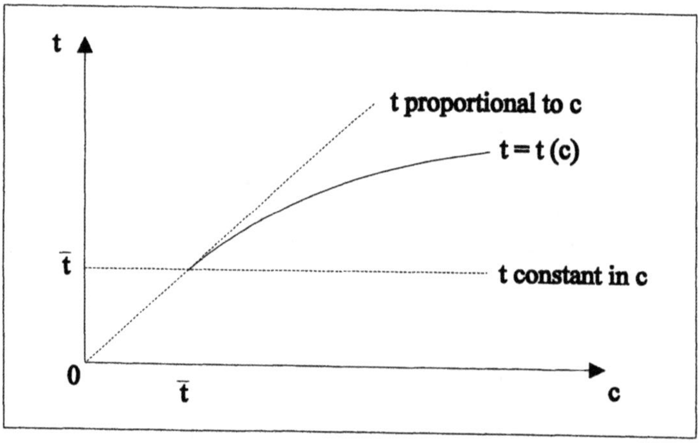

Unfortunately, the data of usual ultimatum bargaining experiments do not reveal the acceptance border t of responders Y since one only observes the actual response to X's offer y and not the whole response strategy. In experiments, which rely on the (monotonic response) strategy method, one can observe the acceptance threshold $\underline{y}$, but up to now neither pie size c nor Y's entitlement have been varied systematically. The value s of the rejection border could be estimated as the highest value below which a high proportion, e.g. 95%, of all offers are rejected.

One might rely on the chosen offer y as an indicator of the acceptance border t which a proposer X expects. Although c varied in many experimental studies of the ultimatum game (see surveys of Güth and Tietz (1990) and

Roth (1995)), the amounts c are naturally rather small (the highest amount c seems to be up to now \$ 200). Within this limited range the first part of the hypothesis could not be confirmed: The offered share y/c for the responder only weakly depends on c and does not decrease significantly with c as predicted. Of course, experimental studies of ultimatum bargaining often vary in strategically inessential aspects which nevertheless exert significant effects on the offered share y/c. To test our hypothesis in a more rigorous way one should perform an experiment which only varies c over some significant range.

3.3 Secondary Concern of Inexperienced Proposers

A proposer X, employing some cognitive model of response behavior to generate his offer y, typically has to imagine how the responder Y will feel when being confronted with a specific offer y and, especially, when being confronted with a "greedy offer" y far below the natural aspiration level $y = c/2$ of responders Y. Imagining the situation of responder Y in such a way can change the proposer's concerns considerably. Irrespective of his primary concern "Will my offer y be certainly accepted?" he may want to avoid that Y can only grudgingly accept the offer y. In other words: Imagining the situation of responder Y might provoke an empathy for responder Y (see figure 3.5 for an illustration). Such a proposer's concern for $Y's$ well-being is called **secondary** since it results from investigating whether proposer's primary concerns are compatible or conflicting.

Fig. 3.5. The emergence of secondary concerns (in case of low offers y proposer X expects Y to be very upset what, in turn, upsets X)

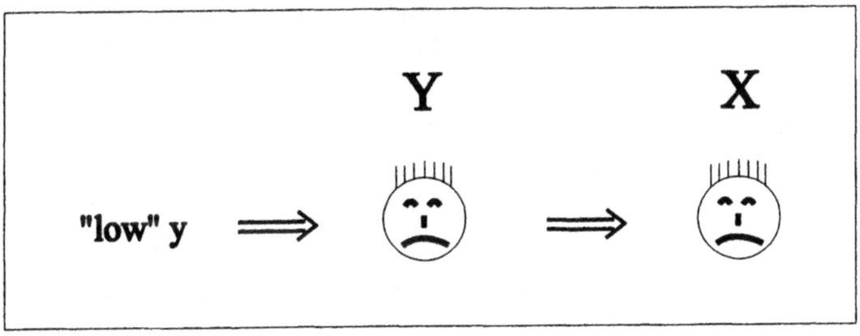

One might object that a secondary concern of proposer X for $Y's$ well-being is indistinguishable from $X's$ fear that an offer $y < c/2$ will be rejected. This, however, is no longer true when one also considers the experimental results of related experiments. In the **no revenge-games** of Güth and Huck (1997) responder Y can either only reject his own payoff y, but not the payoff x of the proposer X, or Y has no veto power at all (see the illustration by figure 3.6). For $c =$ DM 16,- the average offers were DM 5,82 and DM 5,77, respectively. Although these amounts are significantly smaller than the corresponding average offer of DM 7,86 in the ultimatum game, they nevertheless represent significant shares of $c =$ DM 16,-. This convincingly proves that many proposers X develop a (secondary) concern for $Y's$ well-being when considering which proposal to choose.

Fig. 3.6. The no revenge-games (if Y receives y after "no", (s)he has no veto power at all, otherwise Y can reject only y)

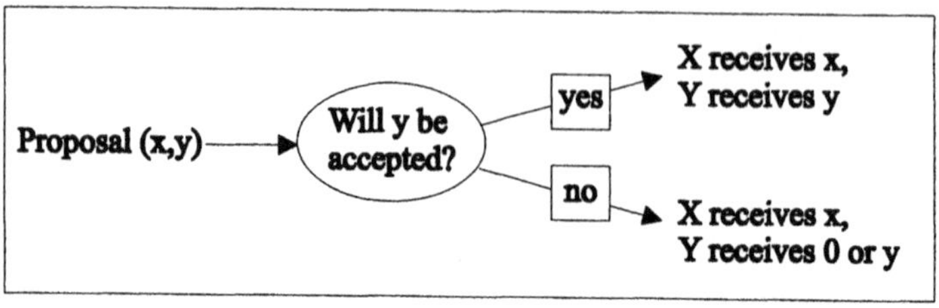

Another possibility to test the strength of $X's$ secondary concern for $Y's$ well-being is to perform an experiment with three groups of participants. One group of proposers X and responders Y play the usual ultimatum game with X and Y deciding simultaneously about the offer y, respectively about the acceptance threshold $\underline{y}$. Another group of proposers X' has to make an offer y' which also must be accepted by a responder Y who, however, does not know that his choice of $\underline{y}$ decides whether y' is accepted and who does not receive y' if it is accepted. Thus X', knowing this, has no reason to be concerned about Y. Of course, also X should not be aware of X'.

In **double blind-experiments** of no revenge games, where not only the partner Y, but also the experimenter cannot observe the offer y of an individual proposer X, one does not observe high average offers (see Hoffman et al. (1994) and Bolton and Zwick (1995)). The trick is that at least for some pairs the pie is $c = 0$ where only the proposer X himself, but neither the responder nor the experimenter knows the true pie size. Güth and Huck (1997) allow for a large (DM 38,-) and a small pie (DM 16,-). Nevertheless 16 out of 42 proposers X with the large pie $c =$ DM 38,- offered more than the small pie (DM 16,-) in at least one of the two no revenge-games, described above. Thus the possibility to "hide behind the small pie" does not prevent all proposers X to care for $Y's$ well-being. We summarize, what is illustrated in figure 3.5, by

Conclusion: When analyzing whether or not a responder Y will accept an offer y in the range $0 \leq y < c/2$, many proposers X develop a (secondary) concern for $Y's$ well-being what inspires more generous offers y.

One has to expect an even more important role of such secondary concerns for $Y's$ well-being when the two parties X and Y interact face to face (one could describe such experiments as zero-blind procedures). In a face to face-interaction most people develop a group feeling what usually rules out unequal and seemingly unfair reward allocations (see Frey and Bohnet (1995)).

3.4 Shaping Behavior by Qualitative Learning

If a proposer plays the ultimatum game repeatedly against changing opponents, he usually will improve his behavior in the light of previous experiences. As demonstrated above the cognitive considerations of the proposer are related mainly to two questions:

"How likely will an offer $y < c/2$ be rejected?"

and

"How much should one offer to Y anyhow?"

Whereas the first question reflects the primary concern that X wants his offer to be accepted, the second question is related to the secondary concern for $Y's$ well-being which some, but not necessarily all proposers will develop.

Qualitative or directional learning (see, for instance, Selten and Buchta (1998)) predicts the direction of better decisions by inferences from previous experiences (see figure 3.7 for a graphical illustration).

Fig. 3.7. The cognitive idea of directional learning (or why looking back when moving forward makes sense)

What one can infer from previous results depends, of course, on the specific experiences as well as on one's cognitive ideas. Naturally a proposer X whose offer $y < c/2$ was rejected will conclude that he should be more generous next time. If an offer $y > 0$ is accepted, one might regret to have offered so much. Thus qualitative learning can be described by the following rules:

Rule (1) : A proposer X, whose offer $y > 0$ has been accepted, will tend to decrease it or keep it constant.

Rule (2) : A proposer X, whose offer $y < c/2$ has been rejected, will increase it next time.

Table 3.1.

			$t-(t-1)$					
		$\Delta y_t = y_t - y_{t-1}$	1-2	2-3	3-4	4-5	5-6	$\sum$
accepted		$\Delta y_t > 0$	5	0	5	1	1	12
y_{t-1}	(*)	$\Delta y_t = 0$	8	10	10	17	14	59
	*	$\Delta y_t < 0$	11	9	7	5	7	39
rejected	*	$\Delta y_t > 0$	0	3	1	1	1	6
y_{t-1}		$\Delta y_t \leq 0$	0	2	1	0	1	4

To analyze the support for the two rules (1) and (2) we use the data of Güth and Van Damme (1998). In their experiment a proposal consisted of three components since a third party Z without strategic influence was included to combine the aspects of ultimatum bargaining and dictatorship. In table 3.1 we only consider those results where $Y's$ information about the proposal was never varied (Y either knows all three components or only the amount offered to him). A "*" indicates correspondence with rule (1), respectively (2), "(*)" stationarity (for rejected y_{t-1} we do not make the distinction because of the small number of observations). The change $\Delta y_t = y_t - y_{t-1}$ in the offer y to responder Y from period $t-1$ to period t is classified according to whether y_{t-1} has been accepted or rejected. If y_{t-1} has been accepted, only $\Delta y_t = 0$ and $\Delta y_t < 0$ confirms rule (1), i.e. 98 of 110 observations. If y_{t-1} has been rejected, rule (2) predicts $\Delta y_t > 0$ what is confirmed by 6 of the 10 observations. Thus we can conclude that rule (1) seems to be empirically valid whereas for rule (2) the number of observations is too small for a final judgement. More generally, the idea of qualitative learning can only be insufficiently confirmed by the data.

In the **full information trials** of Güth and Van Damme (1998) a responder did not only learn which part y of the cake has been assigned to him but also what X has granted to the third, strategically inessential party Z. Here a proposer X might have feared that responder Y will not only protect his own share y, but also, e.g. out of a secondary concern for party Z, the share $z = c - x - y$ of the third party Z. There is, however, little support that Y cares for $Z's$ well-being: Whenever there was a rejection under full information it could be attributed to a low offer $y < c/3$, i.e. responders Y did not sacrifice y simply because z was too low. Furthermore, proposers X quickly learned this and offered more to responders when they know z in addition to y, i.e. proposers X apparently thought it cheaper to bribe Y by increasing y than to grant more to Z. Strong secondary concerns of X for Z's well-being should have induced significant z-shares which were rarely observed.

Although we could validate only Rule (1) how qualitative learning shapes the preferences of proposers who repeatedly play the ultimatum game with changing opponents, the hypothesis, in general, seems intuitively convincing. Since reasonable proposers shy away from greedy offers, one usually (see Kagel et al. (1996) for an exceptional study with a surprisingly high conflict quota) observes not enough conflicts for testing also rule (2). Other studies with surprisingly high frequencies of conflict, e.g. Slembeck (1999), do not rely on one shot-games, but on a partner design (one plays many games with the same partner) where one tries to establish a reputation for being tough in early rounds.

Table 3.2. The information conditions of the cycle mode, Güth and Van Damme (1998)

Round	1	2	3	4	5	6	7	8	9
Information condition	x, y, z	y	z	x, y, z	y	z	x, y, z	y	z

Learning is more complex when a proposer is confronted with many experiences between two successive trials. Instead of discussing this abstractly without data we illustrate this with the help of the data observed by Güth and Van Damme (1998). As mentioned before in their experiment a proposer X had to allocate c among three persons X, Y and Z, i. e. a proposal was a vector (x, y, z) with $x + y + z = c$ and $x, y, c > 0$ (there was a smallest positive money unit). In the **cycle mode** a proposer played altogether 9 games successively against changing opponents which can be subdivided into three cycles. Here a cycle means that the knowledge of Y about the proposal (x, y, z) was varied systematically. Under **full information** Y knew the whole proposal (x, y, z), under **essential information** only y, and under **irrelevant information** only the component z of the proposal (x, y, z). In a cycle one first plays the full, then the essential, and finally the irrelevant information condition (see table 3.2).

message form		$m = (x, y, z)$		$m = y$	
round t - round $t-3$		4-1	7-4	5-2	8-5
y_{t-3}	$\Delta y_t > 0$	12(10)	7(5)	3(3)	4(2)
accepted	(*) $\Delta y_t = 0$	14	15	15	15
	* $\Delta y_t < 0$	9	14	16	17
y_{t-3}	* $\Delta y_t > 0$	1	0	1	0
rejected	$\Delta y_t \leq 0$	0	0	1	0

Table 3.3. in brackets: the number of cases where not only y_t, but also x_t has been increased

According to table 3.3 of the altogether 36 plays of the cycle mode only one began with conflict in the first round (the full information of the 1st cycle). In accordance with Rule (2) this proposer reacted by a more generous offer y to Y when he played the full information again where now, of course, $\Delta y_t = y_t - y_{t-3}$. Of the 35 proposers, whose first proposals were accepted,

9 decreased, 14 kept, and 12 increased their offers to Y when playing the full information condition again. This illustrates that Rule (1) is less reliable when other experiences intervene. Obviously most of the 12 proposers learned between the first two plays of the full information game, i.e. by experiencing the essential and the irrelevant information game, that they have been too generous to Z and that, to be sure of $Y's$ acceptance, also responder Y should profit from treating Z less favourably (in 10 of the 12 cases x increased together with y, twice x was kept constant).

All 36 proposals of the second time of playing the full information game (the 4th round altogether) were accepted. Of these 36 proposers 14 decreased, 15 kept, and 7 increased their offer y to responder Y so that the predictive success of Rule (1) increased from 23/35 to 29/36. Of the 7 allocators, who increased y although their previous offer y was accepted, 5 increased x together with y. Thus the weaker support for Rule (1) can be mostly explained by attempts to "exploit" Z and to "bribe" Y by a larger offer y. According to table 3.3 the results for the essential message $m = y$ are not dramatically different. Actually they are slightly more in line with Rule (1) than the corresponding results for full information $m = (x, y, z)$.

3.5 Conclusions

According to an old anecdote a decision theorist when being confronted with a difficult decision task reacted rather angrily ("Are you kidding? This is serious!") when being helped with the "advice": "Maximize your utility!" What this illustrates is that we are not established with complete preferences telling us what is best. The major problem of decision making is rather to generate a (preference for a) choice what is sometimes easy and sometimes difficult, e.g. when there is conflict between (primary) concerns.

If one wants to discuss the crucial aspects of economic behavior in a way which aims at truly helping in making up one's mind, one can do so in rather general terms (like Güth (forthcoming)) or more specifically. General models can offer a framework by which one can check how the various concepts of behavioral economics fit together. Their disadvantage is, however, that many of their assumptions are at best reasonable conjectures. This can be avoided by focussing attention on special decisions like ultimatum proposals for which a lot of evidence is available.

Here we have concentrated on proposing in ultimatum bargaining. Since the two primary concerns "the own demand x" and "the certainty of having one's offer accepted" are conflicting and since the situation is strategic, a proposer X has to predict how likely a certain proposal will be accepted by responder Y. Thinking about others in such a way may inspire some concern for Y's well-being. We have named this a secondary concern since it typically develops when analyzing whether the primary concerns are conflicting or not. The advantage of not having to speculate without facts was illustrated by investigating how experiences (re)shape preferences for certain choices.

The fact that, especially in case of conflicting concerns, a certain choice has to be generated by an often cumbersome process of cognitive modelling, reevaluating concerns, reinterpreting evidence etc. makes it clear that preferences will hardly ever be complete. On the contrary, one usually will begin by singling out a few relevant decision alternatives when being offered too many as in the usual ultimatum game. How this is done, in general, has not been discussed at great length. Most proposers seem to compare the equal split offer $y = c/2$ with some more or less unfavorable offer $y < c/2$ for responder Y where prominence theory (see, for instance, Albers and Albers (1983)) undoubtedly has a lot to say which offers $y < c/2$ easily come to one's mind.

In our view, the theory of decision emergence is still in a very preliminary state although psychological theories like cognitive dissonance theory certainly provide some guidance. Since there are far too many choice problems, theoretical results for particular decision tasks will not suffice. Our hope is therefore that certain aspects of the process, how ultimatum proposers generate their choices, are of general importance, e.g. how the analysis of primary concerns can generate secondary concerns and how qualitative learning can (re)shape preferences.

References

[1] Albers, W. and G. Albers (1983). On the Prominence Structure of the Decimal System. in: *Decision making under uncertainty*, R.W. Scholz (ed.), Amsterdam, 271-287.

[2] Bolton, G. and R. Zwick (1995). Anonymity Versus Punishment in Ultimatum Bargaining. *Games and Economic Behavior 10*(1), 95–121.

[3] Cameron, L. (1995). Raising the Stakes in the Ultimatum Game: Experimental Evidence from Indonesia. Working Paper 345, Industrial Relations Section, Princeton University.

[4] Festinger, L. (1957). *Theory of Cognitive Dissonance.* Evanston (Ill.): Roar.

[5] Frey, B. and I. Bohnet (1995). Institutions Affect Fairness: Experimental Investigations. *Journal of Institutional and Theoretical Economics 151*(2), 286–303.

[6] Güth, W. (1995). Ultimatum Bargaining Experiments – a Personal Review. *Journal of Economic Behavior and Organization 27*, 329–344.

[7] Güth, W. (forthcoming). Boundedly Rational Decision Emergence. Journal of Economic Psychology.

[8] Güth, W. and E. Van Damme (1998). Information, Strategic Behavior and Fairness in Ultimatum Bargaining – an Experimental Study. *Journal of Mathematical Psychology 42*, 227–247.

[9] Güth, W. and S. Huck (1997). From Ultimatum Bargaining to Dictatorship – an Experimental Study of Four Games Varying in Veto Power. *Metroeconomica 48*(3), 262–279.

[10] Güth, W. and H. Kliemt (1994). Competition or Cooperation – on the Evolutionary Economics of Trust, Exploitation and Moral Attitudes. *Metroeconomica 45*, 155–187.

[11] Güth, W., R. Schmittberger, and B. Schwarze (1982). An Experimental Analysis of Ultimatum Bargaining. *Journal of Economic Behavior and Organization* (367-388).

[12] Güth, W. and R. Tietz (1986). Auctioning Ultimatum Bargaining Positions: How to Decide If Rational Decisions Are Unacceptable? in: *Current Issues in West German Decision Research*, R.W. Scholz (ed.), Frankfurt, 173-185.

[13] Güth, W. and R. Tietz (1990). Ultimatum Bargaining Behavior – a Survey and Comparison of Experimental Results. *Journal of Economic Psychology 11*(3), 417–449.

[14] Hoffmann, E. and M. Spitzer (1985). Entitlements, Rights and Fairness: an Experimental Examination of Concepts of Distributive Justice. *Journal of Legal Studies 14*, 259–297.

[15] Hoffmann, E., K.A. McCabe, K. Shachat and V.L. Smith (1994). Preferences, Property Rights and Anonymity in Bargaining Games. *Games and Economic Behaviour 7*(3), 346–380.

[16] Hoffmann, E., K.A. McCabe and V.L. Smith (1996). On Expectations and the Monetary Stakes in Ultimatum Games. *International Journal of Game Theory 25*(3), 289–301.

[17] Kagel, J., C. Kim, and D. Moser (1996). Fairness in Ultimatum Games with Asymmetric Information and Asymmetric Payoffs. *Games and Economic Behavior 13*, 100–110.

[18] Roth, A. (1995). Bargaining Experiments. in: *Handbook of Experimental Economics*, J. H. Kagel and A. E. Roth (eds.), Princeton, N.J.: Princeton University Press, 253 - 348.

[19] Selten, R. and J. Buchta (1998). Experimental Sealed Bid First Price Auctions with Directly Observed Bid Functions. in: *Games and Human Behavior - Essays in Honor of Amnon Rapoport*, D. V. Budescu, I. Erev, and R. Zwick (eds.), Mahwah, NJ: Lawrence Erlbaum Associates.

[20] Shapiro, E. (1975). Effects of Future Interaction on Reward Allocation in Dyads: Equity or Equality. *Journal of Personality and Social Psychology 31*, 873–880.

[21] Slembeck, T. (1999). Reputations and Fairness in Bargaining – Experimental Evidence from a Repeated Ultimatum Game with Fixed Opponents. Discussion Paper No. 9904, Department of Economics, University of St. Gallen.

[22] Slonim, R. and A. Roth (1998). Learning in High Stakes Ultimatum Games: An Experiment in the Slovak Republic. *Econometrica 66*(3), 569–596.

4 Economic Decisions by Approved Principles

Rules of Thumb as Behavioral Guidelines

Walter Buhr and Thomas Christiaans *

Abstract. We discuss the relevance of the concept of rational behavior in economic theory and suggest, on the basis of modern brain research results, to abstain from this notion and instead to apply behavioral rules of thumb in decision-making, especially if these rules can be derived from rational problem solutions determined by individual economic agents. We give an example for our point of view which refers to a contribution by Baumol and Quandt (1964) on the pricing behavior of a monopolistic firm and which also emphasizes the general importance of dynamic analysis in economics.

4.1 The Concept of Rational Behavior in Economic Theory

In this paper we discuss the relevance of the concept of rational behavior in economic theory and suggest, on the basis of modern brain research results, to abstain from the assumption of rationality in solving economic problems and instead to apply behavioral rules of thumb in decision-making of individual economic agents.[1] From a normative point of view, it is reasonable to find rules that can be derived from rational problem solutions. With respect to positive economics, we argue that, in general, economic agents are not in a position to calculate rationally optimum solutions of their problems. Hence, it is important to investigate whether the implications of positive neoclassical economics are robust with respect to other behavioral assumptions. For our position we give an example which refers to a contribution by Baumol and Quandt (1964).

Substantial parts of economic theory are based on the assumption of rational behavior of human beings. The common understanding of the term *rationality* implies comprehensive information processing, far-reaching capabilities of calculation and sound reasoning that cannot be justified as the results of learning and adaptation (Arrow, 1987, p. 69). An economist's definition is more specific: Under the assumption of certainty, rationality of human

* We thank Hagen Bobzin, Siegen, for his comments on this paper.

[1] We only consider decision rules in relation to human behavior and are aware that rules may also originate from experiences dealing with complicated problems, for example, the increase of labor productivity due to an improved division of labor or the interest of the private sector in a constant and permanent economic policy.

behavior either means internal consistency of decision-making, for example, the realized requirement of transitivity, or reasoned pursuit of self-interest, in both cases the maximization of something (Sen, 1987, p. 69).

Sen (1987, pp. 68, 71) indicates that the interest in the concept of rational behavior stems from two motivations, on the one hand, from the normative question how one could behave rationally in a given situation, and, on the other hand, from the possible positive use of models of rational behavior in explaining and predicting actual behavior. The latter approach starts from the characterization of the implications of rational behavior, being aware that rationality is not a property of the individual alone, but derives its actual significance in the social context, in relation to other basic concepts of neoclassical theory such as equilibrium, competition, and completeness of markets, as Arrow (1987, pp. 71–73) convincingly demonstrates. Following this discussion, actual behavior is based on rational behavior. When we evaluate the unrealism of rational behavior, we should also consider the unrealism of any selected kind of irrational behavior. In general, there is no principle that prevents the formulation of an economic theory founded on assumptions other than that of rationality, although it is not an easy task to find alternatives for the standard hypothesis of rational behavior.

In this context it would go too far to investigate individual economic models whether, to what extent, and in which form they are devised on assumptions other than rationality. Therefore, at first, we should like to point out two mainstreams of economic thinking in the literature that show divergences from the hypothesis of rationality. The first group of models is related to different areas of applied economics and, due to its empirical and practical orientation, there is no major direct concern with rationality hypotheses. Arrow (1987, p. 70) gives practical theories of macroeconomics (in the field of Keynesian theory and monetarism) as examples (specifically cf. Krusell and Smith, 1996). Only by analysis one finds that rationality assumptions are partial and often supplemented by assumptions of a different nature.

The second group of models concentrates on bounded rationality, an approach developed by Simon (1957, 1979). The starting point is rational decision-making which is taken to be subjected to various restrictions (limited time span, uncertainty, market imperfections etc.), the result not being overall maximizing behavior, but a sequence of more or less independent and sometimes inconsistent decisions derived under partial information. A good and simple example is Simon's (1955) well-known *satisficing* hypothesis of behavior, meaning that economic agents perform limited searches over all possible decisions and then accept the first satisfactory alternative. For bounded rationality in economic models cf. Conlisk (1996).

Our aim now is to substantiate an existing third line of economic thinking on the basis of the theory of chemical and biological evolution as emerging from modern brain research. We propose that economic agents interested in optimal solutions follow rules of thumb as behavioral guidelines in decision-making, especially if it is possible to show that these rules can solidly be derived from or founded on models of rational behavior. As we shall argue, this suggestion takes into account the limited capabilities and specific working methods of the human brain. Moreover, given these limited capabilities of the brain, the positive use of models involving rules of thumb seems to be more reliable than using models of rational behavior. The following outline of the interaction of the essential parts of the vertebrate brain has been summarized from Ditfurth (1976), except for other quotations indicated.

4.2 Some Considerations on Human Behavior Based on the Results of Brain Research

Our brain must be understood as a chronologic arrangement in different layers which has developed in the process of chemical and biological evolution, in its course leading to psychic evolution (as general texts on the structure of the brain cf. Popper and Eccles (1977, 1987), Schütz, Caspers, and Speckmann (1982), Faller (1995)). We are confronted with an anachronistic cooperation of the sections of the brain which are of totally different age; in their development they are millions of years apart. The hierarchical setup of the brain has been organized to improve the individual's chances of survival. Subsequently, our interest will be only in the psychic functions of the vertebrate brain and here again mainly in two parts of it. In the core of the brain we find (1) the diencephalon (including the center of vision) following and surrounding the brain stem. The diencephalon is superimposed by (2) the younger telencephalon or cerebrum which comprises seven-eighttth of the mass of the vertebrate central nervous system.

The diencephalon includes the steering centers for inherent motion and the centers for processing information from the outside world. It generates natural instinctive behavior, emotions (feelings, sensations) and desires (instincts), being a storage place for experiences which are millions of years old. They influence our thinking and behavior without our own interference and generally unnoticed. The localization of specific behavior in the diencephalon is still unknown to a wide extent. However, there are certain indications as to the centers of anxiety states, the urge to locomotion, impetus reduction, the feeling of hunger, the rhythm of sleep and wakefullness.

Typical for the functioning of the diencephalon is the provision of a number of lines of conduct each of which appears to be totally natural, emerging from readily available behavior programs (cf. Lorenz, 1975). These programs (instincts, innate experiences) have optimally been adjusted to the environmental conditions in the course of evolution. They concern, for example, personal hygiene, reactions of defense, or provision of forage. Signals of the external world generate - beyond certain thresholds installed - releasing devices to stimulate the behavior programs in the diencephalon.

This part of the brain produces a representation of the world as a section of reality formed by the effectively perceived characteristics of the individual's environment. This representation of the outside world has not been derived by individual experiences, but by experiences of the human kind. There is a total correpondence between the inborne programs and reality of the external world as observed by the diencephalon (cf. also Lorenz, 1974).

The youngest and most progressive part of the brain, the telencephalon, renders possible conscious experiences, rational accomplishments, consciousness, capability of learning, and perception of the objective outer world.

The achievement of the individual's capability of learning which is the decisive step of evolution from the diencephalon to the telencephalon makes possible own experiences of the individual, the perception of the outside world in specific details, and the appearance of the objective world outside in the brain.

Up to the diencephalon the incoming information is concentrated and then, while it moves on to the telencephalon, is extremely dispersed to the different areas of the telencephalon. The areas of the cortex cerebri are uncommitted in the sense that they are not occupied by specific functions, programs, or instincts; they are freely available and give room for personal behavior. The forehead brain (frontal lobes) as most developed part of the telencephalon is the organ of human freedom, meaning that the telencephalon separates the individual from its environment.

The step-by-step development of the vertebrate brain leads to the consequence that all connections between the telencephalon and the external world must pass through the older parts of the brain, the brain stem and the diencephalon. The forehead brain and the rest of the cortex cerebri have no direct access to the outside world. The telencephalon is not a sovereign. Each information heading for the telencephalon must cross the diencephalon governed by its own archaic laws. This fact explains the irrationality, inconsistency and unreasonableness of human behavior (existence of wars, crimes, political narrowness in mind, religious fanatism etc.) which are basically due to the deep gap between the telencephalon and the diencephalon.

Both sections are cooperating parts of the same organ, the brain, considering their antagonistic nature. Thus the human being simultaneously lives in two worlds: on the one hand, it is capable of understanding and reasoning and, on the other hand, it exists in the transition of animal to man. Although the telencephalon has radically changed and improved the conditions and opportunities of man's existence, the diencephalon still plays a decisive role in shaping the thinking and the actions of human beings. To repeat, the diencephalon is incapable of learning and rational reasoning, bound to fixed problems and their solutions.

We are far away from objective rational experiences about this world.[2] We live in a subjective reality determined also by experiences not made by ourselves. Moreover, the capabilities of our senses are limited, our processing of information is characterized by particularities, and the development of the telencephalon in our brain is still in the state of immaturity.[3] In addition, the access to information is restricted so that information is an economic good carrying a positive price and thus leading to procurement costs.

As for empirical evidence, Berk, Hughson, and Vandezande (1996) conduct an interesting test of rational decision theory. They consider the game show *The Price is Right* as a laboratory where the stakes are sufficiently high to ensure an economic incentive to play optimally (the contestants play for prizes worth as much as $60,000). The authors' result is that the players' strategies are transparently suboptimal. Interestingly, Berk, Hughson, and Vandezande (1996) develop simple rules of thumb which explain the observed behavior better than rational decision theory.

The main result so far for our purposes is that we are well advised in economic analysis to give up our pretension to live in an objective, clearly concrete world and thus to drop the assumption of rationality in economic decision-making, a notion that is connected with the end of the information processing line in the telencephalon. (In this context we may question the justification of the term *bounded rationality*! However, this is a different research topic.) We suggest to give up the sole and strict references to the sphere of telencephalon and turn to the functions of diencephalon[4] which are structured in the form of programs. If we interpret a program as a set of rules, we understand the relevance of behavioral rules of thumb in economic decision-making. As a counterpoint to our argument we consider the fact that the now excessive urge to regulate too many aspects of modern private life is the result of growing human anxieties.

Any decision rule implies some type of justification, be it rational or irrational (cf. Etzioni, 1987, whose statements shall not be discussed here). However, decision rules are particularly convincing and valuable, if they can be derived from a rational problem solution. A good example for this third line of economics is the theory of investment evaluation, particularly cost-benefit analysis, and related areas of investment theory (cf., for example, Day, Morley, and Smith, 1974, Ellison and Fudenberg, 1993, Rosenthal, 1993). For the illustration of the wide applicability of our suggestion we shall discuss an example that draws on Baumol and Quandt (1964). This important contri-

---

[2] The claim to rationality is an overweening estimation of man, a form of dehumanization, that corresponds to the reality of human behavior, to the wicked shames of mankind in the sense of Lorenz (1980).

[3] On the interrelationships of information, organization, and incentives cf. Will 1998.

[4] On replacing the idealized, perfectly rational agents by *calibrated* agents who represent actual human behavior cf. Arthur (1993).

bution has widely been neglected as to its importance for neoclassical theory so that it deserves to be revived, especially in the present context; however, it must be corrected in an important aspect, as we shall demonstrate.

4.3 A Stable Rule of Thumb for a Monopolistic Firm

Baumol and Quandt (1964) are the first to analyze the convergence of a *rule of thumb*—a *learning rule*, as they say—to an optimal supply price in a simple model of a monopolistic firm. They consider several types of pricing rules and give a rough classification of such rules.[5] In their Appendix A, they provide analytical proofs of stability for a (linear) discrete time model as well as a continuous time model, which, however, involves an error that is also present in Gandolfo's (1996, pp. 420–421) more general exposition of this model. We present the approach of Baumol and Quandt (1964) and Gandolfo (1996) and show how to reformulate the model in order to avoid this difficulty. We shall demonstrate that the chosen rule of thumb leads to the optimal solution after some time of—possibly cyclic—adjustment.

Although in reality a monopolist adjusts his price at discrete time intervals, we employ a continuous time approach. The following arguments can be given in favor of differential equations.[6]

1. There is no natural discrete unit of time. In this respect, choosing years, months or days is completely arbitrary. Therefore, in employing a discrete time model, it should always be checked whether its main implications depend on the chosen length of time intervals. If they are actually independent of period length, they should also be robust with respect to a change of the time span if it tends to zero, that is when we pass on from difference equations to differential equations.
2. Nonlinear discrete time models tend to show a very complex behavior. They may therefore imply chaos that arises only because of the chosen length of the period. Since a continuous time model can be interpreted as the limiting case of a model with very short periods, it should be observed, however, that a stable continuous model may be unstable in discrete time, if the adjustments do not occur in sufficiently small steps.
3. Even if difference equations are easy to use numerically, differential equations are analytically more tractable.

With reference to the Baumol and Quandt (1964) model we also assume that profit π is given as a twice differentiable, strictly concave function of the

[5] Other types are *markup rules*, *imitative rules*, and *pseudo maximizing rules*, cf. Baumol and Quandt (1964, p. 27).

[6] As for a more general outline of various arguments in favor of differential equations which comprises our arguments 1 and 3 cf. Gandolfo (1996, pp. 547–549). This book is also recommended as a general and comprehensible reference on differential (difference) equations and dynamic systems for economists.

price p satisfying

$$\pi = f(p), \qquad f''(p) < 0 \quad \forall p \geq 0,$$

which has its unique maximum at $\hat{p} > 0$ with $f'(\hat{p}) = 0$.[7] The monopolist does not know this profit function, except for some specific values of the function. Therefore, he uses the following simple rule of thumb: *Raise the price, if the profit change has been positive as a result of an antecedent increase in price, and lower the price, if the profit change has been negative. If the level of profits is stationary, do not change the price.* In other words, the price is changed in the same direction as in the previous period, if the change in profit has been positive, and in the opposite direction, if it has been negative.

The monopolist's application of this decision rule means that he is not obliged to solve explicitly his profit maximization problem in a rational way. He need not even have some notion of his specific market situation. In terms of brain research, the reference to the sphere of the telencephalon, to rational decision-making, may directly be neglected, being substituted by approaching the sphere of the diencephalon. This realm of the brain is governed by rules that are not subject to personal influences of the individual, but for mankind have emerged from the adjustment to the environment in the course of evolution, here to the monopoly situation of all individual suppliers who have ever produced under monopoly. The above given decision rule is particularly convincing and thus lasting, since it implies the convergence to the optimum solution of the monopolist's profit maximization problem, as will be shown.

A formal representation of the rule of thumb now to be discussed more thoroughly is

$$p_{t+1} - p_t = g\left(\frac{\pi_t - \pi_{t-1}}{p_t - p_{t-1}}\right) \tag{4.1}$$

where $g \in C^1(R)$ is a sign-preserving function fulfilling $g' > 0$, that is,

$$g \gtreqless 0 \iff \frac{\pi_t - \pi_{t-1}}{p_t - p_{t-1}} \gtreqless 0.$$

Using a quadratic profit function and a linear function $g(.) = k[(\pi_t - \pi_{t-1})/(p_t - p_{t-1})]$, $k > 0$, Baumol and Quandt (1964) show that the rule of thumb (4.1) implies a linear second order difference equation being characterized by the optimum price as a stable steady state, provided the adjustment speed k is sufficiently small.

In continuous time, their rule of thumb is approximated by[8]

$$\dot{p} = \begin{cases} g(\dot{\pi}/\dot{p}) & \text{if} \quad \dot{p} \neq 0 \\ 0 & \text{otherwise} \end{cases} \tag{4.2}$$

[7] At $p = 0$, the terms $f'(p)$ and $f''(p)$ have to be interpreted as right-hand derivatives.

[8] Baumol and Quandt (1964, p. 43) use again a linear function g.

From the profit function, the authors derive $\dot{\pi} = f'(p)\dot{p}$; substituting this expression into the continuous rule of thumb yields

$$\dot{p} = g(f'(p)).$$

The properties of f and g imply that the function $h(p) := g(f'(p))$ satisfies

$$h(p) \gtreqless 0 \iff p \lesseqgtr \hat{p}, \quad \text{and } h'(p) = g'(f'(p))f''(p) < 0 \ \forall p \geq 0. \qquad (4.3)$$

Baumol and Quandt (1964) conclude on the basis of relationship (4.3) that the profit maximizing price $\hat{p}$ is an asymptotically stable equilibrium of the differential equation $\dot{p} = h(p)$.

This result embodies a serious flaw, however. Equation (4.2) is inconsistent in itself, because it means that $\dot{p}$ can be positive and negative at the same time. For example, if $\dot{\pi} < 0$ and $\dot{p} > 0$ at some point in time, relationship (4.2) implies $\dot{p} < 0$. The reason for this obvious contradiction is a wrong inference regarding the continuous version of equation (4.1). Since this relationship is a second order difference equation, the corresponding differential equation must also be of the second order.[9]

A more reasonable continuous version of (4.1) that fairly well approximates the verbal rule of thumb is the following representation by a lagged differential equation:

$$\dot{p}(t+1) = \begin{cases} g(\dot{\pi}(t)/\dot{p}(t)), & \text{if} \quad \dot{p}(t) \neq 0 \\ g(\ddot{\pi}(t)/\ddot{p}(t)), & \text{if} \quad \dot{p}(t) = 0 \neq \ddot{p}(t) \\ 0, & \text{if} \quad \dot{p}(t) = \ddot{p}(t) = 0 \end{cases} \qquad (4.4)$$

Substituting $\dot{\pi}(t)$, respectively $\ddot{\pi} = f''(p)\dot{p}^2 + f'(p)\ddot{p} = f'(p)\ddot{p}$ in case of $\dot{p}(t) = 0$, into relationship (4.4) eliminates the case distinction and yields the only equation[10]

$$\dot{p}(t+1) = h(p(t)).$$

[9] One obtains a reasonable result despite the faulty approach, because $\dot{p}$ drops from the function g.

[10] Actually, the result of this substitution is

$$\dot{p}(t+1) = \begin{cases} h(p(t)), & \text{if not} \quad \dot{p}(t) = \ddot{p}(t) = 0 \\ 0, & \text{if} \quad \dot{p}(t) = \ddot{p}(t) = 0 \end{cases}$$

Clearly, the monopolist initially has to put the system into motion to get a reasonable rule of thumb, since if he starts with $\dot{p} = \ddot{p} = 0$, the system remains in this situation. If $\dot{p} \neq 0$ at the start, however, then it can be seen from the continuous version (4.5) that $\dot{p}(t) = \ddot{p}(t) = 0$ is possible only if $p(t) = \hat{p}$. Therefore, we do not have to bother about the second case.

To get rid of the lag in this mixed difference-differential equation, subtract $\dot{p}(t)$ from both sides:

$$\dot{p}(t+1) - \dot{p}(t) = h(p(t)) - \dot{p}(t).$$

If the lag is reduced from one period to the fraction θ of this period, the change on the right-hand side should also be diminished to the fraction θ:

$$\dot{p}(t+\theta) - \dot{p}(t) = [h(p(t)) - \dot{p}(t)]\theta.$$

Dividing by θ and taking limits for $\theta \to 0$ yields the continuous adjustment process

$$\ddot{p} + \dot{p} = h(p). \tag{4.5}$$

This second order differential equation can be transformed into an equivalent system of two first order differential equations by introducing the new variable q defined by $q = \dot{p}$:

$$\begin{aligned} \dot{p} &= q, \\ \dot{q} &= h(p) - q. \end{aligned} \tag{4.6}$$

The unique equilibrium of this system is $(\hat{p}, 0)$.

It is important to notice that local stability results are only of a limited value in evaluating a rule of thumb, because such rules are only reliable, if they converge for initial values that are far off from an optimum. Moreover, for the problem at hand it does not make much sense, if the price approaches zero during the adjustment process. In order to meet these requirements, the following version of Lyapunov's second method – which allows for the explicit positivity condition $p > 0$ – is employed to prove the stability of the proposed rule of thumb.

Theorem 1. *Let $f: X \to R^n$ be a continuously differentiable function on the open state space $X \subset R^n$. Suppose that $\hat{x}$ is an equilibrium of the autonomous system $\dot{x} = f(x)$.*[11] *If there is a real-valued continuously differentiable function $V: X \to R$, a constant $l > 0$, and a nonempty and bounded region $D \equiv \{x \in X : V(x) < l\}$ such that*

(a) $V(x) > 0 \;\; \forall x \neq \hat{x},\; x \in D,\; V(\hat{x}) = 0,$
(b) $\dot{V}(x(t, x_0)) < 0 \;\; \forall x(t, x_0) \neq \hat{x},\; x(t, x_0) \in D,$

then the equilibrium $\hat{x}$ is asymptotically stable for all $x_0 \in D$. Every trajectory starting in D remains in D for all $t \geq 0$.

Proof. Cf. Lasalle and Lefschetz (1961), e. g. □

[11] The solution of $\dot{x} = f(x)$ starting at $x(0) = x_0 \in X$ is denoted by $x(t, x_0)$.

Proposition 1. *The equilibrium* $(\hat{p}, 0)$ *of system* (4.6) *is asymptotically stable. Its basin of attraction includes the region* $D = \{(p,q) \in R^2 \;:\; V(p,q) < l\}$, *where* $l = -\int_{\hat{p}}^{0} h(s)\,ds > 0$. *For all initial values in* D, *the price* $p(t)$ *is positive for all* $t \geq 0$.

Proof. The function

$$V(p,q) = \frac{1}{2}q^2 - \int_{\hat{p}}^{p} h(s)\,ds,$$

is a suitable Lyapunov function for $p > 0$. To prove this, observe that $V(p,q) > 0$ for all $(p,q) \neq (\hat{p}, 0)$ according to (4.3), and $V(\hat{p}, 0) = 0$. The derivative with respect to t is

$$\dot{V}(p,q) = q\dot{q} - h(p)\dot{p} = q[h(p) - q] - h(p)q = -q^2 < 0$$

for all $q \neq 0$. This proves $(\hat{p}, 0)$ is asymptotically stable. Now choose $l = -\int_{\hat{p}}^{0} h(s)\,ds > 0$ and define the region D of the theorem as $D \equiv \{(p,q) \in R^2 \;:\; V(p,q) < l\}$. Since conditions (a) and (b) of the theorem are satisfied for D, the proposition is proven, if it is shown that $p > 0$ in the case $(p,q) \in D$. From $V(p,q) < l$ we get

$$\frac{1}{2}q^2 + \int_{p}^{\hat{p}} h(s)\,ds < \int_{0}^{\hat{p}} h(s)\,ds$$

$$\Longleftrightarrow \quad \frac{1}{2}q^2 + \int_{p}^{\hat{p}} h(s)\,ds - \int_{0}^{p} h(s)\,ds - \int_{p}^{\hat{p}} h(s)\,ds < 0$$

$$\Longleftrightarrow \quad \int_{0}^{p} h(s)\,ds > \frac{1}{2}q^2 > 0,$$

which requires $p > 0$ according to (4.3). Thus, $V < l$ implies $p > 0$; since V is decreasing along trajectories, $p(t) > 0$ for all $t \geq 0$. □

Figures 4.1 and 4.2 illustrate the argument by means of an example computed with *Mathematica*.[12] The region D is represented by the interior of the oval in each of the figures. The coordinate axes cut each other at the origin. The function $h(p)$ is affine and cuts the p-axis at the equilibrium value $\hat{p}$. The figures only differ with respect to the initial values of (p,q). It can be seen that the equilibrium is reached asymptotically regardless whether the initial values are inside or outside of D. In the latter case, however, p enters the negative region during the adjustment process.

[12] *Mathematica* is a registered trademark of Wolfram Research, Inc.

Fig. 4.1. The phase plane of (4.6).

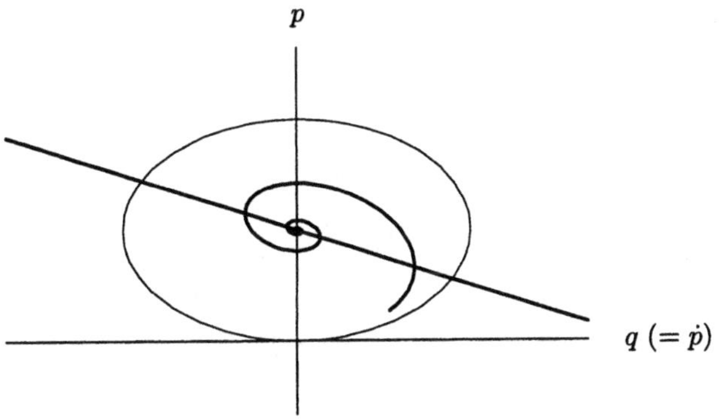

The function $h(p)$ which is affine in this example cuts the p-axis at the unique equilibrium $(\hat{p}, 0)$. If $h'(\hat{p}) < -1/4$, it is a stable spiral, and otherwise a stable node. (The eigenvalues of the matrix A of the linearized version of system (4.6) at the point $(\hat{p}, 0)$ are $\lambda_{1,2} = -1/2 \pm \sqrt{h'(\hat{p}) + 1/4}$. Damped cyclic behavior near the equilibrium can therefore be excluded by choosing g' sufficiently small.) The figure shows a stable spiral. The region enclosed by the oval belongs to the basin of attraction and is defined by $V(p,q) < l$, where $l = -\int_{\hat{p}}^{0} h(s)\, ds > 0$. The trajectory with initial value inside the oval asymptotically approaches $(\hat{p}, 0)$ without leaving the region of positive p-values. (This figure assumes the demand function to be $x = 10 - p$ and the cost function to be $K(x) = x^2$, leading to the profit function $\pi = f(p) = 30p - 2p^2 - 100$. If we choose the function g as $g(f'(p)) = f'(p)$, we get $h(p) = g(f'(p)) = 30 - 4p$.)

It should also be noted that the model offers an explanation for a damped oscillatory movement of the price around its equilibrium value in a monopolistic market, although these oscillations can in principle be excluded by choosing g' sufficiently small (cf. the annotation to Figure 4.1).

The simple rule of thumb formally represented by (4.6) is asymptotically stable and does not violate the positivity condition for p, at least for initial values in $D = \{(p,q) \in R^2 \;:\; V(p,q) < \int_0^{\hat{p}} h(s)\; ds\}$. In other words, a monopolistic firm that uses such a rule of thumb has a good chance to end up in the true optimum without knowing its own profit function. This statement makes it much easier to trust in the results of the simple neoclassical model of monopoly because it is not necessary to assume that the monopolist knows his profit function.

4.4 Concluding Remarks

We have justified the application of behavioral rules of thumb on the grounds of brain research. Specifically, we have shown that a simple rule of thumb

Fig. 4.2. The phase plane of (4.6).

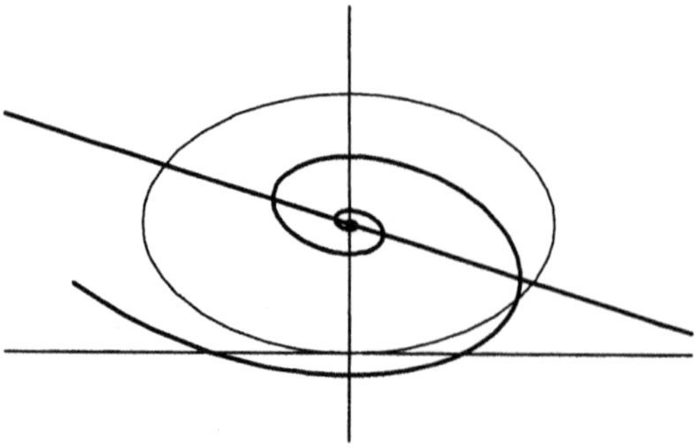

The only difference in comparison with Figure 4.1 is that the initial value of the considered trajectory lies outside the region defined by $V(p, q) < l$. Although the initial value of p is positive and the equilibrium is reached asymptotically, p enters the negative region during the adjustment process.

can be expected to lead to the true optimum of a monopolistic firm. Such results can raise the reliance on the implications of basic neoclassical models. Unfortunately, this model is only a first step considering its simple structure. Although it seems to be possible that similar results could be obtained for other static basic neoclassical market forms such as perfect and monopolistic competition or oligopoly, there is much less hope in formulating suitable rules of thumb for dynamic models. The reason is simple. On the one hand, in a static model we only have to look for some kind of method to find the roots of a (system of) equation(s). This approach resembles analogous mathematical procedures such as Newton's method, although the equations are known in the application of these methods while this is not the case for using a rule of thumb such as the one discussed here. On the other hand, the optimum in a dynamic model is not just a root of a system of equations but a solution of a system of differential equations that constitutes a boundary value problem, which is even difficult to approximate by a mathematical method if the underlying model is completely known. Part of this difficulty stems from the fact that the optimal paths usually are, at best, saddle paths. The slightest error in determining the correct initial values will take the proposed solution away from the optimum solution. Clearly, these problems are reinforced if the true model is unknown.

As Lettau and Uhlig (1999) have shown, agents who are endowed with several (exogenously given) competing rules including the dynamic programming solution may fail to learn that the latter is indeed the optimum rule. This result depends on the so-called *good state bias* in a stochastic environment. If the suboptimal rule is only applicable in good states, whereas the dynamic programming solution is always a possible alternative, it may happen that agents falsely learn that the suboptimal rule is superior. While their assumption on the applicability of several competing rules seems questionable, the results of Lettau and Uhlig (1999) nevertheless indicate that, in an explicitly dynamic setting, it is quite possible that agents choose other solutions than the dynamic programming solution, even if it is one of the given alternatives. The argument of our paper goes a step further. In many applications it seems to be very dubious whether the dynamic programming solution is among the given alternatives at all. Therefore, the implications of such solutions for positive economics could only be relied on, if it would be possible to approximate the optimum solution by some kind of a simple rule.

The Baumol and Quandt (1964) model also points out another important methodological fact. Even if we are looking at basically static models, a dynamic analysis may lead to important additional insights. Since it is likely that a producer does not know the demand schedule he faces, for example, we believe that the use of static models is only really justified after the introduction of additional dynamic considerations. (The reader will observe the resemblance of this argument to Samuelson's celebrated correspondence principle.) Advocates of the neoclassical rationality postulate may object that a quasi-dynamic interpretation of such a basically static model involves conceptual problems, because a static objective function is used in a dynamic setting. This overall problem of repeating static decision problems becomes more significant in the case of dynamic interactions of several suppliers, as in the market form of oligopoly. In view of the results of brain research as well as of other evidence from the literature on bounded rationality, however, it is very doubtful whether economic agents are in a position to formulate a dynamic decision problem accurately at all.

A systematic analysis of neoclassical standard models aiming at the derivation of behavioral rules of thumb that require only a small amount of information is still missing. In view of the importance of dynamic analysis also for analyzing static models of decision making and taking into account that there are many branches of economic theory that are inherently dynamic anyway, we conclude this paper with the observation that dynamic theory should be of central concern in economics now and in the future.

References

[1] Arrow, K. J. (1987). Economic Theory and the Hypothesis of Rationality. See Eatwell et al. (1987, pp. 69–75).

[2] Arthur, W. B. (1993). On Designing Economic Agents that Behave like Human Agents. *Journal of Evolutionary Economics 3*, 1–22.

[3] Baumol, W. J. and R. E. Quandt (1964). Rules of Thumb and Optimally Imperfect Decisions. *American Economic Review 54*, 23–46.

[4] Berk, J. B., E. Hughson, and K. Vandezande (1996). The Price is Right, But Are the Bids? An Investigation of Rational Decision Theory. *American Economic Review 86*(4), 954–970.

[5] Conlisk, J. (1996). Why Bounded Rationality? *Journal of Economic Literature 34*, 669–700.
[6] Day, R. H., S. Morley, and K. R. Smith (1974). Myopic Optimizing and Rules of Thumb in a Micro–Model of Industrial Growth. *American Economic Review 64*(1), 11–23.
[25] von Ditfurth, H. (1976). *Der Geist fiel nicht vom Himmel, Die Evolution unseres Bewußtseins.* Hamburg: Hoffmann und Campe. (reprint 1993).
[7] Eatwell, J., M. Milgate, and P. Newman (Eds.) (1987). *The New Palgrave, A Dictionary of Economics.* London: Macmillan.
[8] Ellison, G. and D. Fudenberg (1993). Rules of Thumb for Social Learning. *Journal of Political Economy 101*(4), 612–643.
[9] Etzioni, A. (1987). On Thoughtless Rationality (Rules of Thumb). *Kyklos 40*(4), 496–514.
[10] Faller, A. (1995). *Der Körper des Menschen, Einführung in Bau und Funktion, neubearbeitet von M. Schünke* (12 ed.). Stuttgart: Georg Thieme.
[11] Gandolfo, G. (1996). *Economic Dynamics* (3 ed.). Berlin: Springer.
[12] Krusell, P. and A. A. Smith, Jr. (1996). Rules of thumb in Macroeconomic Equilibrium: A Quantitative Analysis. *Journal of Economic Dynamics and Control 20*, 527–558.
[13] La Salle, J. and S. Lefschetz (1961). *Stability by Liapunov's Direct Method with Applications.* New York: Academic Press.
[14] Lettau, M. and H. Uhlig (1999). Rules of Thumb Versus Dynamic Programming. *American Economic Review 89*(1), 148–174.
[15] Lorenz, K. (1974). Die stammesgeschichtlichen Grundlagen menschlichen Verhaltens. In G. Heberer (Ed.), *Die Evolution der Organismen*, pp. 572–624. Stuttgart: Gustav Fischer.
[16] Lorenz, K. (1975). Evolution des Verhaltens. *Nova Acta Leopoldina, N. F. 42*(218), 271–290.
[17] Lorenz, K. (1980). *Die acht Todsünden der zivilisierten Menschheit* (11 ed.). München: Piper.
[18] Popper, K. R. and J. C. Eccles (1977). *The Self and Its Brain: An Argument for Interactionism.* Berlin: Springer. The enlarged German version has the title: Das Ich und sein Gehirn, 7. Aufl., München: Piper, 1987.
[19] Rosenthal, R. W. (1993). Rules of Thumb in Games. *Journal of Economic Behavior and Organization 22*, 1–13.
[20] Schütz, E., H. Caspers, and E.-J. Speckmann (1982). *Physiologie, Lehrbuch für Studierende* (16 ed.). München: Urban und Schwarzenberg.
[21] Sen, A. (1987). Rational Behavior. See Eatwell et al. (1987, pp. 68–76).
[22] Simon, H. A. (1955). A Behavioral Model of Rational Choice. *Quarterly Journal of Economics 69*, 99–118.
[23] Simon, H. A. (1957). *Models of Man.* New York: Wiley.
[24] Simon, H. A. (1979). *Models of Thought.* New Haven: Yale University Press.
[26] Will, H. C. U. (1998). *On the Interdependencies among Information, Organization, and Incentives.* Ph. D. dissertation, University of Bonn, Bonn.

5 Fairness, Power and their Relationship

Manfred J. Holler *

Abstract. The discussion of power measures and fairness concepts follows two isolated strings of thought that have rather different traditions. This paper argues that it is exactly this restriction that confuses the discussion. By making use of the theory of power indices and Binmore's theory of justice, this paper illustrates where the problems lie. The paper contains a brief introduction into the theory of power indices such as Shapley-Shubik, Banzhaf, and Deegan-Packel indices, as well as the Public Good Index and the member-MWC index. The monotonicity properties of these measures is analyzed, and it is demonstrated that these properties refer to implicit notions of fairness. In contrast, a critical examination of Binmore's theory of justice suggests that his theory is one of power, with bargaining power, threats, and reciprocity as the main constituents.

5.1 Two Strings of Discussion

Despite power being a catchword in the everyday description of economic relationships, it is a concept that has largely been neglected in economic theory. And while it seems almost impossible to talk about markets without reference to power, industrial organization theory offers but little guidance on the problem. In contrast, fairness has received some treatment in economic theory, although many economists are somewhat hesitant in applying the proposed concepts in the evaluation of economic policies. Moreover, the everyday discussion of fairness – especially with regard to labor relations and social policy reform – does not in general refer to the concepts which economic theory and modern social philosophy developed with such great ambition. This state of affairs obviously calls for more profound research, as it would seem that power and fairness are of equivalent importance for explaining and shaping social interaction as are preferences and efficiency in a more traditional context.

A look at the literature shows that there appears to have been a growing interest in the problems of fairness and power over the last ten years. The increasing number of publications on power indices and their application, and the huge success of Ken Binmore's two recent volumes, *Playing Fair* and *Just Playing* (1994, 1998), illustrate this development. Yet, while the research in these two areas has followed quite different traditions, a closer look reveals that the problems and solutions are closely related – or even inseparably intertwined.

---

* The author wrote the first draft of this paper while he was Malmsten Visiting Professor at the University of Gothenburg, Sweden.

One explanation for why there has been two different and isolated strands to the discussion is perhaps related to the fact that there is neither a straightforward definition of power nor of fairness, which would allow us to combine these two concepts. This paper, however, proposes that it is exactly this restriction that is a source of confusion in the discussion.

In the following pages I will try to illustrate this hypothesis by making use, on the one hand, of the theory of power indices, and Binmore's theory of justice,[1] on the other. The following section contains a brief introduction to power indices. Readers who are familiar with the Shapley-Shubik, Banzhaf, and Deegan-Packel, as well as the Public Good and member-MWC indices can skip this section. In section 5.3, I explain why the discussion has significantly increased during the last decade. In section 5.4, I discuss how this development is related to the problem of fairness and show its relationship to the problem of monotonicity. In section 5.5, I present a critical outline of Binmore's theory of justice, and discuss it with respect to power, inasmuch as bargaining power and reciprocity are its constituents. Section 5.6 relates the monotonicity discussion to the bargaining arguments in Binmore's approach to operationalize fairness.

The essence of the paper is as follows. If we accept the nonmonotonicity results of the power measures and of the bargaining underlying Binmore's theory, and conclude that they indicate structural problems of collective decision making, then we need to try to answer the following questions: (a) What is the cause of the nonmonotonicity results? (b) Can (and should) we restructure social interaction (i.e. society and its institutions) such that the monotonicity is not likely to prevail; (c) Can we accept nonmonotonicity from an alternative perspective, e.g. a wiggish[2] political-philosophical position.

5.2 A Brief Review of Selected Power Indices

This section[3] discusses five power indices: the Shapley-Shubik index (SSI), the Banzhaf index (BI); the Deegan-Packel index (DPI); and the Public Good Index (PGI); and variant of the PGI, the member-MWC-index. These indices have been selected because (a) they have all been fully axiomatized, (b) they represent four different ideas about power and coalition formation, and (c) they satisfy different monotonicity properties. Perhaps one should add that SSI and BI are by far the most popular measures in terms of application.

We will apply these measures to voting games. In this application, the notion of power seems more obvious than in other social situations: it is about

[1] This, of course, is a reference to Rawls (1972) and is supposed to summarize (a possible interpretation of) Binmore's *Playing Fair* and *Just Playing*.

[2] Wiggishness refers to Binmore's political-philosophical position as an English liberal in contrast to the conservative Tories, on the one hand, and the Socialists, on the other hand.

[3] This section is derived from Holler and Widgrén (1999).

winning and losing in voting decisions. The *a priori* voting power results from relationship of the number of votes (i.e. voting weights) and the majority rule (i.e., decision rule) and abstracts from the preferences of the decision-makers. For example, take the voting game $v = (d; w)$ where d represents the majority rule and $w = (w_1, \ldots, w_i, \ldots, w_n)$ describes the voting weights. The sum of the voting weights over all players is 1. A coalition S is a winning coalition if

$$\sum_{i \in S} w_i \geq d \tag{5.1}$$

and it is losing if (5.1) is not satisfied for S. If S is winning, we assign a value 1 to S such that, $v(S) = 1$ and define $v(S) = 0$ if S is losing. Thus, v defines a *simple game.*

We say that player i has a *swing* for coalition S if i can turn S from a winning coalition into a losing one by leaving S. Formally, i is a *swinger* with respect to S if

$$v(S) = 1 \qquad \text{and} \qquad v(S \setminus \{i\}) = 0. \tag{5.2}$$

It is generally accepted that i exerts power in this case. A coalition with at least one *swing player* is called minimum winning coalition (MWC).[4]

The following five measures elaborate on this assumption. They are specified by the coalitions, S, which they take into consideration and about the values which they assign to swing voters.

5.2.1 The Shapley-Shubik Index (SSI)

The SSI is not only the pioneer in the history of power indices, but also serves as a point of reference for the great variety of measures that have since been developed. It is derived from the *Shapley value* proposed in Shapley (1953) as solution concept for cooperative games. Shapley and Shubik (1954) apply this concept to voting games.

The SSI is based on the concept of a *pivot player* which is a special type of swinger. The qualification derives from the specific assumption about coalition formation, i.e. the probability of a coalition to form. For a simple (and proper) game (N, v) the following definition holds:

Definition 1. Player i is *pivotal* if i turns a coalition $S \setminus \{i\}$, which consists of the first $s-1$ elements of an ordering, into a winning coalition S by joining coalition $S \setminus \{i\}$ such that i is the sth element of coalition S. The expression #pivots(i) counts the number of orderings for which i is a pivotal member (i.e. permutations of the elements of the set of payers N).

[4] However, this term is often reserved for coalitions which have *only* swing players, see Widgrén (2000). Below we will define such a coalition to be a minimal decisive coalition (MDC).

Then the SSI is a vector $\Phi(v) = (\Phi_1(v), ..., \Phi_n(v))$ with components defined as

$$\Phi_i(v) = \frac{\#\text{pivots}(i)}{\sum_{j \in N} \#\text{pivots}(j)} \tag{5.3}$$

The value #pivots(i) is specified by:

- (a) the probability that i is pivotal, i.e. that i is in the position to turn a winning coalition into a losing one - or a losing coalition into a winning one - and,
- (b) the normalization of $v(S)$ which implies that $v(S) - v(S \setminus \{i\}) = 1$ if S is a winning coalition and $S \setminus \{i\}$ is a losing one.

Given that all permutations of n players are equal likely, the probability that i is pivotal, is given by:

$$\frac{(s-1)!(n-s)!}{n!} \tag{5.4}$$

where s is the cardinal number of coalition S, i.e. the size of the membership of S, and n is the cardinality of the set of players n. The factorial $n! = 1 * 2 * \cdots * n$ expresses the total number of permutations which can be formed out of an ordered set of n players. Thus, the probability of a specific permutation is 1/n!. Note that each permutation has *one and only one* pivotal player.

Combining (5.3) and (5.4) it follows that SSI is a vector $\Phi(v) = (\Phi_1(v), \ldots, \Phi_n(v))$ such that

$$\Phi_i(v) = \sum_{\substack{S \ni i \\ S \subset N}} \frac{(s-1)!(n-s)!}{n!} [v(S) - v(S \setminus \{i\})] \tag{5.5}$$

That is, to calculate $\Phi_i(v)$ we look at all subsets S of N which have i as an element and ask, for each such S, (a) whether S is a winning coalition and, if *yes*, (b) whether i can turn a winning coalition into a losing coalition by defecting from S. If the answer is again *yes*, then we get $v(S) - v(S \setminus \{i\}) = 1$ for the specific S. Next, we take into account that the SSI is based on orderings and apply (5.4). Finally, we sum the resulting product (of the probability that i is pivotal and the value of i being pivotal) over all subsets S of N which have i as an element.

It is obvious from (5.5) that the SSI values sum up to 1 if the sum is over all players $i \in N$ and for each i over all coalitions which have S as a member. This sum is expressed by the denominator $n!$ of (5.5). Thus we have:

$$\sum_{i \in N} \Phi_i(v) = 1 \tag{5.6}$$

The summation of SSI values to 1. This result is implicit to the definition of the index, and is not the result of an explicit normalization as in other indices that we discuss below. It stems from the fact that each permutation is characterized by exactly one pivotal player.

Example 1. Given a weighted voting game $v^* = (d; w) = (55; 50, 30, 20)$. The set of permutations has $n! = 6$ elements. Player 1, who is characterized by voting weight $w_1 = 50$, is the pivot element of 4 permutations while players 2 and 3 are pivot elements of only one permutation each. The SSI of (N, v^*) therefore is: $\Phi(v^*) = (2/3, 1/6, 1/6)$.

It is not easy to intuitively justify the application of orderings when only coalitions, i.e. unordered sets, seem to matter. This is all the more because as each permutation is taken into account with equal probability, this gives unequal weights to coalitions that have different numbers of members. There are 2^n coalitions which correspond to a set of players of n members, including the null coalition and the grand coalition, while only n! permutations can be derived from this set. The classical story to justify the focus on permutations, given in Shapley and Shubik (1954), is an illustrative bargaining model. It assumes that those players with stronger preferences to form a winning coalition S enter the coalition formation process first, followed by players with weaker preferences. Therefore, the pivotal player i, the last player in the sequence who turns a losing coalition $S \setminus \{i\}$ into a winning coalition S by joining $S \setminus \{i\}$ is the member of S with the weakest preferences concerning this coalition (or its performance). Nevertheless, it is assumed that i will get the undivided coalition value $[v(S) - v(S \setminus \{i\})] = 1$, because the members of $S \setminus \{i\}$ will get "nothing" if i does not join them. The undivided coalition cake thus goes to the pivotal player. However, since no specific information on preferences is given with respect to the various winning coalitions $S \subset N$, all permutations of n players are considered. This amounts to saying that i is only with a certain probability, expressed by (5.4), in the pivotal position with respect to coalition S in which i is a member.

It should be mentioned that alternative and perhaps more convincing stories could be told to justify the SSI, e.g., the probabilistic approach in Straffin (1977).[5] It should, however, be added that Shapley and Shubik (1954, p. 790) themselves considered the arranging of the voters in all possible orderings to be "just a convenient conceptual device".

To conclude we will present:

Example 2. Given a weighted voting game $v' = (d; w) = (55; 51, 48, 1)$. The set of permutations has $n! = 6$ elements. Players 1 and 2, who are characterized by voting weights $w_1 = 51$ and $w_2 = 48$ are the pivot element of 3 permutations each while player 1 is no pivot element. The SSI of (N, v^*) therefore is: $\Phi(v') = (1/2, 1/2, 0)$.

[5] See Widgrén (1995) for an application of the probabilistic approach to the power analysis of the EU Council of Ministers and Owen (1995) for a formal treatment.

A comparison of v^* and v' and $\Phi(v^*)$ and $\Phi(v')$ shows that, going from v^* and v', player 1 loses power although his voting weight increases from 50 to 51.

5.2.2 Banzhaf Index (BI)

The non-normalized Banzhaf index[6] of player i is defined by the number of i's swings divided by the number of coalitions which have i as a member. (The latter number is 2^{n-1} if the number of players is n.)

$$\beta_i'(v) = \frac{\#\text{swings}(i)}{\#\text{coalitions}(i)} = \frac{\#\text{swings}(i)}{2^{n-1}} \tag{5.7}$$

The *normalized* version of the Banzhaf index is:

$$\beta_i(v) = \frac{\#\text{swings}(i)}{\sum\limits_{j\in N} \#\text{swings}(j)} \qquad \text{so that} \qquad \sum_{i\in N} \beta_i(v) = 1 \tag{5.8}$$

$$\text{Obviously,} \quad \beta_i(v) = \frac{\beta_i'(v)}{\sum_{j\in N} \beta_j'(v)}$$

Example 3. Given the weighted voting game $v^* = (d; w) = (55; 50, 30, 20)$ of example 1 above. The (normalized) *Banzhaf index* of $(N, v*)$ is $\beta(v*) = (3/5, 1/5, 1/5)$.

Example 4. Given the weighted voting game $v' = (d; w) = (55; 51, 48, 1)$ of example 1 above. The (normalized) *Banzhaf index* of (N, v^*) is $\beta(v^*) = (1/2, 1/2, 0)$.

Again, a comparison of v^* and v' and $\beta(v^*)$ and $\beta(v')$ shows that, going from v^* to v', player 1 loses power although his voting weight increases from 50 to 51.

5.2.3 The Deegan-Packel Index (DPI)

The *Deegan-Packel index* $\rho(v)$, introduced in Deegan and Packel (1979), is based on $M(v)$, the set of *minimal decisive coalitions* (MDC) - also called the *decisive set.*

Definition 2. $M(v)$, the set of *minimal decisive coalitions* (MDC) - also called *strict minimum winning coalitions* - is defined such that

$$M(v) = \{S \subseteq N | v(S) = 1 \text{ and } v(T) = 0 \text{ if } T \subset S \text{ and } T \neq S\} \tag{5.9}$$

[6] The basic idea of this measure is proposed in Banzhaf (1965) and Coleman (1971). Earlier it has been discussed by Lionel Penrose (see Felsenthal and Machover (1998b)).

In other words, if S is a winning coalition and any coalition T, which is a true subset of S, is a losing coalition, then S is an MDC and thus an element of $M(v)$. That is, all members of coalition S are crucial for S to be winning. S does not contain *surplus players*.

The DPI index assumes that the members of a minimal decisive coalition S share the coalition value $v(S)$ such that each member of S receives a value $v(S)/s$, where s is the number of members of S. Of course, if v is a simple game then $v(S) = 1$. The $v(S)/s$ values of a player i will be summed for all S, which have i as a member, and divided by $1/|M(v)|$, where $|M(v)|$ is the total number of minimal decisive coalitions. We get

$$\rho_i(v) = \frac{1}{|M(v)|} \sum_{\substack{S \ni i \\ S \in M(v)}} \frac{1}{s} \tag{5.10}$$

The multiplier $1/|M(v)|$ assures us that $\sum_i \rho_i(v) = 1$ holds. A probabilistic interpretation of $\rho_i(v)$ is straightforward. It is implicit in (5.10) that each $S \in M(v)$ is formed with equal probability and the payoff of $i \in S$ is $1/s$. Then the expected value of i equals $\rho_i(v)$.

Example 5. Given a weighted voting game $v' = (d; w) = (51; 35, 20, 15, 15, 15)$. Then the DPI of (N, v^*) is

$$\rho(v') = \left(\frac{18}{60}, \frac{9}{60}, \frac{11}{60}, \frac{11}{60}, \frac{11}{60}\right).$$

Although player 2 has the second largest voting weight it has a smaller power value than players 3, 4, or 5. That is, the DPI is *not* monotonic in voting weights, i.e. it violates *local monotonicity*.[7]

5.2.4 The Public Good Index (PGI)

The *Public Good Index*[8] is based on the concept of *minimal decisive coalitions* (MDC). This specification is supported by the fact that the coalition value is considered to be a public good. If the players in a winning coalition consider the value $v(S) = 1$ as a public good, there should be no *rivalry in consumption* and each member of S will enjoy this value if the coalition is formed. Further, in absence of entry or transaction costs of coalition formation, S will be formed - given that S is a coalition in $M(v)$ so that no possibility of free-riding exists.

Nonrivalry in consumption and the *exclusion of free-riding* are the core elements from which the public good index is derived.

[7] A formal definition of local monotonicity is given in section 5.4 below.

[8] This index has been introduced in Holler (1982) and axiomatized in Holler and Packel (1983). In a recent publication Napel (1999a) completes the axiomatization.

Definition 3. Let $c_i(v)$ express the *decisiveness* of player i, i.e., the number of coalitions S so that $S \in M(v)$ and $i \in S$ in the simple game (N, v). Then the value of the Public Good Index (PGI) for player i is defined by

$$h_i(v) = \frac{c_i(v)}{\sum_{j=1}^{n} c_j(v)} \qquad \text{so that } \sum_{i=1}^{n} h_i(v) = 1 \tag{5.11}$$

If S is not an MDC then it is assumed that, because of the potential of free-riding, it will only be formed by "luck"[9] - and not because of the power of its members - or that the outcome of S is *identical* with a $T \subset S$, and T is an MDC. In the latter interpretation, it leads to double counting, if S is taken into consideration.

If the power of the coalitions in the set $M(v)$ are assumed to be equal, then we can conclude that the larger the number c_i of MDCs of which i is a member, the larger will be i's power in the game. This number, however, is not monotonic in voting weights, i.e. it also violates *local monotonicity.* This is demonstrated in the following example, taken from Holler (1982).

Example 6. Given the vote distribution $w = (35, 20, 15, 15, 15)$ and a decision rule $d = 51$, the corresponding values of PGI are equal to:

$$h(v') = \left(\frac{16}{60}, \frac{8}{60}, \frac{12}{60}, \frac{12}{60}, \frac{12}{60}\right).$$

Note that it is not always the case that the DPI and PGI show identical results for identical games. An example would be the voting game.

Because of the *basic principles* underlying the PGI (nonrivalry in consumption and exclusion of free-riding) it is obvious that only minimal decisive coalitions (i.e. strict minimum winning coalitions) should be considered when it comes to measuring power. All other coalitions are either nonwinning or contain at least one member which does not contribute to winning. If coalitions of the second type are formed, then it is by luck, similarity of preferences, tradition, etc. - *but not because of power.* It should be noted that the PGI does not maintain that only minimal decisive coalitions will be formed.

5.2.5 The member-MWC Index

In a recent publication, Brams and Fishburn (1995) present a member-MWC index, which is *formally identical* to the PGI.[10] The member-MWC index assumes that only strict minimal decisive coalitions, i.e. MDCs, *will form.* Correspondingly, the member-MWC index can be used to express expectations.

[9] For an explicit distinction of power and luck, see Barry (1980).

[10] For a further elaboration of the member-MWC index, see Fishburn and Brams (1996). For a discussion of the relationship of member-MWC indexand PGI, see Holler (1998).

This is clearly different from the story behind the PGI, and the interpretation of power which is derived from it suggests that only minimal decisive coalitions should be *considered* if the coalition value is a public good.

Brams and Fishburn apply the member-MWC index to *categories* of member-MWC (i.e. minimal decisive coalitions). In this context, a category is a set of member-MWC that can be derived from a specific stylized game: there exist voting weights for each player that yield exactly the MDCs which form the category. For example, in the case of $n = 3$ players with $N = \{1, 2, 3\}$ and an order of voting weights $w_1 \geq w_2 \geq w_3$, there exist two vectors of "feasible weights", i.e. (2,1,1) and (1,1,1), which summarize the coalition formation possibilities. Alternative weight distributions create identical sets of member-MWCs for $n = 3$. Vector (2,1,1) implies category $\{\{1,2\},\{1,3\}\}$ and vector (1,1,1) implies category $\{\{1,2\},\{1,3\},\{2,3\}\}$. In total, there are five member-MWCs describing the case $n = 3$; player 1 is member in four member-MWCs while players 2 and 3 are members in three member-MWCs. The *member bargaining power* (M_i) of players $i = 1, 2$, and 3 is therefore $M_1 = 4/5$, $M_2 = 3/5$, and $M_3 = 3/5$ or $m = (0.4, 0.3, 0.3)$ if normalized such that index numbers m_i sum to 1.

Obviously, member-MWCs enter the calculation of member bargaining power M_i with equal weights. This can be considered as a problem because, given simple majority voting, category $\{\{1,2\},\{1,3\}\}$ is valid only if the voting weight of player 1 equals the sum of the voting weights of players 2 and 3. In general, it seems more likely that a vote distribution concurs with "feasible weights" (1,1,1) and the category $\{\{1,2\},\{1,3\},\{2,3\}\}$. The number of possible categories rapidly increases with the number of players. In the case of 6 players, 116 categories have to be analyzed. The results show that an inverse relationship between weight and bargaining power cannot be excluded if the number of players is larger than 4.

The different stories behind the member-MWC index and the PGI demonstrate that it is not enough to apply a specific index. We have to decide what to measure in order to give an adequate interpretation of the result.

5.3 Trends in Power Index Theory and its Applications

In recent years, publications on power indices and coalition formation have multiplied. The application of power indices to political institutions, more specifically, to the analysis of the European Union, has become increasingly popular. And it should be noted that there are also new theoretical instruments and perspectives that support these applications. In the first place, there is the probabilistic model of coalition formation, which is made operational by the multilinear extension of the characteristic function form of coalition games. This instrument triggered off a reinterpretation of existing power indices[11] and the formulation of new ones. This development is accompanied by an intensive discussion of the concept of power in general - what do we measure when we apply power measures? - and the properties that an adequate measure of power has to satisfy. In this discussion the various monotonicity properties which the alternative power indices do or do not satisfy, play an important role. For a number of authors, some monotonicity properties are inseparably related to their specific notion of power.

Details of this discussion and its relationship with the fairness problem will be postponed to the next section. Instead we need to have a closer look at the fact that there is an increased tendency towards weighted voting in committees. Yet, there is the widely shared intuition that voting weights are a poor proxy for the impact that the various decision-makers have on the outcome. Nevertheless, weighted voting has been applied in presidential elections in the United States (see the pioneering study of Shapley and Shubik (1954)), in the United Nation's Security Council (see, again, Shapley and Shubik (1954), and Coleman (1971)), and in the governing board of the International Monetary Fund (see Dreyer and Schotter (1980)), as well as in various second chambers of federal systems, e.g., the *Bundesrat* of the Federal Republic of Germany (see König and Bräuninger (1996) for a recent study). Indeed, most parliaments in western democracies operate like weighted voting, given the strong links of its members to party factions and of the party factions to coalitions. But it was the Council of Ministers of European Union and its status in the EU decision-making process that brought weighted voting on a more general research agenda. There are numerous publications related to EU decision making which give evidence of this development.

Interestingly, it seems that these studies have come to the attention of a wider audience and are even apparently read by a number of politicians. It also seems that there are researchers who apply power indices with technocratic or emancipating tendencies – the kind who attempt to engineer or stimulate informed change of political institutions instead of being confined to the "ivory tower". In this vein, Johnston (2000) strongly argues that researchers of power indices should ensure that this research informs debates about the structure in which political life is played-out. And in this regard, the EU arena is a fascinating playground. König and Bräuninger (2000) study the intergovernmental choice of European voting rules with respect to the interaction of the Commission, the Council of Ministers and the European Parliament. The study focuses on an absolute notion of power that takes into consideration the *inclusion* of member states in winning coalitions under various voting rules.

The growing importance of weighted voting, especially in relation to the implementation of the 1987 EU Single Act and the 1997 Treaty of Maastricht

[11] Straightforward probabilistic interpretations of the Shapley value and the non-normalized Banzhaf index are already given in Shapley (1953) and Dubey and Shapley (1979), respectively

seems to be the reason why a younger generation of researchers dedicates so much effort to theoretical and applied work in this area. Much of this work is characterized by a straightforward application of power indices to the analysis of voting bodies (such as the Council of Ministers) and the effects of institutional changes as reflected by new decision rules and changes in the vote distribution. This approach carries over to discussing the effects of alternative institutional settings, in the tradition of *mechanism design*, and flows into propositions of institutional reform. We have also, therefore, started to speak of *institutional design*, something which Shapley and Shubik (1954, p. 791) were aware of: "power index computations may be useful in the setting up of norms or standards, the departure from which will serve as a measure of, for example, political solidarity, or regional or sociological factionalism, in an assembly."

Yet, it should not be ignored that there is fair amount of opposition to the application of power indices. Garrett and Tsebelis[12] have repeatedly argued that their use in evaluating power in the European Union is inappropriate on the grounds that they ignore preferences. If we look, however, at the EU Council of Ministers, which consists of representatives of 15 member states, then it is far from clear as to (a) what their preferences are and, (b) what their preferences will be in the near future. Without doubt, these preferences depend on national factors such government popularity and election results. If we recall the 1957 Treaty of Rome, on the one hand, and consider the expected extension of the EU in the not-too-far-off future, on the other, it remains uncertain who in fact is playing the EU voting game. The assumptions, therefore, of specific preferences appears rather dubious. In this and other cases of analyses of *institutional design*, it seems more natural to rely on power measure that abstracts from specific preferences in order to distill some general results on the power relations at work within the EU decision-making body.

This is not to deny that some preferences are more likely than others for a given problem at a specified time. This seems to be relevant if we want to derive expectations on decisions and not analyze institutions. Hosli (2000) takes preferences of EU members into account and analyzes the power distribution on the basis of likely coalitions. Her paper provides calculations of the normalized Banzhaf index and the Shapley-Shubik index for connected coalitions.

Nurmi, Meskanen, and Pajala (2000) analyze the power in the EU Council of Ministers "in the spirit of the voter calculus outlined by Buchanan and Tullock in their *Calculus of Consent*". They conclude EU enlargement will, *ceteris paribus,* lead to a fractionalization and loss of the collectivity to act.

Laruelle and Widgrén (2000) quantify the extent to which the development of decision-making procedures in the EU has changed the division of

[12] See, e.g., Garrett and Tsebelis (1996, 1999) and Tsebelis and Garrett (1996, 1997). See also Holler and Widgrén (1999b) for a comment.

power among its main organs: the Council of Ministers, the Commission, and the European Parliament. They use probabilistic measures of a priori voting power in order to analyze the dynamics of the EU voting process, implied by the alternative decision procedures such as consultation, cooperation, and co-decision, as a sequence of cooperative games.

This study is an example of the research which benefits from the probabilistic interpretation of power indices based on the multilinear extension of the characteristic function form of coalition games. The multilinear extension concept was introduced in Owen (1972) and first applications are contained in Straffin (1977, 1988) and Owen (1975). It triggered off a re-interpretation of existing power indices, the formulation of new indices, and, more recently, a series of applications[13] and also further theoretical work. The standard result with respect to voting power is that the Shapley-Shubik index is adequate if voters are homogeneous and vote "yes" with equal probabilities and these probabilities are uniformly distributed on the interval $[0, 1]$. The Banzhaf index applies if voters are independent and each has an expected value of 0.5 to vote "yes". If some voters are homogeneous and others are independent, then we have a case of partial homogeneity and the application of a partial homogeneity index, which is a combination of SSI and BI, seems adequate.

An example for recent theoretical work is Widgrén (2000) which analyzes the probabilistic relationship of the PGI, h_i, and the normalized BI, β_i. Widgrén demonstrates that the normalized BI index can be written as a linear function of the PGI such that

$$\beta_i = (1 - \pi)h_i + \pi\varepsilon_i \qquad (5.12)$$

where $(1 - \pi)$ represents the share of minimal decisive coalitions (MDC), i.e. strict minimum winning coalitions (see (5.9) above), compared to all MWCs, i.e. coalitions that contain at least one swinger; and ϵ_i expresses the share of minimum winning coalitions which have i as a member, but are not strict, compared to the number of all MWCs which are not strict, i.e. which are not in the set $M(v)$ defined by (5.9), but contain at least one swing player. Obviously, the larger these two shares the more β_i and h_i deviate from each other.

Widgrén interprets the part of the function that is independent of the PGI, $\pi\epsilon_i$, as an expression of a special type of luck in the sense of Barry (1980). If the institutional setting is such that minimal winning coalitions form which are not strictly minimal, and the corresponding coalition goods are produced, then the normalized BI seems an appropriate measure and, at least, local monotonicity is guaranteed with respect to the power to influence the outcome. This implies that the institutions are such that the fundamental free-rider problem (of which the PGI takes care) does not apply. There is a large set of enforcement mechanisms available—the Groves Mechanism[14] is

[13] See, e.g., Widgrén (1994, 1995).
[14] See Green and Laffont (1979).

one—that constrain incentives for free-riding. In general, it is assumed that these mechanisms are designed and implemented by public agents (i.e. the state). An iteration of the decision situation "with unforeseeable end" such that the Folk Theorem applies could have similar effects. If, however, the institutional setting does not support the formation of coalitions with surplus players, and thus allow for MDCs only, then $\pi = 0$, the constrained normalized BI ends up giving the same results as the PGI. As consequence, this version of BI satisfies neither global nor local monotonicity.

5.4 The Monotonicity Discussion

The increasing interest in the application of power measures and the emergence of both new indices or variants of established ones is, perhaps, the main reason for the very intensive debate about the adequacy of the measures and what properties disqualify an index as measure of power. Needless to say, this has once again triggered off the discussion about the nature of power. And here, monotonicity seems to be the decisive property separating the adequate from the inadequate measures.[15] Yet, there are numerous concepts of monotonicity, and the relationship between these concepts cannot always be brought into a hierarchical order. In this regard, Turnovec (1998) discusses various indices with respect to the following concepts of *monotonicity* applied to weighted voting games.

Definition 4. A power index $\pi(v) = (\pi_1(v), \ldots, \pi_n(v))$ satisfies *local monotonicity* for voting games of type $v = (d, w)$ if $w_i > w_j$ implies $\pi_i \geq \pi_j$.

Definition 5. A power index $\pi(v) = (\pi_1(v), \ldots, \pi_n(v))$ satisfies *global monotonicity* for voting games if given two voting games $v^* = (d, w^*)$ and $v' = (d, w')$ such that $w_i' > w_i^*$ and $w_j^* \geq w_j'$ for all j implies $\pi_i' \geq \pi_i^*$.

If a measure fails to satisfy global monotonicity, then the Donation Paradox applies: a player can increase his power value by giving away votes (i.e. reducing his voting weight).[16]

The main results of Turnovec's study are that the SSI satisfies both local and global monotonicity properties, the normalized BI satisfies only local monotonicity, while the PGI satisfies neither local nor global monotonicity. The latter result follows straightforwardly from example 5 and applies also for the DPI as we can see from example 4 above.

A comparison of the monotonicity properties of various indices also forms the heart of a recent book by Felsenthal and Machover (1998b). As a consequence of these kind of studies, we have more substantial information on the properties of power indices than we had before. However, these studies

[15] See, e.g., Felsenthal and Machover (1995), Felsenthal, Machover, and Zwicker (1998), Freixas and Gambarelli (1997) and Machover (1999).

[16] See Felsenthal and Machover (1995), (1998b, p. 252).

also inspired us to ask about the properties of power and the social outcome that is related to it, e.g. whether the social outcome is a public good that satisfies properties of nonrivalry in consumption and nonexclusiveness; or is it a club good that offers nonrivalry to members of the group and excludes nonmembers from consumption; or is a private good which has to be distributed before consumption. In the latter case, bargaining plays a major role. Our hypothesis is that the more important the role of bargaining, the stronger is the demand for monotonicity because monotonicity reflects the requirement of fairness. So it is useless worrying that the PGI satisfies not even local monotonicity.

Technically speaking the PGI's nonmonotonicity results from the fact that it takes exclusively *strict* minimum winning coalitions, i.e. minimal decisive coalitions (MDCs) as defined in (5.9), into consideration. Levínský and Silárszky (2000) discuss an index that builds on the idea of bargaining and consequently considers decisive sets with minimal numbers of members only. This index satisfies *local monotonicity* and even *global monotonicity*. Moreover, it is identical to an index that has been independently introduced by Napel and Widgrén (1999). They also give an axiomatization of this measure that is based on the concept of inferior players, i.e. players who can be played off by potential coalition partners as they mutually underbid themselves in order to have some influence on the outcome. This study, as many others, shows that axioms and (monotonicity) properties as well as assumptions on coalition formation are not independent from each other, and that axioms and properties are often close substitutes. Thus, rankings of the various power indices which are based on axioms or satisfying the various monotonicity properties have to be taken up with care, and do not always give an adequate answer to question of the "right index".[17]

Furthermore, we do not know of any study that systematically discusses the properties of *distribution* of resources that guarantees that the local monotonicity property is satisfied - analogously to global monotonicity and the constraints it implies for changes in the distribution of voting weights.[18] Obviously, if there are n voters and $n-2$ voters are dummies, then the local monotonicity property will not be violated by any of the known power measures, including the DPI and the PGI. Further, it follows from the studies of Brams and Fishburn (1995) and Fishburn and Brams (1996) that the PGI does not violate local monotonicity when the number of players is not larger than $n = 4$ and the (voting) game is decisive. The same result seems to hold for the DPI. So we can conclude that neither the PGI nor the DPI violates a constrained local monotonicity definition that considers voting games with a maximum of four non-dummy players only.

---

[17] This refers to "Power, Luck and the Right Index", Holler and Packel (1983). See also Nurmi (1998, p. 172–176) and Nurmi, Meskanen, and Pajala (2000).

[18] There is work in progress on *constrained monotonicity*, see Holler, Ono, and Steffen (1999).

It is of note that the PGI satisfies a monotonicity property that the SSI and the BI do not: if player i is in more strict minimal winning coalitions than player j, then the power value of i is larger than the power value of j. Whether this is an important property, I do not know. Obviously this monotonicity property is similar to *price monotonicity* property proposed by Felsenthal and Machover (1998a). This property says that the power value of i is larger than that of j if and only if the number of winning coalitions which are minimal with respect to i is larger than the number of winning coalitions which are minimal with respect to j. Needless to say, the BI index satisfies this monotonicity property while the SSI, DPI, and PGI do not.

When it comes to monotonicity of power with respect to voting weights, it is important to note that none of the existing measures guarantees that the power measure of a player i will *not* decrease if the voting weight of i increases. Fischer and Schotter (1978) demonstrate this result (i.e., the *paradox of redistribution*) for the SSI and the normalized BI. The paradox stresses the fact that power is a social concept: if we discuss the power of an individual member of a group in isolation from his or her social context, we may experience all sorts of paradoxical results. Sociologists appear to be quite aware of this problem and nonmonotonicity of an individual's power with respect to his or her resources comes as no surprise to them (see, e.g., Caplow (1968)).

Machover (1999) writes in his forthcoming critique of Holler and Widgrén (1999a): "Any mathematical measure of voting power must be based on some intuitive pre-formal notion of what voting power is. A given measure can be considered reasonable only if it passes two kinds of test. First, the underlying preformal notion must be reasonable and coherent. Second, the mathematical properties of the measure must be reasonable for the intuitive notion it supposed to formalize." In Felsenthal and Machover (1998b) we read: " ... to say that a given index of voting power suffers from a paradox in the strongest sense is tantamount to saying that that index fails to satisfy an intuitively compelling condition, and is therefore ineligible as a reasonable measure of voting power" (p.196).

I have discussed power measures and intuition elsewhere Holler3 (1984)). A possible response to Machover's position is the following, lifted from the classic Ayer (1936), *Language Truth and Logic* – in this case substituting "geometry" for "power index theory": " ... while the view that pure geometry is concerned with physical space was plausible enough in Kant's days, when the geometry of Euclid was the only geometry known, the subsequent invention of non-Euclidean geometries has shown it to be mistaken. We see now that the axioms of geometry are simply definitions, and that the theorems of a geometry are simply the logical consequences of these definitions. A geometry is not in itself about physical space; in itself it cannot be said to be 'about' anything. But we can use a geometry to reason about physical space. That is to say, once we have given the axioms a physical interpretation, we can proceed to apply the theorems to the objects which satisfy the axioms. Whether a geometry can be applied to the actual physical world or not, is an empirical question which falls outside the scope of the geometry itself. There is no sense, therefore, in asking which of the various geometries known to us are false and which are true. In so far as they are all free from contradiction, they are all true. The proposition which states that a certain application of a geometry is possible is not itself a proposition of that geometry" (Ayer, 971, p.110).

An alternative reaction is to clarify the social situations in which monotonicity matters and then to discuss the kind of monotonicity that is of importance. Needless to say, an adequate concept of fairness could be of great help in solving these problems. For example, if a player loses power although he gains resources (i.e. votes) then this seems inherently unfair. Now, either power is an "unfair social relation" or the power measure is inadequate. What, however, is a fair social relation? In order to answer the question, we will take a look at Ken Binmore's theory of justice published as *Playing Fair* (1994) and *Just Playing* (1998).

5.5 Theory of Justice or Theory of Power

Let me first briefly summarize Binmore's rather complex theory, with the risk that I may be too selective, somewhat subjective, and over-simplified.[19] Binmore's theory builds up on two metaphors: the *Game of Life* and the *Game of Morals.* The rules of the *Game of Life* are determined by physical, biological, and other context-specific constraints and cannot be changed by individual players. In the *Game of Life,* people (i.e., the members of the society under consideration) interact with infinite time horizon or unforeseeable end. The Folk Theorem tells us that there exist multiple equilibria and the (social) problem is to select an efficient one and to coordinate social behavior accordingly. Binmore argues that - in the medium run - people solve this equilibrium selection problem by face-to-face bargaining that results in a self-enforcing outcome (and can be described by a Rubinstein game[20]).

In the short run, however, people will apply a fairness norm in order to avoid bargaining costs. The fairness norm is the result of the *Game of Morals,* which assumes *hypothetical bargaining* in a Rawlsian *original position*, i.e., people imagine that they meet behind a *veil of ignorance* that covers the role identity in the underlying real bargaining problem and use their *empathetic preferences.* Here it is assumed that people think they might end up in any identity with equal probability when the veil of ignorance is finally lifted.

If the empathetic preference of an individual i is represented by E, then we can say that i prefers to be individual j in situation x to being individual

[19] The following three paragraphs are derived from Holler (1999). For a more detailed review of Binmore's Theory of Justice, see Napel (1999a).

[20] See Rubinstein (1982) for the original model.

k in situation y by $(x, j)E(y, k)$. If such binary relations can be formed for all situations $x, y, z, \ldots$, including risky prospects (i.e. lotteries over situations) and all individuals $i, j, k, \ldots$, in a society, then cardinal utilities can be derived such that individual i can determine how much better or worse he/she feels when identifying with j or k over a particular situation. From this we get cardinal utility functions that imply trade-off relations U_i/V_i and U_j/V_j for individuals i and j. In the *evolutionary equilibrium,* all individuals will apply the same empathetic preferences, such that $U_i/V_i = U_j/V_j = U/V$ holds for each pair of members i and j. Thus, the value ratio U/V is valid for all members $i, j, k, \ldots$ of the society under consideration. Individuals with idiosyncratic valuations will not successfully be replicated, they will "die out" because of alienation and perhaps social sanctions, or revise their values and patterns of behavior so that they are consistent with the common standards defined by *evaluation equilibrium* U/V. Yet, why is that so?

Fig. 5.1. The social value equilibrium

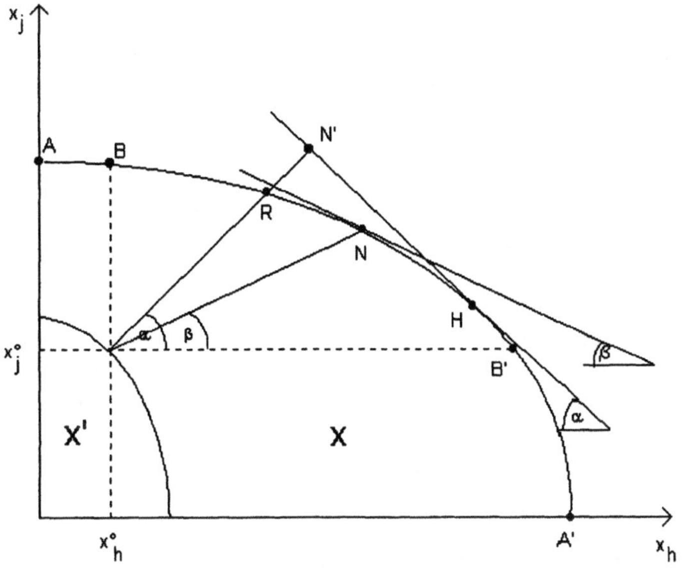

Binmore assumes that U/V will be determined by the outcome of real face-to-face bargaining and social evolution in the *medium run.* In the *short run,* U/V represents the fairness norm for application in daily life. Behind the veil of ignorance, the common U/V standard implies that a *proportional bargaining solution* with weights U and V (in terms of *co-operative game theory*) is used in these decisions. However, people are free to repeatedly call for re-negotiations with respect to the U/V ratio after the veil of ignorance has been lifted. Figure 5.1 illustrates the interaction of the *Game of Life* and the *Game of Morals*.

5.5.1 The Proportional Solution and the Bargaining Approach

In figure 1, the set X expresses the total of payoff pairs (x_j, x_h) which the society can achieve in this game, i.e. it is the payoff space of the *Game of Life*. Since the set of social outcomes may contain lotteries (i.e. events with a positive probability lower than 1), we assume that the utility functions x_j and x_h are of Von Neumann and Morgenstern type, and therefore satisfy the expected utility hypothesis. The standardization on positive values, $x_j > 0$ and $x_h > 0$, has therefore no deeper meaning because the Von Neumann and Morgenstern utility function can be submitted to any linear order-preserving transformation and still express the same preferences as prior to the transformation. However, the Pareto frontier[21] AA', which contains the efficient payoff pairs, illustrates that a fundamental asymmetry is assumed for this game: the *Game of Life* is basically unfair inasmuch it discriminates between the members of the society.

The payoff pair $(x_{j^\circ}, x_{h^\circ})$ describes the status quo. Since $(x_{j^\circ}, x_{h^\circ})$ is not an element of the Pareto frontier, it is clear that the payoffs of all members of the society can be improved.[22] However, the set of Pareto efficient and individually rational payoff pairs, illustrated by the segment of the Pareto frontier between points B and B', is large; and it is not straightforward that the members of the society can coordinate their actions so that an element in this set, often called *bargaining set*, will describe the evaluation of the result of these actions.

This is where the *Game of Morals* and its reference to fairness enters the stage. Empathetic preferences assure that the preferences of agents j and h can be ordered so that, assuming Von Neumann and Morgentern utilities, payoffs x_j and x_h can be defined and Bayesian decision theory applies.[23] The reference to the original position allows us to derive a ratio U_i/V_i, such that $V_i x_j = U_i x_h$. If an *evaluation equilibrium* exists and U_i/V_i generalizes to U/V then we write $Vx_j = Ux_h$ instead. If this *indifference condition* is applied to select a payoff pair from the Pareto frontier, the Rawlsian point R results. Given the status quo $(x_{j^\circ}, x_{h^\circ})$, then $V(x_j - x_{j^\circ}) = U(x_h - x_{h^\circ})$ holds for R. This implies that, given the social evaluation U and V, it is

[21] The Pareto frontier contains all payoff pairs (x_j, x_h) such that there is no (y_j, y_h).

[22] We can think of $(x_{j^\circ}, x_{h^\circ})$ as the outcome of an *earlier* society characterized by a payoff space X' such that X' is a true subset of X.

[23] In this context, it is sufficient to summarize Bayesian decision theory by its implication that "a rational decision-maker will behave *as though* he had attached subjective probabilities to the events about which he is uncertain and were seeking to maximize the *expectation* of a Von Neumann and Morgenstern utility function relative to these probabilities", Binmore (1994, p. 52).

not profitable for j to trade position with h and versa. Thus in point R the agents should not envy each other. Only if j does not think in terms of the evaluation equilibrium U/V he might prefer h's position in R to his own. If there is an evaluation equilibrium U/V, then the allocation in R is *envy-free* and *efficient* and thus satisfies Varian's notion of *fairness* (see Varian (1974)).

Now, if a member of the society is unhappy with the result described by R and does not want to be alienated he or she will, according to Binmore, enter into face-to-face bargaining with the people he or she interacts with. It is assumed that this process can be described by a Rubinstein game and its result therefore is self-enforcing if it coincides with the game's subgame perfect equilibrium.

It is a standard result that the subgame perfect equilibrium of the Rubinstein game converges to the outcome of the Nash bargaining game if the time preference of the players are identical and the corresponding discount factor converges to 1 (see, e.g., Owen (1995, p. 201–208) for this result). It seems plausible to assume that these conditions hold for the original position and thus for the *Game of Morals.*

We have already noted that if R is selected, and the value ratio U/V and the status quo $(x_{j^\circ}, x_{h^\circ})$ are acknowledged by all members of the society, then neither j nor h can do better by choosing the other's position and personality. Rawlsian point R is therefore an equilibrium position. This is the twist which allows Binmore (1994, p. 53) "to pull a maximin rabbit out of a hat into which only Bayesian decision theory is placed." The utilitarian outcome, marked by H in figure 1, which results from maximizing the weighted sum of the payoffs of the members of the society, $S = Ux_j + Vx_h$, puts h in a favorable position so that j will envy him. However, fairness is by-and-large identified with the absence of envy and efficiency.[24] So, if j had a chance he would choose to be h. We conclude that H is not an *equilibrium* in the *Game of Morals.*

5.5.2 On Monotonicity of Bargaining Solutions

The *proportional solution* which, at least technically, determines R has the nice property that it is monotonic in the sense that it will never be the case that a player will achieve a smaller solution payoff in game (X, c) than in (Y, c) if Y is a subset of X. we want to restate this property because it is often applied for the evaluation of bargaining solutions with respect to fairness.

Definition 6. Given any two bargaining games (X, c) and (Y, c) such that $Y \subset X$, then the bargaining solution f is monotonic if $f_i(X, c) \geq f_i(Y, c)$ for each agent i who is a player in (X, c) and (Y, c).

Kalai (1977b) surprisingly demonstrates that the proportional solution is the only solution for cooperative game which satisfies this monotonicity

[24] Varian (1974) defines an allocation as fair if it is efficient and equitable (i.e. envy-free) so that no agent prefers the bundle of any other agent to his own.

property. The monotonicity property of the proportional solution does not, however, guarantee monotonic results if the U/V ratio changes in the course of time. Inasmuch as Rubinstein bargaining and therefore the Nash (bargaining) solution are the core of the *Game of Morals*, which determines (together with the invisible hand of evolution) the U/V ratio, it is quite likely that U/V will change when the payoff space P of the game changes. Note that, for a two-person game, the Nash solution $u^* = (u_1^*, u_2^*)$ implies that the ratio $-(u_1^* - c_1)/(u_2^* - c_2)$ equals the slope of the Pareto frontier of P at point (u_1^*, u_2^*), where (c_1, c_2) is the conflict point. This result also holds for more than two players.

In order to illustrate this result, it suffices to reconsider the definition of the Nash solution in the case of two players.

Definition 7. Given a bargaining game (X, c) where X represents the payoff space and c describes the conflict point, the Nash solution selects a payoff pair $u^* = (u_1^*, u_2^*)$ such that $u^* = argmax(u_1 - c_1)(u_2 - c_2)$ subject to $u^* \in P$ and $u_1 > c_1$ and $u_2 > c_2$.

In figure 1, the Nash solution describes a payoff pair which is represented by a point N, situated on the utility frontier AA' between the points R and H. Point N' represents the Nash solution if unconstrained side payments are feasible in the society. In this case the Nash solution coincides with the proportional solution and monotonicity is assured even for face-to-face bargaining. In case of side payments utilities are transferable and the game can easily be transformed into a symmetric one for which the Nash and the proportional solution coincide.[25]

If, however, side payments are excluded, it is immediate from this result that the Nash solution – *which is at the heart of Binmore's notion of social contract* – does not have the monotonicity property in accordance to *Definition refdefinition:d5-1*: it can be the case that a player will achieve a smaller solution payoff in game (X, c) than in (Y, c) if Y is a subset of X. If we apply this result to the real-world situation, then it could well happen that some (or a group of) agents will be worse of than before, although the over-all situation of the society has been improved in such a way that everybody could be made better off - but to make everybody better off violates the *Game of Morals* and Binmore's notion of fairness as implied in face-to-face bargaining and summarized in the Nash solution. Those who are disfavored by the latter may no longer accept the rules embedded in the *Game of Morals* and try to implement a U/V ratio which works in their favor.

In this context, formation of a coalition (i.e. collusive behavior) might be a decisive step to change the rules of the game. Binmore (1994, p. 78)

[25] An asymmetric Nash solution (see Kalai (1977a)) of the game $(X, (x_{j^\circ}, x_{h^\circ}))$ could result in the payoff pair R. either this is by coincidence or we assume that the R-point defines the a-parameters of the asymmetric Nash solution $u^*(a) = argmax(u_1 - c_1)^a(u_2 - c_2)^{1-a}$. In the latter any Pareto efficient and individual rational payoff pair could be justified as a Nash bargaining outcome.

is quite aware that "a less sympathetic critic may feel" that his inability to cope adequately with the problem of coalition formation makes his attempts to theorize about social contract questions "like putting to sea in a half-built boat". Without doubt, cartels, political parties, ethnic groups, etc., have a strong influence on the shaping of societies and the social outcome.[26] According to Galbraith (1967, p. 320) it is characteristic for the *New Industrial State* that the techno-structure of a large corporations "extends to shaping the demand for its particular product or range of products". Similarly, other larger organizations and social groups successfully shape the preferences of the individuals, i.e. manipulate the U/V ratio, and perhaps even benefit from the nonmonotonicity of the Nash solution in the *Games of Morals*. Moreover, as it is well known from the economic theory, collusion such as price cartels can destabilize invisible hand equilibria and lead to socially inefficient outcomes. If collusive behavior in the *Game of Morals* carries over into the *Game of Life*, it could well be that the Pareto frontier will not be reached in the latter game.

5.5.3 Power and the Theory of Justice

I have argued elsewhere (Holler5 (1999)) that Binmore's *Theory of Justice* lacks coherence (or completeness) in two of its major building blocks: (i) the generalization of the *small world behavioral assumptions* about bargaining and fairness to a the *larger society* and (ii) the relationship between the *short-term* rule of thumb solution and the *medium-term* bargaining perspective. However, here I am not interested in the completeness or consistency of his theory but about its motivation and interpretation.

I argue that Binmore's theory is not primarily a theory of fairness or justice, but a theory of power: his theory relies heavily on reciprocity and the threat potential of repeated social interaction when it comes to coordinating social activities; and the implementation of the Rawlsian point R relies on iteration within the *Game of Life*. But, these iterations can only bind the agents if each of them is threatened to by a smaller payoff than in R if he (or she) deviates from the behavior that supports R. For example, the well-known trigger strategy prescribes that all agents choose a strategy which leads to the conflict point, here given by the status quo $(x_{j^\circ}, x_{h^\circ})$, if one of the agents chooses a pattern of behavior that violates R.

On the other hand, when it comes to Rubinstein bargaining there is an obvious first mover advantage which, however, vanishes in the case that time period between two offers shrinks or, alternatively, the discount factor converges to 1. Still, the face-to-face bargaining in the Rubinstein game is not based on any fairness principle and its subgame perfect equilibrium relies on the fact that the agents are threatened by the "shrinking of the cake". As a

[26] E.g., Holler (ed., 1984) contains a collection of articles on "coalition formation and collective actions".

consequence, player j is willing to accept a share of the cake today which is smaller than player h's share who made the offer as, in equilibrium, j will not better off if he makes the next offer which gives him a larger share but of a smaller cake. The more a player might suffer from the shrinking of the cake, i.e. the lower his discount factor, the smaller will be his share of the cake. This is how the threat of disagreement works in this context.

In the presentation of his solution, Nash (1950) explicitly assumes equal bargaining skills with the consequence that the payoffs of the players should be identical if the game is symmetric. However, since the payoffs are Von Neumann Morgenstern utilities and open to order-preserving linear transformation, the equality of payoffs does not imply that both players are equally happy with the outcome. In fact, a player might be very unhappy with the outcome of the Nash solution, but still better off than when an agreement has not been achieved and the conflict point applies. Nash suggests that "we may think" of the outcome on which the players agree "as fair bargains" (p.158). This is a rather weak reference to fairness.

The reference of the Nash solution to the conflict point is more explicit. This point expresses the threat if players disagree. As it is obvious from the formal presentation of the Nash solution in *Definition 7*, a modification of the conflict point has direct impact on the bargaining outcome: the conflict point and the solution point are the only two points that are *relevant* for the Nash solution. This is somewhat peculiar because the conflict point will never prevail because the cooperative conceptualization of the Nash solution presupposes that an agreement will be achieved.

The dependence of the outcome of the Nash solution on the threat point is even more explicit if the conflict payoffs are not exogenously given but subject to variable threats which are proposed by the bargainers. The corresponding threat game has the property of a constant-sum game (Nash (1953)),[27] and thus reflects pure *conflict of interest* between the bargainers on that level.

5.6 Monotonicity and Fairness

To Binmore, morality is merely a means of coordination: "Just as it is actually within our power to move a bishop like a knight when playing Chess, so we can steal, defraud, break promises, tell lies, jump lines, talk too much, or eat peas with our knives when playing a morality game. But rational folk choose not to cheat for much the same reason that they obey traffic signals", Binmore (1998, p. 5). Binmore argues that a fairness norm is valid as long as nobody can profit by deviating from it in his/her behavior. He believes that this describes social reality at least for small scale societies. He strongly suggests that this experience should be used for the organization of

[27] Thus it is equivalent to a zero-sum game for which the Nash equilibrium coincides with the condition "maximin equal to minimax" which Von Neumann and Morgenstern (1947) elaborated for non-cooperative games.

the society on a larger scale and maintains that his model verifies that fairness is universal coordination tool and not confined to small groups. The empirical basis of Binmore's theory is, unfortunately, weak even for small groups; and the theoretical model is incomplete. In particular, if we accept both Binmore's naturalistic and relativist point of view, we have to admit that people have something else in mind than coordination when we speak of fairness. My witnesses are Kant, Harsanyi, Rawls, Varian, and the host of others who have developed a "substantial theory of fairness". Of course, this does not exclude that fairness works as a coordination device. However, what people have in mind as being fair does not, in general, help to coordinate their behavior; and only in very selected cases does it help to resolve conflicts. It seems that more often than not fairness leads to disagreement. The voluminous and rather controversial literature on fairness may serve as a proxy for such a potential.

There is, no doubt, the possibility that we are only aware of fairness when "it" *fails* to solve our coordination and conflict problems. Yet, social experience and introspection tells me that there are hardly any socially relevant decisions that are not reflected by the parties with respect to some fairness concept. You only have to go to a used car market and listen to the verbal representation of the ongoing bargaining to get to grips with the problem. Because of the multitude of fairness concepts it is, in general, not difficult to find arguments which justify one's bargaining proposal or decision as fair and judges the arguments of the other party as unfair if, e.g., one "feels unhappy" or wants to ask for compensation, re-negotiation, etc.

The fact is, human beings do not seem to have a "natural" sense of fairness. And it seems, too, that human beings also lack a "natural" sense of power. The multitude of power measures should not, therefore, come as a surprise. Combining the discussion of fairness and power in the proposition of monotonicity is unlikely to deliver straightforward answers about which concepts are suitable – and which are not. It seems a very interesting project, because it provides additional insights about the properties of the various concepts and their possible relationships which should be very helpful to evaluate their applications to theoretical as well as real-world problems.

References

[1] Ayer, A. (1971, first print 1936). *Language, Truth, Logic.* Harmondsworth: Penguin Books.

[2] Banzhaf, J. F. (1965). Weighted Voting Doesn't Work: A Mathematical Analysis. *Rutgers Law Review 19*, 317–43.

[3] Barry, B. (1980). Is it Better to be Powerful or Lucky: Part I and Part II. *Political Studies 28*, 183–194 and 338–352.

[4] Binmore, K. (1994). *Playing Fair, Game Theory and the Social Contract, vol. I.*, Cambridge, Mass., and London: The MIT Press.

[5] Binmore, K. (1998). *Just Playing, Game Theory and the Social Contract, vol. II.*, Cambridge, Mass., and London: The MIT Press.
[6] Brams, S. and P. Fishburn (1995). When is Size a Liability? Bargaining Power in Minimal Winning Coalitions. *Journal of Theoretical Politics 7*, 301–316.
[7] Caplow, T. (1968). *Two Against One: Coalitions in Triads.* Englewood Cliffs, N.J.: Prentice Hall.
[8] Coleman, J. (1971). Control of Collectivities and the Power of a Collectivity to Act. in: B. Lieberman (ed.), *Social Choice*, New York: Gordon and Breach.
[9] Deegan, J. J. and E. Packel (1979). A New Index of Power for Simple n–Person Games. *International Journal of Game Theory 7*, 113–123.
[10] Dreyer, J. and A. Schotter (1980). Power Relationships in the International Monetary Fund: The Consequences of Quota Changes. *Review of Economics and Statistics 62*, 97–106.
[11] Dubey, P. and L.S. Shapley (1979). Mahematical Properties of the Banzhaf Index. *Mathematics of Operations Research 4*, 99–131.
[12] Felsenthal, D. and M. Machover (1995). Postulates and Paradoxes of Relative Voting Power: A Critical Review. *Theory and Decision 38*, 195–229.
[13] Felsenthal, D. and M. Machover (1998a). The Bicameral Postulates and Indices of A Priori Voting Power. *Theory and Decision 44*, 83–116.
[14] Felsenthal, D. and M. Machover (1998b). *The Measurement of Voting Power. Theory and Practice, Problems and Paradoxes.* Cheltenham: Edward Elgar.
[15] Felsenthal, D., M. Machover, and W. Zwicker (1998). The Bicameral Postulates and Indices of A Priori Voting Power. *Theory and Decision 44*, 83–116.
[16] Fischer, D. and A. Schotter (1978). The Inevitability of the Paradox of Redistribution in the Allocation of Voting Weights. *Public Choice*, 49–67.
[17] Fishburn, P. and S. Brams (1996). Minimal Winning Coalitions in Weighted–Majority Voting Games. *Social Choice and Welfare 13*, 397–417.
[18] Freixas, J. and G. Gambarelli (1997). Common Internal Properties Among Power Indices. *Control and Cybernetics 26*, 591–603.
[19] Galbraith, J. (1967). *New Industrial State.* London: Hamish Hamilton.
[20] Garrett, G. and G. Tsebelis (1996). An Institutional Critique of Intergovermentalism. *International Organization 50*, 269–299.
[21] Garrett, G. and G. Tsebelis (1999). Why Resist the Temptation to Apply Power Indices to the EU. *Journal of Theoretical Politics 11*, 321–331.
[22] Green, E. and J.-J. Laffont (1979). *Incentives in Public Decision-Making.* Amsterdam: North-Holland.
[29] Holler, M. J. (1978). A Priori Party Power and Government Formation. *Munich Social Science Review 1*, 25–41. reprinted in: M.J. Holler (ed.) (1982), *Power, Voting, and Voting Power*, Würzburg and Vienna: Physica-Verlag.
[23] Holler, M. (1982). Forming Coalitions and Measuring Voting Power. *Political Studies 30*, 262–271.
[32] Holler, M. J. (ed.) (1984). *Coalition Formation and Collective Action.* Würzburg and Vienna: Physica-Verlag.
[30] Holler, M. J. (1997). Power Monotonicity and Expectations. *Control and Cybernetics 26*, 605–607.
[31] Holler, M. J. (1998). Two Stories, One Power Index. *Journal of Theoretical Politics 10*, 179–1990.
[24] Holler, M. (1999). Review of 'K. Binmore (1998), Just Playing, Game Theory and the Social Contract, vol. II, Cambridge, Mass., and London: The MIT Press'. *Journal of Economics (forthcoming).*

[25] Holler, M., R. Ono, and F. Steffen (1999). Constrained Monotonicity and the Measurement of Power. paper submitted.
[26] Holler, M. and E. Packel (1983). Power, Luck and the Right Index. *Zeitschrift für Nationalökonomie (Journal of Economics) 43*, 21–29.
[27] Holler, M. and M. Widgrén (1999a). The Value of a Coalition is Power. *Homo Oeconomicus 15*, 497–512.
[28] Holler, M. and M. Widgrén (1999b). Why Power Indices for Assessing EU Decision Making? *Journal of Theoretical Politics 11*, 291–308.
[33] Hosli, M. (2000). Coalition Formation and Voting in the Council of the European Union. in: M.J. Holler and G. Owen (eds.), *Power Indices and Coalition Formation.* Boston, Dordrecht and London: Kluwer. (forthcoming).
[34] Johnston, R.J. (2000) Power Indices and the Design of Electoral/Constitutional Systems. in: M.J. Holler and G. Owen (eds.), *Power Indices and Coalition Formation.* Boston, Dordrecht and London: Kluwer. (forthcoming).
[35] Kalai, E. (1977a). Nonsymmetric Nash Solutions and Replication of Two–Person Bargaining. *International Journal of Game Theory 6*, 126–133.
[36] Kalai, E. (1977b). Proportional Solutions to Bargaining Situations: Interpersonal Utility Comparisons. *Econometrica 45*, 1623–1630.
[37] König, T. and T. Bräuninger (1996). Power and Political Coordination in American and German Multi–Chamber Legislation. *Journal of Theoretical Politics 8*, 331–360.
[38] König, T. and T. Bräuninger (2000). Decisiveness and Inclusiveness: Two Aspects of the Intergovernmental Choice of European Voting Rules. in: M.J. Holler and G. Owen (eds.), *Power Indices and Coalition Formation.* Boston, Dordrecht and London: Kluwer. (forthcoming).
[39] Laruelle, A. and M. Widgrén (2000). Voting Power in a Sequence of Cooperative Games: The Case of EU Procedures. in: M.J. Holler and G. Owen (eds.), *Power Indices and Coalition Formation.* Boston, Dordrecht and London: Kluwer. (forthcoming).
[40] Levínský, R. and P. Silárszky (2000). Global Monotonicity of Values of Cooperative Games: An Argument Supporting the Explanatory Power of Shapley's Approach. in: M.J. Holler and G. Owen (eds.), *Power Indices and Coalition Formation.* Boston, Dordrecht and London: Kluwer. (forthcoming).
[41] Machover, M. (1999). Notions of A Priori Voting Power: Critique of Holler and Widgrén. *Homo Oeconomicus (forthcoming).*
[42] Napel, S. (1999a). Game Theory and the Evolution of Fairness: A Review Article. *Homo Oeconomicus 15*, 581–588.
[43] Napel, S. (1999b). The Holler–Packel Axiomatization of the Public Good Index Completed. *Homo Oeconomicus 15*, 513–520.
[44] Napel, S. and M. Widgrén (1999). Inferior Players in Simple Games (in progress).
[45] Nash, J. (1950). The Bargaining Problem. *Econometrica 18*, 155–162.
[46] Nash, J. (1953). Two–Person Cooperative Games. *Econometrica 21*, 128–295.
[47] Nurmi, H. (1998). *Rational Behaviour and the Design of Institutions: Concepts, Theories and Models.* Cheltenham, UK, and Northampton, MA: Edward Elgar.
[48] Nurmi, H., T. Meskanen, and A. Pajala (2000). Calculus of Consent in the EU Council of Ministers. in: M.J. Holler and G. Owen (eds.), *Power Indices and Coalition Formation.* Boston, Dordrecht and London: Kluwer. (forthcoming).

[49] Owen, G. (1972). Multilinear Extensions of Games. *Management Science 18*, 64–79.

[50] Owen, G. (1975). Multilinear Extensions and the Banzhaf Value. *Naval Research Logistics Quarterly 22*, 741–750.

[51] Owen, G. (1995). *Game Theory* (3rd ed.). San Diego: Academic Press.

[52] Rawls, J. (1972). *A Theory of Justice.* Oxford: Oxford University Press.

[53] Rubinstein, A. (1982). Perfect Equilibrium in a Bargaining Model. *Econometrica 50*, 97–111.

[54] Shapley, L. (1953). A Value for n–Person Games. in: H. Kuhn, A.W. Tucker (eds.), *Contributions to the Theory of Games* II, Princeton: Princeton University Press.

[55] Shapley, L. and M. Shubik (1954). A Method of Evaluating the Distribution of Power in a Committee System. *American Political Science Review 48*, 787–792.

[56] Straffin, P. D. (1977). Homogeneity, Independence and Power Indices. *Public Choice 30*, 107–118.

[57] Straffin, P. D. (1988). The Shapley-Shubik and the Banzhaf Power Index as Probabilities. in: A.E. Roth (ed.), *The Shapley Value: Essays in Honor of Lloyd S. Shapley*, Cambridge: Cambridge University Press.

[58] Tsebelis, G. and G. Garrett (1996). Agenda Setting Power, Power Indices, and Decision Making in the European Union. *International Review of Law and Economics 16*, 345–361.

[59] Tsebelis, G. and G. Garrett (1997). Why Power Indices Cannot Explain Decisionmaking in the European Union. in: D. Schmidtchen and R. Cooter (eds.) *Constitutional Law and Economics of the European Union*, Cheltenham, UK: Edward Elgar.

[60] Turnovec, F. (1998). Monotonicity and Power Indices. in: T.J. Stewart and R.C. van den Honert (eds.), *Trends in Multicriteria Decision Making, Lecture Notes in Economics and Mathematical Systems* 465, Berlin et al.: Springer-Verlag.

[61] Varian, H. (1974). Equity, Envy, and Efficiency. *Journal of Economic Theory 9*, 63–91.

[62] Von Neumann, J. and O. Morgenstern (1947). *The Theory of Games and Economic Behavior* (2nd ed.). Princeton: Princeton University Press.

[63] Widgrén, M. (1994). Voting Power in the EC and the Consequences of Two Different Enlargements. *European Economic Review 38*, 1153–1170.

[64] Widgrén, M. (1995). Probabilistic Voting in the EU Council: The Cases of Trade Policy and Social Regulation. *Scandinavian Journal of Economics 97*, 345–356.

[65] Widgrén, M. (2000). On the Probabilistic Relationship Between Public Good Index and Normalized Banzhaf Index. in: M.J. Holler and G. Owen (eds.), *Power Indices and Coalition Formation.* Boston, Dordrecht and London: Kluwer. (forthcoming).

6 Solidarity

Friedel Bolle and Alexander Kritikos

Abstract. For many people the word Solidarity has become a meaningless slogan - to often used without leading to any economic consequences. This is not always true. We show in this paper under which conditions solidarity can be a powerful instrument. We call an action a solidarity action when a group of individuals is willing to contribute to this action which aims for a reallocation of scarce resources within a society. The willingness to contribute is mainly caused by the efficiency of the target of the solidarity action and is enhanced by feelings of mutual exchange (solidarity) within a group.

"If Terry walks in,
we walk in with him".
Dockers in the movie
'On the waterfront'.

6.1 Introduction

People are demanded every here and there to behave in solidarity with somebody or something. Often nobody pays any attention anymore to such calls. But there are also incidences that solidarity is a powerful instrument which can change complete societies. Reviewing its history sheds a glance on the multiple connotations connected with solidarity.

In ancient societies the commitment to solidarity was a matter of death or survival. The struggle against the uncontrollable power of nature forced individuals into mutual cooperation. As Gide (1987) exemplifies, the necessity of contending with the Nile floods compelled all the inhabitants of Egypt to solidarity in labour and cultivation.

History shows that due to its necessity, solidarity became gradually institutionalized. Examples for the different grades of institutionalization are co-operatives which were built over the last centuries to share common properties or tools among their members, and which culminated in the 20th century to the enlarged civil, public and social order of a society. Within these rules modern liberalism propagates 'everyone for himself' as central behavioral conception. At the downstage of the 21st century, therefore, there is an increasing number of 'pop-liberals' who doubt the necessity to pay any attention to a word on which the whole doctrine of their strongest antagonist, the communist society, was based on.

Solidarity, in the sense of 'each for all and all for each', is the opposite to a society which is governed by individualism within the given social rules. In the communist societies, solidarity was to be achieved in particular between the communist party and the working class. The target of this unity was to realize the 'historic mission' of 'outrunning without overtaking the capitalist society'. Leading ideologists stressed that i) solidarity will be the strongest existing motive power of the working class due to its social position, its historic task, and its intellectual power, and that ii) there is a class division of solidarity due to this particular motive in the working class[1] (cf. Universallexikon (1988)). In actual socialism, however, it proved that the working class did not show any willingness to realize the communist targets so that the desire for solidarity was substituted by obligatory cooperation to which the working class resigned itself as to fatality - with all the known consequences for the communist economies.

It is an historical irony that one important voluntary social movement among the communist societies - the polish trade union "Solidarnosz" - struggled *against* the communist doctrine of solidarity, the unity of state, party and working class. This movement showed that communist parties were not successful in representing the interests of the working class and that solidarity may be rather target- than class-dependent.[2] The actions of Solidarnosz are, moreover, central to explain the roots of the systemic transformation of socialist into pluralist societies.

The Polish "Solidarity" showed that the principle power resource of the weak is their collective mobilization into social movements. Such movements based on solidarity motives may have tremendous economic consequences: the transition of the communist into capitalist economies is nothing else than the dramatic switch from one set of social rules to another, so it induced one of the most important economic changes in the world of the 20th Century - and this deserves further analysis.

However, the Polish movement is only one mosaic where the idea of solidarity was successfully stressed in modern times. Solidarity was also an important motivation in the trade unions of capitalist countries. Mainly in Sweden, but also in central Europe and in the United States, the "Solidarity Wage Policy" of the 1960s and 1970s was the attempt of the main unions to reduce the wage dispersion by using the economic power of well organized strikes[3]. In particular in Sweden wage inequalities were substantially narrowed (cf. Edin and Holmlund (1993)).

[1] In order to make sure that the working class exhibits that particular solidarity, workers had to pay less taxes than other employees even if they earned the same amount of money.

[2] Solidarnosz closed the gap between the narrowly defined classes, since the unity was built between the working class and professionals like e.g. engineers, cf. Kennedy (1991). For a historical introduction into the early years of this movement, cf. Touraine et al. (1983).

[3] For a detailed discussion on relation between strikes and solidarity, esp. in England, cf. Church and Outram (1998).

The trend decline in wage inequality was broken in the mid-1980s and wage differentials were widened again when right-winged governments came into legislative power in most of these countries. Nevertheless, the solidarity wage bargaining lasted for more than 20 years driven by the egalitarian ambitions of strong and coordinated trade unions, reducing the wage differentials among workers. At the end, however, they were confronted with the reproach that their wage policy was counterproductive to the whole economy in general and to the less educated workers in particular - those who should profit from the solidarity wage policy. Many of these workers are assumed to have lost their jobs because their productivity increase was more than overcompensated by their wage increase.

Solidarity caused another dramatic change in the (former West-)German economy. In particular under the impression of the Harrisburg and Tzernobyl events, weekly demonstrations and riots - rather reminding of a civil war - at places where nuclear waste should be deposited brought the question of an optimal energy policy mix into attention to the broad public. This movement succeeded in stopping the building of a reprocessing plant (in Wackersdorf, lower Bavaria) in particular, and it also confirmed the decision not to build any new nuclear power plants.

A kind of institutionalization of this movement was realized when the Green party was founded which twenty years later achieved governmental power. It is quite ironic to see that, once elected, the party has much more difficulties to carry out its goal, i.e. the exit from the nuclear energy production. One reason may be that the anti-nuclear movement seems to have stopped the support on the streets. They might had the feeling that there was no more need for solidarity actions outside the parliament after the electoral success of their party.

There are examples of less voluntary solidarity movements. The people's solidarity feelings are challenged when they are obliged to co-operate through tax payments or coercive insurance in order to finance the solidary welfare states, like in Scandinavia, Germany, France or England.[4] Nowadays, after the fall of the iron curtain, income-tax payers in Germany are forced to pay an excess solidarity tax in order to finance the reconstruction of the East German infrastructure. Solidarity is even endeavoured to explain why poorer *countries* should receive monetary compensation from the richer countries - within the European Community e.g. by the 'structural fonds' or within Germany by the so called 'Länderfinanzausgleich'.

Meanwhile, these welfare states are facing economic problems which arise from such coercive payments. Moreover, the mere citation of the word solidarity is often used to cover battles and disputes over redistributive advantages of those who benefit from the financial compensations, while those who are obliged to pay, rather call that kind of solidarity exploitation.

[4] For an overview, cf. Baldwin (1990).

One may question the concept of solidarity in situations where it has neither economic nor political, not even personal consequences. Innumerable solidarity addresses were sent to extorted workers in third world countries who even did not get to know that there were some fellows somewhere in Europe whose minds were full of solidarity feelings towards them.[5] However, persons who did not contribute to these solidarity addresses because they charged them as meaningless, were often attacked as incompassionate or cynical.

Above all these possible applications of solidarity, the state can be regarded as the highest form of social solidarity. Within the social contract between the state and its citizens, "solidarity will gain a high moral value when it is understood, accepted, and desired by men, when it becomes the basis of duty, and when men endeavour to realize freely that moral good will be the desire to be and behave as members of a common humanity", Gide (1987). In the course of evolution the adherence to the collective rules of a society by the vast majority of its citizens became a spontaneous order.[6] It is the main prerequisite for building effective market and non-market institutions allowing human societies to reach a high level of economic development.

When the pieces of mosaic are put together, we have a dazzling image of what solidarity could be. One of the important movements in world history, Solidarnosz, aimed to change the social order of an economic system which was based on coercive solidarity. In western countries, strikes and wage policies based on solidarity were not viable because they led to wages disadvantageous to those who were supposed to benefit from this specific wage. Solidarity movements which gained administrative power lost their influence after their institutionalization. If solidarity is connected with a system of coercive payments, those who have to pay often feel exploited and not to behave solidarily. Volunteered solidarity, however, often has no consequences either, at least for those who were supposed to benefit from the solidary action.

One rather simple explanation for the confusion might be that the concept of Solidarity was often (mis-)used as a slogan. However, this is an explanation for solidarity addresses without any consequences or for movements which aim to cover their real targets by overemphasizing solidarity feelings. Another explanation is that solidarity actions - once voluntarily provided - may have lost their justification because the circumstances changed.

The explanation we will offer in this paper is derived from the first statement - solidarity as a matter of life or death - which will explain any rise and fall of solidarity actions. If we try to transform matters of life and death into today the best approximation might be social efficiency. We will show that, usually, an action will be realized with higher probability the more efficient

[5] And sometimes the evoked international solidarity was nothing else than an euphemism for the financial support of terroristic alliances which was organized at the same time.

[6] For an explanation of this central hypothesis of human behavior, cf. Sugden (1986).

this action is. This also means that any support of solidarity actions which lost efficiency over time will be reduced when the loss of efficiency is realized by its contributors. In addition, we will show that solidarity has even vanished in a world in which people are no longer dependent on one another, i.e. where fewer socially efficient actions are possible.

This paper aims to shed some light on the economics of solidarity by introducing a decision theoretic approach. However, in the next section we will try to describe solidarity. We will classify different degrees of solidarity which depend on who will benefit from a solidary choice under which conditions and to which extent he will benefit, and who will have to contribute so that the solidarity action will be effective. In section 6.3 we will elaborate a dynamic utility function for a general class of solidarity games which allows to explain the conditions for an individual to be willing to contribute to a solidarity action. Section 6.4 concludes.

6.2 Solidarity and its Economic Consequences

In Economics the notion of solidarity is often used in a similar confusing ad-hocness as in politics and colloquial speech. There seems to be no agreement on a clear definition. E.g. Selten and Ockenfels (1998) assert in their experiment on the solidarity game that "subjects can show solidarity in the sense that they are willing to help *others* who by chance came to a much worse position than they themselves". In contrast to this, Orbell et al. (1988) assert that solidarity is measured when contributions to a public good where the *own* group (i.e. the group of contributors) benefits are compared with contributions to a public good where the benefits go to others. Therefore, approaches from other sources may be more helpful.

The noblest illustration of solidarity is given by St. Paul who suggested that "we all are members of one body". However, economics science is not particularly famous for analyzing noble behavior and the majority of individuals seem to be far from behaving in a noble way.

A general description of solidarity is the following. It is an "implicit agreement of many individuals as of a group. [It calls for] complete unity as of opinion, purpose and interest" (Webster's (1980)) which may lead to *mutual dependence* among the individuals of the group.

Gide (1987) emphasizes "that the larger part of the great inventions tend to increase these relations of *mutual dependence* which exist between men, and make them vibrate throughout the universe in the community of the same emotions". And further: "It compels to our attention to all that happens to our fellow-creatures, whether fortunate or not, since all that concerns them concerns us."

In accordance with this assertion the 'school of solidarity' – founded by a rare combination of Christian socialists, positivists and evolutionist socialists – stated in its doctrine that this growing *interdependence* of individuals and peoples is a harmonic law, and that the solution of the social question must be sought in the continual development of solidarity, especially in *cooperation* in all its forms.[7]

These descriptions and illustrations tend to be rather normative. They suggest that individuals *should* act in a solidary way, but not when, why and with which target such actions do really arise. Nevertheless, it is possible from these descriptions to implicitly derive two different kinds of solidarity actions.

6.2.1 Solidarity in the Sense of Cooperation and Donation

1) Solidarity may exist *within* a group of two or more persons; all members of the group are expected to make a certain contribution in order to reach a *superior state* which could not have been reached without the contribution.[8] We will call this kind of relationship *cooperation.*[9] This first kind of solidarity is based on a relationship of expected reciprocity. Since this kind of cooperation is confronted with the problem of the social dilemma, its restriction is the defection of some (or even all) group members whose individual payoffs are then increased at the cost of the whole group. A typical example for this kind of solidarity is a strike.

2) Solidarity may also exist in a group which is willing to make a certain contribution in order to help a *second* group because the situation of the second group was worsened by unforeseen occurrences. This kind of solidarity is called *donation.* This second kind of solidarity is an altruistic choice of many individuals and is often formed by the richer or luckier part in a population to *help* the poorer or unlucky part of the same or another population. A typical example is the contribution to victims of earthquakes.

Thus, we assume that a solidarity action can arise in both ways, with the aim to increase the benefit of the own group (cooperation) as well as

---

[7] Typical objections of individualistic approaches to this doctrine are that 'the only solidarity discoverable in the world is that of mutual exploitation' and that this doctrine is in opposition to competition - the basis of economic development in capitalist economies.

[8] This means at the same time that we do not have in mind aspects of solidarity which are explained as 'multiple-win-situation' for all participants where contributions are or seem to be individually rational, like within clans, cf. Ouchi (1980). Typical examples are xenophobia (cf. Kulczycki (1994)), quotas, or public contracts with a loyal party (and not with the lowest cost offer) which is usually called corruption. Although we do not explicitly exclude in our approach all group formations which aim to restrict economic competition at the cost of third parties, we will not discuss this topic any further.

[9] Lindenberg (1988) asserts that poorer groups in a society are more ready to make use of the mobilization of solidarity movements because they have less access to public goods.

of another group (donation). Under a long-term perspective or if we assume that it is decided under the veil of ignorance concerning one's position in the world, donation is simply an aspect of cooperation. As we will see in section 6.3, donation is from the contributor's point of view (at least for those who think in terms of efficiency) the limiting case of cooperation.

6.2.2 Coercive Versus Voluntary Contribution

There are more dimensions to the solidarity question than met by the above distinction. An important dimension is whether the solidary choice is done voluntarily or coercively.[10] Nevertheless, voluntary and coercive contributions are strongly connected, at least with respect to the observance of the basic laws. By sufficient education the obedience to certain collective rules may be turned into spontaneous cooperation because educated individuals may feel morally committed to this kind of cooperation.[11]

When solidarity is connected with obligatory contributions it often concerns social insurances like the statutory health insurance.[12] In terms of misfortune's consequences, all members of a common risk pool stand equal, while contributions to this kind of insurance are often positively related to the income of the insured members. The typical problem of these insurance systems is that they completely lack incentive compatibility.

On the one side, it results in the commonly known behavior of moral hazard and of adverse selection.[13] As a result economists attempted to develop improved insurance systems which save the idea of solidary contributions but which do not suffer from these problems. In this paper, however, we focus on another effect that arises when the solidary feeling of contributing to a social security system is substituted by the above mentioned disputes among the participating groups: The advantages of redistribution induce a constant renegotiation of the social contract, and as a consequence solidarity, originally introduced as the driving force of the contribution, is curtailed to a meaningless slogan. This certainly shows that the original aim of the solidarity action has been achieved and that individuals might have stopped to support the solidarity action if contributions had been voluntarily. In the following, we

[10] There are also hybrid forms like peer group lending where the solidarity action is connected with an incentive compatible contract. For more details, cf. Kritikos (1999). For a distinction between co-operatives and peer group lending, cf. Krahnen and Schmidt (1994).

[11] For a model discussing possible influences of education on social norms, solidarity behavior and the voluntary adherence to collective rules, cf. Kritikos and Meran (1998) who describe how the compliance to social norms (which ought to correspond to the basic laws of a society) generates utility.

[12] A progressive income tax may also be established for reasons of solidarity. However, there are other explanations for these tax-systems as well, like richer persons using public goods more than poorer persons.

[13] For the basic theories on this topic, cf. Arrow (1963) and Akerlof (1970).

will, therefore, restrict our analysis to voluntary contributions to a solidarity action.

Beyond these two main distinctions, cooperation and donation, voluntary and coercive contribution, we will characterize within this specified setting three more dimensions. This is necessary because an individual's participation in a solidarity action depends on the outcome of this kind of action and not on any willingness for 'warm glow giving'.[14] We, therefore, have to consider possible aims of a solidarity action.

6.2.3 Three Orders of Public Goods

First of all, the aim of the solidary action itself, in general the provision of a public (or group) good, has to be analyzed. The public good can be of three different kinds. When the group aims to collect contributions in order to produce a productive public good – e.g. a road – it is called a *first order* public good. When the group aims to coordinate on an action in order to change a third party's uncooperative into cooperative behavior by a (threat of a) punishment – a strike or a demonstration against employers, regimes or governments, a boycott of a certain product which is offered by an extortionate monopolist, or which is produced under inhuman conditions – it is called a *second order* public good. When the group aims to redistribute scarce resources in order to achieve a just distribution – e.g. in a social health insurance – it is called a *third order* public good.

The evaluation of the *first order public good* is straightforward. It should be provided, if, by sufficient contribution, its production directly increases the utility of the users of the public good. Thus, the willingness to contribute is opened by the efficiency of the target. And if—as assumed in all experiments conducted on the private provision of a public good[15]—the marginal return from the public good is constant with increasing contributions, efficiency increases with the number of contributors, with the amount every person is willing to contribute and with the marginal return from the public good. Thus, contributions to a first order public good are related to their efficiency which can be measured in terms of utility or even monetary increase. (Nevertheless, contributors are in a social dilemma as long as the individual marginal return from the public good is smaller than one.)

The *second order public good* is somewhat more complex because the utility function of contributors to a second order public good may contain two components: The first component concerns a successful punishment of a

[14] For a more general discussion to which extent warm glow is an important behavioral pattern, cf. Andreoni (1995).

[15] For an excellent overview over the experiments on public goods, cf. Ledyard (1995). An important experiment on this kind of public good provision was conducted by Isaac et al. (1994) who tested the willingness to contribute in large groups and found that this willingness increases as the number of participants in a group is increased.

third party by a sufficiently solidary behavior of the group. This may lead to an increase of the subjective utility of its members. However, the aim of the punishment (mostly) is to change the behavior of the third party in a way that the punishers have access to a state of 'more efficiency'. Therefore, the second component is the expected utility increase of the group when it can harvest the fruits of the third party's behavioral change.[16]

There are further differences between first and second order public goods. The contribution to a second order public good and the success of such a movement does not only depend on monetary support but in particular on the degree of participation. The cost of participation has, therefore, to be measured in opportunity costs. Moreover, in contrast to the provision of the first order public good which contains only the risk of (too) low contributions of others, the provision of the second order public good is connected with more risk dimensions. Essentially, punishment should be a behavioral threat which need not be carried out. Credibility, however, is strongly connected with obligation and self-obligation. In the long run, credibility requires that threats, if necessary, are carried out (see also Bolle (1995)). On the one side, the credibility of punishment is not easy to calculate, not only because the individuals concerned might not have sufficient information about the total number of potential participants which can be activated in a movement, but also because the threshold of effective punishment is, due to a lack of information, not a calculable quantity of action. Therefore, it is important for a successful provision of a second order public good that actions are coordinated, as the introducing citation of the paper implies.

Moreover, political movements against governments, regimes or tyrants face an additional risk which is negatively correlated to the degree of solidarity existing among the population of a society. The less successful the movement is (and the less democratic the regime is) the higher is the probability that the members of a movement will get punished by the executive power of the regime. They may not only face dramatic economic consequences such as a loss of job, but also persecutions, tortures, killings, sentences to prison or even to death.

And even many democratic governments use the tool of denunciation in order to break off solidarity movements and to be able to punish individual members of such movements. Effective resistance against denunciation could only be realized if all members refuse to denounce their fellow members and know that all other members refuse, as well. Only one person willing to denounce his fellows could have negative economic and personal consequences for those who were denounced.[17]

[16] Employers may raise the wages or give employment guarantees. Governments may change their policies in favour of the demonstrators, regimes may resign. Monopolists may decrease their selling prices. Producers may change their production methods.

[17] One famous example during the McCarthy era is the case of the film director Elia Kazan who denounced a dozen script writers and has justified his doing

Thus, the subjective utility of solidarily behaving persons is increased only with a certain probability – i.e. if the threat of punishment was successful.[18] If the threat fails to reach its aim, the participants face the cost of their solidarity behavior and possibly also the cost of being punished by those they aimed to influence. It is, therefore, reasonable to conclude that the utility increase of a solidarity movement is riskier if it does not only contribute to the production of a certain generally welcomed item, but if it is pointed against a third party.

In the case of a *third order public good*, the major aim of the movement is to achieve a just distribution. This might not improve efficiency, but might increase the welfare of a state if accordingly defined. Examples for third order public goods are donations for the victims of earthquakes (not only for personal support but also for the reconstruction of the destroyed infrastructure), or strikes by labour unions which increased wages of the lower paid workers.

6.2.4 Solidarity and its Similarity to Reciprocity and Altruism

Similar to reciprocal exchanges between two persons there is also a mutual relationship between potential contributors to a solidarity action. While a reciprocal relationship between two persons usually concerns the mutual exchange of a *private* good against another, group cooperation can be characterized either as a contribution to a *public* or a *group* good to which some or all potential contributors have access, or as a cyclical instead of a mutual exchange. Reciprocal feelings may arise to the extent that the decision of a person to contribute may depend on the contribution of others.

An isolated solidarity action can hardly be distinguished from altruism: For donation this is more apparent than for cooperation because the temporal distance between giving and (possibly) receiving is larger.

---

in his film "On the waterfront" where Marlon Brando denounces the corrupt behavior of the dockworkers' union, explaining his behavior with the words "I was ratting on myself all those years and I didn't know it." Most of the authors (denounced by Kazan) were, however, not corrupt but members of the communist party and they were for the rest of their life not able to sell one more script to any film studio. We mention this particular example because it exemplifies the tremendous consequences which a whole group tied together by solidarity has to face if the preferences of only one person have changed. (Of course it is one thing to change the preferences and to leave a solidarity group and another to deliver the fellow players into the hands of their 'enemy'). However, the possibility of a preference change underlines that there are always subjectively (rather than objectively) 'good' targets which tie together a group to a solidarity movement against a subjectively bad behaving third party. We will return to this important question in the final discussion.

[18] For the necessary conditions of an effective punishment , cf. Polinksy and Shavell (1991).

Thus, altruism between members of a group *supports* solidarity actions or, in a two-members group, reciprocity.[19] But is altruism *the same* as solidarity? Certainly not! While altruism can be one-sided (e.g. from parents to children), solidarity requires, to a certain extent, mutuality. In section 6.3 we try to describe, by means of a dynamic process, what patterns of mutuality are required for solidarity.

6.2.5 Subjective and Objective Utility

What induces individuals to contribute to a solidarity action if they could easily shirk? It has become to a certain extent a common practice to split a utility function into an objective and a subjective part. If persons are pure egoists their utility function contains only the objective part, usually personal income, which often results in non-cooperation and inefficiency. If individuals are altruists who also consider the impact of their action on other individuals' utility and/or if they are reciprocally motivated individuals who make their decision dependent on the decision of others, then we may observe cooperation and efficiency (from the point of view of objective utility). Such behavior can be individually motivated by an additional subjective part of the utility function. As a matter of fact, the total utility of such individuals is increased when they make an altruistic or a reciprocal choice even if their (isolated) monetary payoff is reduced by such an action. Taking into account similar motivations and decisions of others, however, also the overall monetary payoff will increase.

Under the impression of the introductory sentence that a solidarity action, i.e. a contribution to a public good was the necessary prerequisite for survival, the question of what is an individually rational choice may be posed anew. The necessity to survive makes it a rational decision to contribute – at least to a certain extent – to a public good. If every individual decides prima facie under this perspective, the objective utility is increased because the produced public good increases the payoff for each individual (compared to the outcome without the public good production). If we go one step further one can even argue that in the course of evolution only those groups survived where (a majority of) individuals contributed to a public good.

On the other hand, larger groups face the same difficulties that arise in two-person cooperations. How to exclude the possibility of cheating? There are two solutions to this problem and they are the same as in the literature on two-person cooperations. First, there may be sufficient ex-ante information about the behavior or the utility function of the group members. In this case, the dynamic process in section 6.3 describes learning because the success of the group depends on the individual's to contribute to an efficient action even if the individual marginal return of the contribution is smaller than one.

[19] For a definition of altruism and reciprocity in two person games, cf. Kritikos and Bolle (1999). Here, we also show how these two concepts are linked with each other.

In addition to former behavior of the same kind, other signals may be produced, in particular in situations where unanimity is of utmost importance. Members (or persons who aim to become members) of a solidarity movement may make gifts to their fellow members in order to signal their commitment to the specific norms of the movement (cf. Bolle (1999)).[20] These norms usually aim for the mitigation of the social dilemma.

Second, such a success is possible if deviating behavior is punished by the fellow members such that free riding does not pay, like a direct or indirect exclusion from the benefits of the solidarity action.

6.3 Solidarity: A Model on Group Exchange

6.3.1 Solidarity Within a Group and its Similarity to Reciprocity

What are the differences if we regard mutual exchange *within a group* instead of regarding a reciprocal one-to-one relation? In order to discuss these issues we may first distinguish between a small and a large group, and, second, between strategic and non-strategic behavior.

For a small group with individual knowledge of one's companions and with observability of the origin of income transfers we might think that there is no difference to one-to-one relations. This is not completely true if actions have consequences for all members of a group. A typical example is the distribution of non-durable food of which some members have an oversupply. Thus, small groups can be viewed as intermediary between a large group and a one-to-one relation.

A large group may be characterized by anonymous relations. Every member has an idea what consequences his action would have for the group as a whole but he does not know how much an individual member gains or loses. On the other hand, he has an idea how much he gains or loses by the action of the group as a whole but he does not know the influence of an individual member. A typical example is—as discussed in the last section—the provision of a public good within a large group.

If the members of a group do not care about the behavior of others but decide on the basis of a present or an expected state of the world they act non–strategically. Such behavior is more likely to be observed in large than in small groups.

We, therefore, almost completely restrict the following thoughts on a mutual exchange within a group to the case of non-strategic behavior.

[20] A special kind of making gifts is the exchange of hostages. As we showed in Kritikos and Bolle (1998) posing a hostage may lead even to a self-enforcing contract between bargaining parties.

6.3.2 A Small Group with Non-Strategic Behavior

In all periods $t = 0, 1, \ldots$ the individuals $i = 1, \ldots, n$ of a group have the choice between two decisions which effect their own income E_i as well as the income of others, i.e. E_j , $j \neq i$. Individual i can decide to "do nothing" which leaves the income of all group members unchanged, or he can decide to carry out an action which adds constant transfers $T_i = (T_{ij})_{j=1,\ldots,n}$ to the income vector of the individuals. In general, T_i is chosen by an ex ante random process. Individual i carries out his choice under the knowledge of T_i. For the moment, however, let us assume that T_i is constant, i.e. T_i^t is the same for all t. T_{ij} may be larger or smaller than 0, i.e. positive as well as negative consequences are possible for all members. If $T_{ii} < 0$ we would call the action an altruistic act.

i's behavior is guided by an interdependent utility function

$$U_i^t = \sum_j a_{ij}^t E_j^t \tag{6.1}$$

where $a_{ii}^t = 1$ is a normalization. This implies the assumption that the non-normalized a_{ii}^t are positive. All other a_{ij}^t may be positive or negative.

(6.1) implies that i decides to "do nothing" if[21]

$$\sum_j a_{ij}^t T_{ij}^t < 0, \tag{6.2}$$

otherwise he carries out the action with consequences T_i^t . We indicate i's choice by

$$\mathbf{1}_i^t = \begin{cases} 0 & \text{for doing nothing} \\ 1 & \text{for action} \end{cases} \tag{6.3}$$

Mutual exchange is introduced as a dynamic process which changes the coefficients a_{ij}, $j \neq i$, with respect to the behavior of the other group members.

$$a_{ij}^{t+1} = \delta_i a_{ij}^t + \gamma_i T_{ij}^t \mathbf{1}_j^t \tag{6.4}$$

$j \neq i$, with

$$0 < \delta_i < 1 \tag{6.5}$$

and $\gamma_i > 0$.

So, the coefficients a_{ij} underlie depreciation und updating. The latter may be positive or negative and depends on the transfer T_{ji} of group member j to i.

[21] Note that in the case of indifference, the action is chosen.

(6.1), ... , (6.5) describe solidarity as a mutual exchange within a group, and the motives underlying this mutual exchange are described as dynamic altruism.

For given $\mathbf{1}_i^t$ the process (6.4) converges because of $0 < \delta_i < 1$. If, *in a steady state*, the sum from (6.2) is not equal to 0 for any i, then the same is true for a "small enough" neighborhood of the steady state. Within this neighborhood (6.3) will not change while the a_{ij} are approaching the steady state via (6.4). Thus, we can be sure that in the neighborhood of a steady state, (6.4) "almost always" converges. For $T_{ii} < 0$, $a_{ij} = 0$ for all i, j is always a stable steady state.

Let us now have a closer look at **steady states**. Setting $a_{ij}^{t+1} = a_{ij}^t = a_{ij}$ in (6.5) we get

$$a_{ij} = \frac{\gamma_i}{1 - \delta_i} T_{ij} \mathbf{1}_j \tag{6.6}$$

for $j \neq i$.

Positive transfers evoke positive feelings of mutual exchange or altruism and vice versa. So $\mathbf{1}_i = 1$ requires

$$T_{ii} + \frac{\gamma_i}{1 - \delta_i} \sum_{j \neq i} T_{ji} T_{ij} \mathbf{1}_j \geq 0. \tag{6.7}$$

An implication of (6.7) is: If T_{ij} and T_{ji} have the same sign, then the likelihood of $\mathbf{1}_i = 1$ and $\mathbf{1}_j = 1$ is increased, and vice versa. For positive transfers, this is advantageous from the point of view of i and j while, for negative transfers, $\mathbf{1}_i = \mathbf{1}_j = 0$ would be preferred.

With a lot of negative T_{ij} the interaction may result in a revenge-state, even if the T_{ii} are negative (costly revenge). With positive T_{ii} and negative T_{ij} this is more like a Prisoner's Dilemma equilibrium.

In a *public good situation*, i.e. with negative T_{ii} and positive T_{ij}, $j \neq i$, on the average it is more likely that the action will be chosen the more efficient the action is. In this case, we may reach a solidarity-state where everybody sacrifices income for the improvement of the group income.

But is it really always an improvement? From a *superior individual point of view* only oneself's income counts. The inclusion of other people's income in oneself's utility function guides behavior but is not an appropriate measure of success. From a *social point of view*, the sum of incomes may be the appropriate valuation. Even better, we may take the discounted sum of incomes over all future periods in order to evaluate different situations. If

$$\beta_i = \frac{\gamma_i}{1 - \delta_i} \tag{6.8}$$

is too large, then it may happen that some or all members of the group choose "action" although their choice of "action" is inefficient, i.e. $\sum_j T_{ij} < 0$.

On the other hand, β_i should not be too small because, in that case, we may be caught in a state with no action while $\sum_j T_{ij} > 0$.

It is impossible, however, to determine ex ante and without further information an optimal value β_i. As an example, let us regard a very simple structure, namely

$$T = (T_{ij}) = \begin{pmatrix} -1 & \alpha & \cdots & \alpha \\ \alpha & -1 & \cdots & \alpha \\ \vdots & \vdots & \ddots & \vdots \\ \alpha & \alpha & \cdots & -1 \end{pmatrix}. \tag{6.9}$$

This situation may be interpreted as the private supply of a public good. Efficiency requires to choose the "action" alternative if and only if

$$\alpha_0 \geq \frac{1}{n-1}, \tag{6.10}$$

$\alpha_0 = \frac{1}{n-1}$ is the limiting case. On the other hand, (6.7) requires

$$-1 + \beta_i(n-1)\alpha_0^2 \geq 0. \tag{6.11}$$

Thus "action" and "efficiency" coincide if

$$\beta_i = \frac{1}{(n-1)\alpha_0^2} = n-1. \tag{6.12}$$

In this example, the ex ante (without knowledge of the parameter a) optimal β_i depends on the group size. In more complex examples it will depend on the structure of the T_{ij} and it will be different for different individuals i.

The question is completely different, if we do not only regard steady states but also the question of stability in the face of "mistakes". Then it is apparent that b_i should probably be larger than a static optimum like (6.12) because a single "mistake" could induce the system to converge to $a_{ij} = 0$ although $\sum T_{ij} > 0$.

Let us come to a more general model where the **Tij differ from period to period** according to a random process. For the sake of simplicity, let us assume the structure of the T_{ij} to be (6.9) and let us assume that, in addition,

$$\alpha = \begin{cases} \bar{\alpha} > \frac{1}{n-1} & \text{with Prob } = \frac{1}{2} \\ \underline{\alpha} < \frac{1}{n-1} & \text{with Prob } = \frac{1}{2} \end{cases} \tag{6.13}$$

If we could choose β_i, now, it may not be wise to take $\beta_i = n-1$. Why? If once or several times in a row $\alpha = \underline{\alpha}$ occurred, this could lead to a_{ij} so small that, even in the case $\alpha = \overline{\alpha}$, all members of the group choose the no action alternative. Then, the system will inevitably converge to the state with $a_{ij} = 0$ for all i, j.

Such an "accident" is excluded if β_i (and, therefore, the a_{ij}) is large enough so that even if $\alpha = \underline{\alpha}$ permanently occurs the action alternative would be chosen. The least requirement for the optimality of such a β_i is

$$\frac{\underline{\alpha}+\overline{\alpha}}{2}(n-1)-1>0. \tag{6.14}$$

But not in every case a large β_i is optimal. Let us assume β_i to be only so large that, starting from the steady state (6.6), the event $\alpha^1 = \underline{\alpha}$ would lead to the choice of the no action alternative but $(\alpha^1, \alpha^2) = (\underline{\alpha}, \overline{\alpha})$ would result in indifference in the second period (in which case we assumed that the action alternative were chosen). Now the a_{ij}^t converge to the old steady state value again as long as $\alpha^t = \overline{\alpha}$. If, however, one additional time $\alpha^t = \underline{\alpha}$ occurs then the a_{ij} will fall below the critical value in the second period and so, in all future periods, the no action alternative will be chosen. The social value connected with such a β_i is easy to calculate. β_i may not be optimal from a social point of view but it may be superior to a very large one.

In the appendix, we show that the discounted social value connected with such a "medium" b_i is

$$\overline{V} = \frac{1}{2} * \frac{(n-1)\overline{\alpha}-1}{1-\rho+\rho^2/4} \tag{6.15}$$

with $0 < \rho < 1$. ρ is the discount factor.

A sufficiently large β_i would result in

$$V = \frac{1}{2} * \frac{1}{1-\rho}\left[(n-1)\overline{\alpha}-1+(n-1)\underline{\alpha}-1\right]. \tag{6.16}$$

As $(n-1)\underline{\alpha}-1$ is negative it is apparent that, for certain parameter values, we may find $\overline{V} > V$.

6.3.3 Strategic Behavior

The first question is whether it is necessary to base decisions on interdependent utility functions when behavior is strategic. Couldn't the members of a group simply coordinate on efficient behavior? The problem then is that we might be caught in a Prisoners' Dilemma situation. One advantage of non-zero a_{ij} is the commitment which is incorporated in such a valuation.

There is another, even more severe, difficulty. Above we described short-term preferences. Which are the long-term preferences that guide behavior in such a situation? We easily enter discussions about second order preferences (Sen (1977), Bolle (1983)).

For the sake of simplicity, we, therefore, adopt the "doer-planer" model of Thaler and Shefrin (1981). In this model, the doer decides on "action or not" on the basis of short-term preferences like (6.2). The planer wants to maximize the discounted income of the individual. He has only internal means at his disposal, for example, he may be able to increase or decrease a_{ij} in every period by an arbitrary amount α_{ij} with

$$-\varepsilon < \alpha_{ij} < \varepsilon. \tag{6.17}$$

Such a device gives Robert Frank's (1987) hypothetical question "If Homo Oeconomicus could chose his own utility function, would he want one with a conscience?" a concrete meaning.

An instrument like this might make it possible to leave a suboptimal steady state of (a_{ij}) by the joint decision of some of the group members to increase their a_{ij}. Then the rest of the group may be forced into altruism/reciprocity by the process (6.5). And if all contribute we may arrive at a socially advantageous state which no member can leave, even if he chooses $\alpha_{ij} = -\varepsilon$.

6.3.4 Free Riding and Damaging Behavior

A free rider may be defined as someone who chooses the "no action" alternative (because $T_{ii} < 0$) although $\sum_j T_{ij} > 0$. A damager may be defined as someone who chooses the "action" alternative (because $T_{ii} > 0$) although $\sum_j T_{ij} < 0$.

It is less probable that one of these socially unwarranted types j is (in this case: indirectly) punished in an environment with constant T_i and without strategic actions than under the possibility of strategic actions. It seems to be probable (although there may be exceptions) that at least those who suffer from the choices of the social defectors will not try to keep a positive level of a_{ij} for those j who diminish their income (which may be strategically advisable if the choices are efficient).

But even without strategic actions, a Free Rider or a Damager is jeopardized to suffer from "action" decisions of those whose choice of no action is efficient. Let us give two examples. In both examples there is a group of three individuals and, in both examples, it is socially desirable that individual 1 chooses "action" and individual 2 "no action". In Example 1, individual 3 should choose "no action" and, in Example 2, he should choose "action". It is plausible that, if individual 3 sticks to these choices then also 1 and 2 will follow the socially optimal (and also for 3 advantageous) plan.

$$(T_{ij}) = \begin{pmatrix} 1 & 1 & 1 \\ 0 & -1 & -2 \\ -1 & -1 & 1 \end{pmatrix}$$

Table 6.1. Example 1

$$(T_{ij}) = \begin{pmatrix} 1 & 1 & 1 \\ 1 & 0 & -2 \\ 1 & 1 & -1 \end{pmatrix}$$

Table 6.2. Example2

If, however, 3 decides to deviate he is in danger. Let us first regard Example 1, where he could choose the action alternative in order to increase his income by one unit. In the long run, this will make a_{13} and a_{23} negative. While the incentive of 1 to choose "action" will probably be maintained, the incentive of 2 can easily change. From the negative a_{22} he has always an incentive to avoid the "action" alternative but the increasingly negative a_{23} may, at last, change 2's preferences and then 3 will suffer!

In Example 2, Individual 3 might avoid the action alternative in order to save one unit. Then, if the initial a_{23} was positive, a_{23} will decrease although it will keep positive values. When it is small enough, 2 will switch to the "action" alternative in order to do individual 1 a favour. Again, 3 will suffer from his suboptimal choice.

There ist no *guarantee* in this process that 3 will be punished for inefficient behavior. And there is no guarantee that 3 will not suffer even if he decides socially correct. If, in Example 2, T_{21} is larger than 2 individual 2 will choose "action" anyway. Then, on the other hand, there is no longer an incentive for 3 to sacrifice income by his choice.

If 3 has the possibility to act strategically, he should choose the action alternative in Example 2. If 2 has the possibility to act strategically, he should choose the no-action alternative in the case that $a_{21} > 2$ and $1_3 = 1$.

6.3.5 A Large Group with Non-Strategic Behavior

In a large group, an individual cannot distinguish between different sources of income. So, in order to use the above model as an description of a large group we take

$$a_{ij} = a_i \qquad \text{for } j = 1, \ldots, n \tag{6.18}$$

$$a_i^{t+1} = \delta_i a_i^t + \gamma_i \sum_{j \neq i} T_{ji} \mathbf{1}_j^t. \tag{6.19}$$

Steady states are now

$$a_i = \beta_i \sum_{j \neq i} T_{ji} \mathbf{1}_j^t. \tag{6.20}$$

In such a steady state, $\mathbf{1}_j^t = 1$ is connected with

$$T_{ii} + \beta_i \left(\sum_{j \neq i} T_{ji} \mathbf{1}_j^t \right) \left(\sum_{j \neq i} T_{ji} \right) \geq 0 \tag{6.21}$$

It is even clearer and simpler than in the case of a small group that the mutual exchange offers tremendous social advantages but is also connected with the danger of a "revenge-state". If everybody else litters then I litter, too. And I make this decision not only because I do not care but also because I aim to reduce other people's utility. So, even if there is a bin box in the reach of my arm I throw my waste on the street.

However, usually we should expect the T_{ij} to be positive (T_{ii} negative) and, thus, reach (nearly) efficient behavior.

Although these are all simple structures we get extremely diverse developments and interesting stories, if we allow T_{ij} to vary stochastically in every period. This, however, is another paper.

6.4 Conclusion

We distinguished between voluntary and coercive contribution to a solidarity movement as well as between donation and cooperation. As we saw in section 6.2, the most puzzling piece of solidarity movements is when *cooperation* is to be "organized" *voluntarily*. It is basically this kind of solidarity action which contains more dimensions. With respect to voluntary cooperation we showed that there are different orders of public goods which may be aimed to be provided by a "coordinated" solidarity movement and which constitute the willingness to contribute to a solidarity action. Each order of public good is connected with different risks and utility assessments which basically influence the decision whether or not to contribute to a solidarity action.

In section 6.3 we analyzed how a process of mutual beneficial actions is enhanced, for example when a public good is supposed to be provided by a group which is tied together by solidarity feelings. We assumed that these feelings are expressed in a dynamic utility function by an additional term proportional to the income of others. In the long run, the strength of this term is determined by the average income transfers due to the (beneficial) actions of others. One "dark side" of this usually beneficial process is that, under unfortunate circumstances, it may result in an inefficient revenge state. But under many (most?) scenarios we can expect that the dynamic process describing solidarity is efficiency enhancing. In certain situations, it even implies punishment for socially unwarranted behavior.

We certainly have not touched all aspects of solidarity in our paper. Based on our discussion, a number of further issues—as puzzling as those mentioned in section 6.1—could be raised. Let us mention only two examples, namely the normative aspect of solidarity and a dangerous measure to develop solidarity feelings.

The normative point of view of solidarity movements touches the conflict of why a certain target of a movement is a 'good' target which is here implicitly set equal to an efficiency increase and why the present situation is 'bad'. This brings into attention that there are sometimes subjectively good targets which tie together a group to a solidarity movement against a subjectively bad behaving third party, and that it depends always on oneself's point of view whether a movement increases welfare.

But there are more problems than this one. As we have emphazised, coordination is important, in particular in fighting a third party. One solution to the problem of coordination is leadership which, however, also has an ugly face. The producers of the film 'On the Waterfront' launched the film as a story which shows how 'self-appointed tyrants can be defeated by right-thinking people in a vital democracy'. Anderson (1955, pp. 71f) rather asserts that "the conception... seems to be implicitly (if unconsciously) Fascist: Friendly's [the old master's] hold is broken. The dockers have it in their power to be their own masters. Yet, instead of rising to the occasion, they turn like leaderless sheep in search of a new master. 'If Terry walks in, we walk in with him'. If there is any principle expounded here, it is surely not that of Democracy. The people collectively are shown as incapable of either self-government or mutual aid."

There are not only solidarity movements which turned the set of social rules from hierarchic to democratic rules but also the other way round. This shows that the third party is not always an autocratic regime (as mentioned in the introduction) but has historically often been a wealthier but weaker minority (like the Jews in prewar Germany or the Armenians in Turkey) which was systematically persecuted and killed by a movement which was guided by the enlightening fact that things get better (more efficient) when the respective minority which was responsible for all kinds of evil in a population or even in the world, is 'extinguished'.[22]

It is a well established fact that an action against a common enemy (which we neutrally called the third party) can strengthen the ties of a solidarity movement. Thus the invention of enemies may become a political instrument. This is a paradoxical measure: solidarity towards part of the society is sacrificed in order to strengthen the solidarity feelings of the rest. [23]

Appendix

1. The Calculation of $\overline{V}$

$\overline{V}$ is the social value of a medium b_i, as described in the case belonging to (6.15). In every period with a history of only $\overline{\alpha}$ events this social value is the same. In every period with a history of one $\underline{\alpha}$ event and otherwise only

[22] cf. Bolle2 (1991). Of course also these movements were able to realize an increase of their objective utility by redistributing the property of the persecuted wealthy minority.

[23] With that we would enter the discussion on the psychology of the masses which contains more aspects than raised here. For an excellent introduction into this theme cf. Le Bon (1895) who claimed that such movements adhere to the law of the mental unit of the masses (loi de lœnité mentale des foules) so that from a certain point the mere participation in such a group may already lead to an increase of utility.

$\overline{\alpha}$ events, the social value is denoted by $\underline{V}$. In every period with a history of two or more $\underline{\alpha}$ events, the social value is zero. Thus, we get

$$\overline{V} = \frac{1}{2}\left[(n-1)\overline{\alpha} - 1 + \rho\overline{V}\right] + \frac{1}{2}\rho\underline{V} \tag{6.A1}$$

$$\underline{V} = \frac{1}{2}\left[(n-1)\overline{\alpha} - 1 + \rho\underline{V}\right] \tag{6.A2}$$

and therefore

$$\overline{V} = \frac{1}{2} * \frac{1}{1-\rho+\rho^2/4}\left[(n-1)\overline{\alpha} - 1\right]. \tag{6.A3}$$

2. The Calculation of V

Sufficiently large b_i result in choices of "action" independent of the event. Thus, we get

$$V = \frac{1}{2}\left[(n-1)\overline{\alpha} - 1\right] + \frac{1}{2}\left[(n-1)\underline{\alpha} - 1\right] + \rho V \tag{6.A4}$$

and therefore

$$V = \frac{1}{2}\frac{1}{1-\rho}\left[(n-1)\overline{\alpha} - 1 + (n-1)\underline{\alpha} - 1\right] \tag{6.A5}$$

References

[1] Akerlof, G. (1970). The Market for Lemons. *Quarterly Journal of Economics 84*, 488–500.

[2] Anderson, L. (1955). The Last Sequence of 'On the Waterfront'. *Sight and Sound*, 70–76.

[3] Andreoni, J. (1995). Warm Glow Versus Cold Prickle: The Effects of Positive and Negative Framing on Cooperation in Experiments. *Quarterly Journal of Economics 110*, 1–21.

[4] Arrow, K. (1963). Uncertainty and the Welfare Economics of Medical Care. *American Economic Review 53*, 941–973.

[5] Baldwin, P. (1990). *The Politics of Social Solidarity.* Cambridge Univ. Press.

[6] Bolle, F. (1983). On Sen's Second Order Preferences, Morals, and Decision Theory. *Erkenntnis 20*, 195–205.

[7] Bolle, F. (1991). On Love and Altruism. *Rationality and Society 3*, 197–214.

[8] Bolle, F. (1995). Emotionen und Vernunft – keine Gegensätze. *Homo Oeconomicus 12*, 125–154.

[9] Bolle, F. (1999). Why to Buy Your Darling Flowers: On Cooperation and Exploitation. *Theory and Decision*, in print.

[10] Church, R. and Q. Outram (1998). *Strikes and Solidarity.* Cambridge Univ. Press.

[11] Edin, P.-A. and B. Holmlund (1993). The Swedish Wage Structure: The Rise and Fall of Solidarity Wage Policy. NBER Working Paper #4257.

[12] Frank, R. (1987). If Homo Economicus Could Choose his Own Utility Function, Would he Want One with a Conscience? *American Economic Review 77*, 593–604.

[13] Gide, C. (1987). Solidarity. in: J. Eatwell, M. Milgrate, P. Newan (eds.): *The New Palgrave - A Dictionary of Economics*, Macmillan London, Vol. III, 421.

[14] Isaac, R., J. Walker, and A. Williams (1994). Group Size and the Voluntary Provision of Public Goods: Experimental Evidence Utilizing Large Groups. *Journal of Public Economics 54*, 1–36.

[15] Kennedy, M. (1991). *Professionals, Power and Solidarity in Poland.* Camb. Univ. Press.

[16] Krahnen, J. and R. Schmidt (1994). *Development Finance as Institution Building.* Westview Press.

[17] Kritikos, A. (1999). Kleinkredite mit anreizgesteuertem Solidareintritt. *Kredit und Kapital 32*, 393–425.

[18] Kritikos, A. and F. Bolle (1998). Indenturing Banknotes as a Mechanism to Induce Cooperation. *Journal of Economic Behavior and Organization 34*, 279–294.

[19] Kritikos, A. and F. Bolle (1999). Approaching Fair Behavior: Inequality Aversion Versus Reciprocity and Altruism. Disc. paper, Frankfurt (Oder).

[20] Kritikos, A. and G. Meran (1998). Social Norms, Moral Commitment and Cooperation. *Homo Oeconomicus 15*, 71–92.

[21] Kulczycki, J. (1994). *The Foreign Worker and the German Labour Movement. Xenophobia and Solidarity in the Coal Fields of the Ruhr, 1871-1914.* Oxford/Providence: Berg.

[22] Ledyard, J. (1995). Public Goods: A Survey of Experimental Research. in: J. Kagel and A.E. Roth (eds.): *Handbook of Experimental Economics*, 111-194.

[23] Lindenberg, S. (1988). Contractual Relations and Weak Solidarity: The Behavioral Basis of Restraints on Gain–Maximization. *Journal of Institutional and Theoretical Economics 144*, 39–58.

[24] Orbell, J., A. van de Kragt, and R. Dawes (1988). Explaining Discussion–Induced Cooperation. *Journal of Personality and Social Psychology 54*, 811–819.

[25] Ouchi, W. (1980). Markets, Bureaucracies, and Clans. *Administrative Science Quarterly 25*, 129–141.

[26] Polinksy, A. and S. Shavell (1991). A Note on Optimal Fines When Wealth Varies Among Individuals. *American Economic Review 81*, 618–621.

[27] Selten, R. and A. Ockenfels (1998). An Experimental Solidarity Game. *Journal of Economic Behavior and Organization 34*, 517–539.

[28] Sen, A. (1977). Rational Fools: A Critique of the Behavioral Foundations of Economic Theory. *Philosophy and Public Affairs 6*, 317–344.

[29] Sugden, R. (1986). *The Economics of Rights, Cooperation and Welfare.* Oxf. Univ. Press.

[30] Thaler, R. and H. Shefrin (1981). An Economic Theory of Self–Control. *Journal of Political Economy 89*, 392–406.

[31] Touraine, A., F. Dubet, M. Wieviorka, and J. Strzelecki (1983). *Solidarity.* Cambridge Univ. Press.

[32] Universallexikon (1988). Volume 5, p. 50. Leipzig: VEB Bibliographisches Institut. Printed in the German Democratic Republic.

7 What is a Game?

The Winner Takes it All

Arnis Vilks*

7.1 Introduction

More and more, game theory is becoming the basic tool of economic theory, and it is increasingly found useful in other disciplines such as philosophy, political science, computer science, and even formal logic.

However, many basic notions and assumptions of game theory remain puzzling, and give rise to sometimes heated controversy among acknowledged experts in the field. The present contribution aims at formulating several interrelated questions concerning the foundations of game theory not all of which have received the attention they deserve. The questions are these: What is a game? What is an option? And: How should we model knowledge and belief? While there is a body of literature on the latter of these questions, I believe that its connection with the first two – which do not often seem to be recognized as worthwhile questions at all – has or should have important consequences for modeling knowledge and belief.

Let me begin with the observation that the very notion of a game remains somewhat ambiguous. To be sure, there are unambiguously defined mathematical concepts which are often identified with the concept of game: The concepts "n-player game in strategic form", "extensive game", "coalitional game without transferable utility", and similar ones can be defined with all the clarity that is expected in pure mathematics. However, the fact that game theorists discuss the question of whether two different extensive games "represent the same strategic situation" (Osborne and Rubinstein, 1994, p. 204), or the question whether the "extensive form" or the "strategic form" of a game represent the strategically relevant features of the envisaged situation, points to an underlying idea of "strategic situation" which is only imperfectly captured by the existing formal definitions.

Intuitively, a game is defined by its rules, and the players' preferences among the possible outcomes. In what follows, we will treat players' preferences as more or less unproblematic, and focus instead on the notion of "rules of the game".

* This paper was written while I was visiting the Center for the Study of Language and Information (CSLI) at Stanford University.

7.2 What Are the Rules of a Game?

For the paradigmatic cases of parlor games, the notion of "rules" seems relatively straightforward. The rules of a parlor game are typically available in an explicit form: As a list of sentences saying what may be done by which player in any particular situation of a play of the game. For a parlor game, the list of rules is typically available to, and understood by, all the players.

If one is interested in analyzing a particular parlor game, such as bridge or chess, one can typically disregard the fact that players can violate the rules of any such game, or that they can systematically try to influence the outcome of the game by doing things which are not regulated by the games' written rules. After all, in analyzing a particular parlor game one will typically not be interested in what happens when players contemplate, or carry out actions which are not permitted or not mentioned by the explicit rules. As a matter of fact, however, it is obviously not true that the players of a parlor game never consider breaking the rules or trying in some way to modify them. The history of poker, or of chess, for instance, contains many examples where players did violate the explicitly stated rules, or tried to influence the opponent's play by behavior which is not covered by the written rules.

Conversely, as it were, a game such as chess is well known for having variants or "openings" – such as the King's Gambit, Ruy Lopez, or Giuoco Piano – defined by certain opening moves or a particular position that has to be reached in the course of the play in order to classify it as an instance of that variant. Of such an opening one can ask whether two players who are playing, for instance, the King's Gambit, or have agreed to do so, are still playing, or are about to play, chess. At least in everyday language it seems perfectly natural to say that they are playing *both* chess *and* the King's Gambit at the same time – after all they are not violating the rules of either. On the other hand, for a game-theoretic analysis of "King's Gambit" one is inclined to disregard the opening moves d2-d4 and d7-d5 as "irrelevant" – one tends to disregard all moves whereof it is somehow taken for granted that they will not be made.

Now, in those "games" that are most relevant for economists the observations just made may well turn into problems. Except, perhaps, in the case of auctions, where applied game theory has been remarkably successful, explicit rules typically do not exist prior to game-theoretic modelling. For a typical oligopoly, for instance, there quite obviously do not exist explicitly written rules defining "the game" that is played by the oligopolists - unless the economist analyzing the market decides to use a particular game-theoretic model to describe the market interaction. To be sure, some rules of a market – most notably the rules of law - may be available in an explicit form independently of an economist analyzing the market, but they typically do not include most of the restrictions a game theorist would want to specify.

And even when a game theorist has produced a model of a particular case of interdependent decision-making, that model will typically not be available to, let alone understood by, all the agents described by the model. In such a case, "breaking the rules" or taking actions not covered by the rules will just correspond to taking actions which do not appear in the game-theorist's model. Similarly, the game-theoretic model may contain actions which the agents themselves do not contemplate, or it may distinguish between actions which are not distinguished by the agents. To be sure, a posteriori such phenomena can always be blamed on inadequate modeling. If the agents have chosen to do things which were not represented by the model, or if they have failed to consider options which were available to them in the model, one can try to improve the model by adding options one had previously neglected, or by dropping options which were not considered by the agents themselves. The question remains, however, whether there are criteria for the adequacy of a formal game-theoretic model. After all, one is often not so much interested in giving an a-posteriori explanation for what has actually happened, but rather in predicting the likely behavior of interacting real agents.

Now, while it is sometimes doubtful whether a particular move should or should not be included in a game-theoretic model of some particular strategic situation, there is typically tacit agreement among game theorists about clear cases of "irrelevant" moves. Clearly, most of the actions which are physically possible for the agents under consideration – which they were able to carry out, if only they chose to – would never be explicitly included in a game-theoretic model of a real strategic situation, and even the attempt at doing so would be ridiculous: No reasonable model of an oligopoly will include the "moves" of donating one's company to a competitor, or of shooting all market participants – even though there is little doubt that such actions are "possible", "available", or "feasible" in an objective or absolute sense.

It is thus only natural to argue that a game should be modeled as perceived by the players. (Cf. Rubinstein (1991).) Now, during the last 15 years there has been growing interest among game theorists in epistemic conditions for game-theoretic solution concepts[1], that is, in conditions about the knowledge and/or beliefs of the players that would ensure that the game will actually be played according to a particular solution concept, and it seems that the conceptual and formal tools developed for this purpose should also allow one to make explicit what the players perceive "the game" to be. To be sure, different players may have different beliefs about the game that is played, and if the envisaged situation is of this sort, if might be modeled as a game of incomplete information. But the conceptual tools for describing players' knowledge seem to also provide the tools for describing what they "consider possible": Not knowing that an event E does not obtain, is both plausibly and routinely interpreted as "considering E possible". (Cf. for instance, Binmore (1992), Fagin et al. (1995), Samet (1996), or Dekel and Gul (1997).)

[1] Cf., for instance, Bacharach (1987, 1994), Aumann (1995), Aumann and Brandenburger (1995).

Let us focus on the consequences of such an attempt.

7.3 A "Triviality of Choice" Result

There is a tension between the standard construal of "considering possible" and standard assumptions of game theory, which can be explained informally as follows. Such standard assumptions - for instance rationality and intelligence of the players, or common knowledge thereof – are motivated by the wish to predict the outcome – the actual play of the game. Typically, such standard assumptions will imply not only a particular play, but also that the players themselves can predict the actual play. Now, if this includes a specific prediction of one's own behavior, such standard assumptions will imply that a player knows of all other options he might have, that they will not be actually chosen. But then he knows of any option but the one he will choose that he will not choose it. Which flatly contradicts that he does not know he will not choose it.

Actually, this problem arises in the simplest case – one-agent games. It has been discussed in the philosophical literature (cf. Schick (1988, 1999), Levi (1991)) for the one-agent case, and it may be instructive to reformulate the verbal argument in the formal framework of information structures. Imagine Robinson Crusoe on his island, before he meets Freitag. To formulate the relevant "game" here just amounts to formulating Robinson's relevant optimization problem, that is, to specify the set of feasible options – for short, the feasible set – and his preferences. To focus on our question, let us disregard Robinson's preferences for the moment, and just ask ourselves what the feasible set should be.

Let P be the set of all actions which are *physically* possible for Robinson – the set of all those actions which he could carry out, if only he chose to. Again, this set will include many things Robinson would never seriously consider – such as stirring the ocean waves with a teaspoon. It will also include many actions Robinson is not aware of, and maybe some whereof he mistakenly believes that they are *not* physically possible. Even if we now assume that Robinson's preference relation $\succ$ on P is available, it seems clear that one can hardly hope to specify the set P in a way that would allow one to actually solve the resulting optimization problem $(P, \succ)$. But quite apart from such considerations of tractability, it seems clear enough that $(P, \succ)$ would be quite inadequate as a description of Robinson's problem of choice.

In fact, it seems much more adequate – and also more in line with actual economic modeling - to include only those actions in Robinson's feasible set which he actually considers possible – that is, according to the reading we want to consider, only those actions whereof he does not already know that he will not choose them anyway.

Now, the standard way of describing what an agent knows is by means of an information structure or knowledge system. (A recent state-of-the art survey is given by Aumann (1999)). For our purpose, a knowledge system can be taken to consist of a state space Ω, a function $f : \Omega \to P$, and a correspondence $\wp$ from Ω to Ω such that $\omega \in \wp(\omega)$ for all $\omega \in \Omega$, and where the collection $\{\wp(\omega) : \omega \in \Omega\}$ is a partition of Ω. The state space is meant to consist of all (objectively) possible states of affairs or "possible worlds", the function f tells us which action Robinson would carry out, if a particular possible world were the actual one, and $\wp(\omega)$ is meant to consist of all possible worlds which our agent Robinson considers possible, if the actual world is ω. In world ω, Robinson knows that the actual world is in $E \subset \Omega$, or "knows that E" for short, if all worlds he considers possible are in E, that is, if $\wp(\omega) \subset E$. Denoting the set of all worlds where Robinson knows that E by K(E), this can be summed up by the following definition:

$$\omega \in K(E) : \wp(\omega) \subset E.$$

In words once again: At world ω, the agent knows that event E obtains, if and only if all worlds which the agent considers possible at ω, belong to E.

It is well known (and easy to check) that the knowledge operator K has the following properties (we write $\sim E$ for $\Omega \setminus E$):

(1) $K(\Omega) = \Omega$
(2) $K(E) \subset E$ (this is called the "Truth" or "Veridicality" axiom)
(3) $E \subset F$ implies $K(E) \subset K(F)$
(4) $K(E) \subset K(K(E))$ ("positive Introspection")
(5) $\sim K(E) \subset K(\sim K(E))$ ("negative Introspection")
(6) $K(E \cap F) = K(E) \cap K(F)$

For any potential action $a \in P$, let us write $[a]$ for the event that Robinson carries out a. Formally:

$$[a] := \{\omega \in \Omega : f(\omega) = a\}.$$

From what we said above, it appears that an action $a \in P$ should be considered an option for Robinson at a world ω, if and only if he "considers it possible", that is, if and only if he does not know at ω that he will not choose a. Accordingly, define Robinson's "feasible set" $F(\omega) \subset P$ by:

$$F(\omega) := \{a \in P : \omega \in \sim K \sim [a]\}$$

Assuming for simplicity that P is finite, that Robinson is never indifferent between any two distinct actions, and denoting his (strict) preference relation on the set P by $\succ$, we can now describe Robinson's optimization problem at ω as the problem of choosing the most preferred action from those in $F(\omega)$. The assumption that he actually does optimize at world ω, is accordingly expressed by the conditions

$$\begin{aligned} &f(\omega) \in F(\omega) \\ \text{and} \quad &\{b \in F(\omega) : b \succ f(\omega)\} = \emptyset. \end{aligned}$$

As (2) implies that $[a] \subset \sim K \sim [a]$, it is easy to see that the first of these conditions is always satisfied, so that the assumption that Robinson optimizes, is captured by the second condition alone. It is also easy to verify that this second condition holds for ω, if and only if ω belongs to the following "rationality" event:

$$R := \bigcap_{a \in P} \bigcap_{b \in P : b \succ a} \sim ([a] \cap \sim K \sim [b])$$

If we denote the most preferred action from $F(\omega)$ by $a^*(\omega)$, we can alternatively write

$$R = \{\omega \in \Omega : f(\omega) = a^*(\omega)\}.$$

So far, so good. We have done nothing else than writing down alternative formal representations of the event that Robinson chooses the most preferred action from the set of actions he considers possible. But now recall that each $F(\omega)$, together with Robinson's preferences $\succ$, defines a game – although a very simple one. To these very simple games we should certainly be able to apply those "standard" assumptions which are used for the analysis of much more complicated games.

One such standard assumption is that there is common knowledge of rationality. In our particularly simple case, this assumption boils down to the seemingly much more harmless one that the isolated agent we consider knows that he is rational. In this one-agent case, property (4) of the knowledge operator ensures that knowledge and common knowledge coincide. Thus, consider the event K(R). It has the following property, which we call "triviality of choice":

(Triviality of Choice) $\quad \omega \in K(R)$ implies $F(\omega) = \{a^*(\omega)\}$.

Proof. By property (2), $\omega \in K(R)$ implies $\omega \in R$. As we already know that $f(\omega) \in F(\omega)$, it follows that $a^*(\omega) \in F(\omega)$. To see that $F(\omega)$ cannot contain other actions, assume that $b \in F(\omega)$, and $b \neq a^*(\omega)$. For this b, it must be the case that $a^*(\omega) \succ b$. Thus

$$R \subset \sim ([b] \cap \sim K \sim [a^*(\omega)]).$$

By property (3), we get

$$KR \subset K\Big(\sim ([b] \cap \sim K \sim [a^*(\omega)])\Big).$$

As $\omega \in \sim K \sim [a^*(\omega)] \subset K(\sim K \sim [a^*(\omega)])$ (by property (5)), $\omega \in KR$ implies

$$\omega \in K\Big(\sim ([b] \cap \sim K \sim [a^*(\omega)])\Big) \cap K\Big(\sim K \sim [a^*(\omega)]\Big)$$

,

which by property (6) implies

$$\omega \in K\Big(\sim ([b] \cap \sim K \sim [a^*(\omega)]) \cap \sim K \sim [a^*(\omega)]\Big).$$

As $\sim ([b] \cap \sim K \sim [a^*(\omega)]) \cap \sim K \sim [a^*(\omega)] \subset \sim [b]$, property (3) implies $\omega \in K(\sim [b])$, which contradicts the assumption $b \in F(\omega)$. QED

In a sense, this triviality of choice result is easy to interpret: If Robinson knows that he is rational, he is rational. As rationality means he will choose $a^*(\omega)$, he must consider $a^*(\omega)$ possible. By negative introspection, he must then know that he considers $a^*(\omega)$ possible, and he can combine this knowledge with his self-knowledge of rationality to rule out any other action b. For all he knows, no other action than the optimal one is possible.

Also in a sense, it is easy to see the reason for the triviality of choice result: Our rational Robinson will probably consider possible some non-optimal actions *before* he reflects on his rationality and on what he is going to do, but *after* he has made up his mind, he does not really have a "problem" to solve. Given that (according to the properties of our knowledge framework) he has then drawn all inferences from his self-knowledge of rationality, and does not have the slightest doubt about what he is going to do, one might well say that then, for all that he knows, it is not possible that he will act non-optimally.

Alternatively, we might want to distinguish between what the agent knows and considers possible *before* he has taken his rationality into account, and what he knows and considers possible *afterwards*. If we use only one knowledge system to describe an agent's knowledge in both situations, we get into trouble.

7.4 What do Players not Know? And when?

For a one-agent choice problem, it is easy to circumvent the triviality of choice problem. In order to predict Robinson's choice, it suffices to assume that he is rational. There is no need to assume that he knows himself to be rational. But if there is real interaction between two or more players, we have to face the fact that a player will typically make inferences from his knowledge or beliefs about his opponents' rationality.

In some very simple situations such as the one of Figure 7.1, the assumption that players know about their own rationality, can still be avoided. If we assume that player I is rational and considers both a_1 and d_1 possible, we just have to add the assumption that player I knows of II that he is rational and considers both a_2 and d_2 possible (if his node is reached). The prediction that player I moves "down" then follows, while the players themselves do not know this.

Certainly, one would like to make the stronger assumption that both players know that all our above assumptions hold. This stronger assumption,

Fig. 7.1.

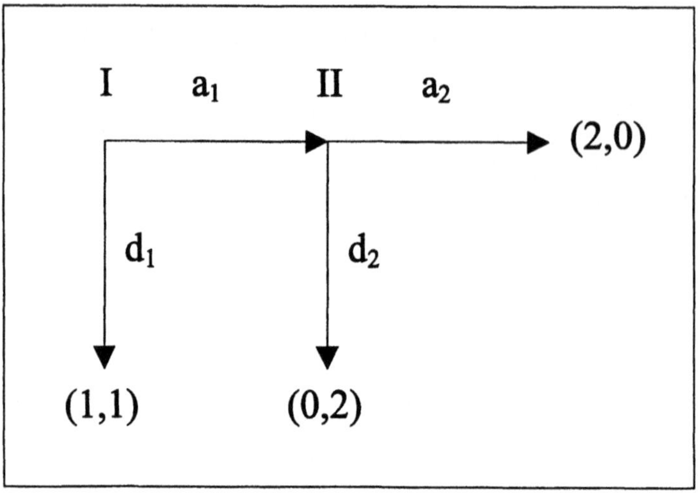

however, is just inconsistent, for it would imply that player I knows that the event $[a_1]$ does not obtain, but that he still considers it possible.

Now, one may react to the problem by insisting that $\sim K_I \sim [a_1]$ should not be read as "player I considers a_1 possible", and that the relevant notion of subjective feasibility must be a different one for which it is consistent to assume that a player knows he will not make a particular move, and that this move is nevertheless feasible. After all, Robinson may know he will not stir the ocean waves with a teaspoon, but still regard this as a feasible action. This may be so, but we would hardly want to include all such feasible, but apparently "silly" actions in the "relevant" description of Robinson's problem. The reason seems to be the very fact that they are "silly" – or, in other words, the fact that they are clearly non-optimal. But if one is allowed to exclude "clearly non-optimal" actions from the description of the relevant game, one must also be allowed to exclude a_2 from the description of the relevant game between I and II. Applying the analogous argument to the resulting tree, we end up with a trivial game again: The relevant game then seems to consist of d_1 alone. For only slightly more complex games such a procedure is hardly acceptable – after all, one would not expect, for instance, the backward induction play in a game of perfect information, if players are ignorant about their opponents' rationality.

Thus, where explicit "rules of the game" are missing, it seems that we always exclude many physically possible actions from the description of the relevant game because of rationality considerations, but that we are reluctant to do so in other cases. The reason seems to be that the property of being "clearly" non-optimal is a matter of degree. If a long chain of reasoning is required to see that a move is non-optimal, we cannot take it for granted that the respective player will actually reason that way. In the case of "silly" actions no reasoning at all seems to be required before one knows one will abstain from carrying them out. Only a short chain of reasoning is required to "solve" the game of Figure 7.1, but in the case of a more complicated game tree, actual players may have to reason for some time before they know what they will do. In order to regard an action as "relevant", there should at least be – or have been – a moment of time where it was not known to some player that it will not be taken.

From the standard model of knowledge, reasoning as a time-consuming process is strikingly absent. Instead, the knowledge of the partition model (and in fact, of more general Kripke-style models) is the knowledge of agents who have already drawn all conclusions they can draw from whatever they know. If we use it to describe players who have already solved any interactive decision problem they may have perceived, we should not be surprised that they do not face a "problem" anymore, and that no traces of the ignorance that defines "having a problem to solve" can be found in that knowledge.

If we want a description of players' knowledge and/or beliefs which allows one to make explicit assumptions about how the players reduce initial ignorance by means of reasoning, more refined models seem to be required[2].

7.5 Conclusion?

It was the questions we wanted to emphasize. We have no definitive conclusions to offer. Tentatively, it seems to us that a game should be modeled "as perceived by the players", and that this must include a specification of both what the players know, and what they do not know. It seems utterly impractical to include all physically possible actions in the "relevant" game, and hardly less impractical to include all actions which the respective players consider physically possible. A more promising criterion seems to be that the relevant game should only include actions whereof some player at some point during his reasoning process was uncertain whether they will be carried out. However, if one wants to describe and analyze how the players reduce this ignorance by means of reasoning, and, in some cases at least, arrive at a prediction, the currently predominant "static" models of information, knowledge, and belief may have to be refined or supplemented by explicitly "procedural" ones.

References

[1] Aumann, R. (1995). Backward Induction and Common Knowledge of Rationality. *Games and Economic Behavior 8*, 6–19.

[2] Some steps in this direction can be found in Vilks (1997, 1999), and Clausing (1999).

[2] Aumann, R. (1999). Interactive Epistemology I: Knowledge. *International Journal of Game Theory 28*, 263–300.
[3] Aumann, R. and A. Brandenburger (1995). Epistemic Conditions for Nash Equilibrium. *Econometrica 63*, 1161–1180.
[4] Bacharach, M. (1987). A Theory of Rational Decision in Games. *Erkenntnis 27*, 17–55.
[5] Bacharach, M. (1994). The Epistemic Structure of a Theory of a Game. *Theory and Decision 37*, 7–48.
[6] Binmore, K. (1992). *Fun and Games: A Text on Game Theory.* Lexington: D.C. Heath.
[7] Clausing, T. (1999). *The Logical Modelling of Reasoning Processes in Games.* Doctoral Dissertation. Leipzig Graduate School of Management (HHL).
[8] Dekel, E. and F. Gul (1997). Rationality and Knowledge in Game Theory. in: *Advances in Economics and Econometrics: Theory and Applications Volume I*, D.M. Kreps and K. F. Wallis (eds.), Cambridge: Cambridge University Press.
[9] Fagin, R., J. Halpern, Y. Moses, and M. Vardi (1995). *Reasoning about Knowledge.* Cambridge, MA: MIT Press.
[10] Levi, I. (1991). Consequentialism and Sequential Choice. in: *Foundations of Decision Theory*, M. Bacharach and S. Hurley (eds.). Cambridge, MA: Blackwell.
[11] Osborne, M. and A. Rubinstein (1994). *A Course in Game Theory.* Cambridge and London: MIT Press.
[12] Rubinstein, A. (1991). Comments on the Interpretation of Game Theory. *Econometrica 59*, 909–924.
[13] Samet, D. (1996). Hypothetical Knowledge and Games with Perfect Information. *Games and Economic Behavior 17*, 230–251.
[14] Schick, F. (1988). Self–Knowledge, Uncertainty, and Choice. in: *Decision, probability, and utility*, P. Gaerdenfors and N.-E. Sahlin (eds.). Cambridge: Cambridge University Press. (Reprinted from The British Journal of Philosophy, 30: 1979.).
[15] Schick, F. (1999). Surprise, Self–Knowledge, and Commonality. in: *Spinning Ideas: Electronic Essays Dedicated to Peter Gaerdenfors on His Fiftieth Birthday* , Halldén, S., B. Hansson, W. Rabinowicz, N.-E. Sahlin (eds.). http://www.lucs.lu.se/spinning/.
[16] Vilks, A. (1997). A Player's Reasoning Process as a Sequence of Propositional Calculi. in: *Epistemic Logic and the Theory of Games and Decisions*, M. Bacharach, L.A. Gerard-Varet, P. Mongin, and H. Shin (eds.). Boston: Kluwer.
[17] Vilks, A. (1999). A Logic for Changing Beliefs with Applications to Reasoning About Choices and Games. in: *Spinning Ideas: Electronic Essays Dedicated to Peter Gaerdenfors on His Fiftieth Birthday* , Halldén, S., B. Hansson, W. Rabinowicz, N.-E. Sahlin (eds.). http://www.lucs.lu.se/spinning/.

8 Monopolistic and Oligopolistic Imperfect Demand Competition
Preferences of Suppliers for Demanders

Jochen Schumann*

8.1 Introduction

The traditional literature on imperfect competition concentrates on suppliers competing about demanders who have preferences for certain suppliers. One could say that, by the preferences of demanders, every supplier may act like a monopolist within certain limits - the limits being due to the fact that the products offered by suppliers are, in demanders' opinion, narrow substitutes. Every supplier sells one specific variant of the product, which is determined by demanders' preferences. There is, thus, product differentiation on the supply side of the market, and there are, on the rule, different profit maximizing prices set by suppliers for the specific but similar variants of the product. This description applies to the models of many suppliers' "monopolistic competition" by Chamberlin (1965), of "imperfect competition" by Robinson (1933) and of "polypolistic competition" by Gutenberg (1979) as well as to models of a few suppliers' heterogenous oligopolistic competition in the tradition of Launhardt (1885) and Hotelling (1929).

In this paper, we wish to apply arguments of the models of imperfect monopolistic and oligopolistic suppliers' competition to situations of imperfect demanders' competition. Demanders compete about suppliers who have preferences for certain demanders. By the preferences of suppliers, a demander may act like a monopsonist within limits - the limits being due to the fact that the products wanted by demanders are narrow substitutes. Every demander buys a specific variant of the product, which is determined by suppliers' preferences. There is product differentiation on the demand side of the market and there are, on the rule, different profit maximizing prices set by demanders for the specific but similar variants of the product.

We will firstly discuss a model of many demanders' monopolistic competition applying arguments in the Chamberlin-Robinson-Gutenberg tradition; and we will secondly dispute a model of few demanders' oligopolistic competition using arguments along the Launhardt-Hotelling tradition. We have,

* I am very grateful to contribute to this volume in honour of Horst Todt. We have been closest friends since the beginning of our second decade of life. High school at Aschaffenburg, studies of economics at Frankfurt University and at Innsbruck University - we shared all stations of juvenile life, of adventures and of learning. When he went to Hamburg and I went to Münster, it was not more than a local diversification.

preliminarily, hinted to models of this type in a textbook (cf. Schumann (1992, chapter IV.C.3 and D.4)).

Instead of "demanders' monopolistic competition", we might also speak of "monopsonistic competition"; and instead of "demanders' oligopolistic competition", the term "oligopsonistic competition" might be used. We shall, however, not use this terminology.

We will assume that demanders are firms demanding factors of production. As examples for the models of demanders' competition, we will frequently refer to the labour market. This means that either many or few firms act as demanders of labour-services, and the labourers supplying the services have preferences in working for certain firms. The examples are not more than illustrations but suggest that the translation of models of suppliers' competition into models of demanders' competition is more than an arbitrary theoretical exercise.

8.2 Monopolistic Imperfect Demand Competition

A market of monopolistic imperfect demand competition may be portrayed by the following asssumptions:

- There are many suppliers and demanders, everyone having only a small share in total supply or demand.
- Imperfect demand competition means that suppliers are not indifferent as to which demander buys their product or labour-service. A supplier has preferences for certain demanders, he is even ready to accept a somewhat lower price from a demander preferred by him.
- Demanders are well informed about the supply of the product or labour-service and about the preferences of suppliers on the market. Suppliers have either perfect or restricted information about the prices set by demanders.

It may be advisable to discuss the meaning of suppliers' preferences as elements of imperfect competition. In the Gutenberg model of suppliers' polypolistic competition, there are locational, personal and physical preferences of demanders for certain suppliers or their product. Applied to the labour market, we may fomulate the following preferences of suppliers for demanders:

Locational preferences: Labour suppliers prefer nearly situated labour demanding firms to save time and cost of transportation.

Personal preferences: There are long-term personal relations between suppliers and demanders. Labour suppliers profit from a firm's culture and reputation.

Physical preferences: Labour suppliers prefer a firm which combines labour with modern machines in a clean environment.

There may, however, be further preferences of labour suppliers for certain firms which are not attributable to one of the three types of preferences mentioned. It is, in particular, the firm's corporate identity, the specific cultural and social equipment the firm has invested in, which attract competent labour and which creates the preferences of labour for this firm. These preferences connect a supplier to a certain demander - even if other conditions of the labour contract, for example wage payments, would be a little bit better with other demanders. In such a market of non-price competition, there can, of course, be different wages set by different demanders. Demanders' non-price competition on the labour market is, however, particularly important if wage-rates are not individually bargained between every demander and supplier, but are the result of collective bargaining between firms and unions.

Generalizing from labour markets to all kinds of markets, our argument is that quite frequently demanders invest in creating suppliers' preferences. In the usually discussed scenario of suppliers' competition, the suppliers invest in sellers' marketing in order to create demanders' preferences. In the presently discussed scenario of demanders' competition, demanders invest in what we like to call buyers' marketing, which is destined to create suppliers' preferences.

In the Chamberlin-Robinson-Gutenberg models of imperfect supply competition, a supplier by sellers' marketing may shift the demand curve for his product (as seen by him) to the right. Considering the influence of marketing expenses on the cost curve and on the shift of the demand curve, a supplier may compute the sales marketing budget and the sales price which will maximize his profit. - In the scenario of imperfect demand competition, a demander may by buyers' marketing shift the supply curve for the product or labour-service (as seen by him) to the right. Considering marketing cost and the shift of the supply curve, a demander may determine the buyers' marketing budget and the price which maximize his profit. If the buyer's price is given to him by the collectively bargained labour wage-rate, he may compute the profit maximizing marketing budget.

Under the conditions of monopolistic imperfect demand competition, every demander's share in total demand being small, the influences of a single demander's price or wage-rate setting and buyers' marketing actions on other demanders' market position are negligible. A demander, therefore, will not react on other demanders' actions. (This is different in oligopolistic imperfect demand competition to be treated in the next section).

In the following analysis of a representative demander's position, we exclude collective price or wage-rate bargaining, and we assume given buyers' marketing budgets and a given supply curve (as seen by the demander). To discuss some details of this supply curve, we transform Gutenberg's arguments for his double kinked demand curve (cf. Gutenberg (1979, chapter 6.III.B)). Because a representative supplier has buyer's marketing-created preferences to sell his good or labour-service to the demander considered, this demander will not loose all of his suppliers if he reduces the price or wage-rate. Some suppliers will move to other demanders or will withdraw from the market, but preferences will bind most of the suppliers to this demander if the reduction is relatively low. The stronger the price- or wage-rate-reduction, the more suppliers will quit the demander. There is a lower limit of the price or wage-rate where the demander would lose all supply.

The demander will, on the other side, not continously gain additional supply if he pays a higher price or wage-rate. Some suppliers will overcome their preferences for other demanders and change over to the price or wage-rate increasing demander, and some additional suppliers will enter the market. The higher the price or wage-rate increase, the more additional supply turns to the demander considered. There is an upper limit of the price or wage-rate, which is high enough to secure to the demander every quantity of supply within his range of capacity.

These arguments are sufficient to construct the double kinked supply curve (as seen by the demander) in figure 8.1. r is the quantity supplied to the demander, q is the price or wage-rate. q' is the price or wage-rate from which we started our argument. At the lower limit q_l and the upper limit q_u the supply curve is parallel to the abszissa. In between these limits the supply curve has a positive slope; it is similar to a monopsonist's supply curve. We may apply Gutenberg's term of a supplier's monopolistic range on the demand curve, which here is, of course, a demander's monopolistic - or monopsonistic - range of the supply curve.

Fig. 8.1. Supply curve for representative demander

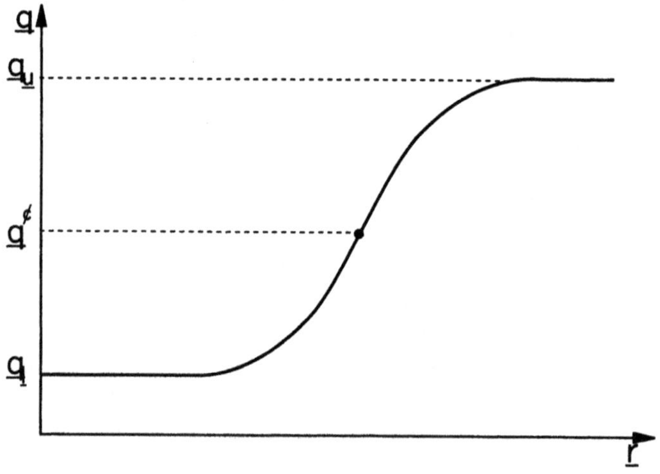

Supply curves in monopolistic imperfect demand are destined only by type. Instead of the two kinks there may be gradual transitions to the limits. Instead of limits completely parallel to the abszissa there may be slightly raising lower and upper limit prices or wage-rates. The extent of the monopolistic range and its positive slope depend on the comparative strenght of suppliers' preferences for other demanders and on the potential of market entrance and exit of suppliers. The weaker the preferences for other demanders and the more elastic market entrance and exit, the lower the positive slope.

Now we want to determine the demander's profit-maximizing price or wage-rate setting and the quantity he will buy in this situation. In a firm's sales market the Cournot formula "marginal cost of production = marginal revenue from sales" would be a first order condition of the profit-maximum (to be supplemented by the second order condition saying that the slope of the marginal cost curve must be greater than the slope of the marginal revenue curve). In a firm's buyer market the corresponding first order condition is "marginal cost of the good or service supplied = marginal value of the good or labour-service in production" (with a similar second order condition).

Fig. 8.2. Profit-maximizing price and quantity of representative demander

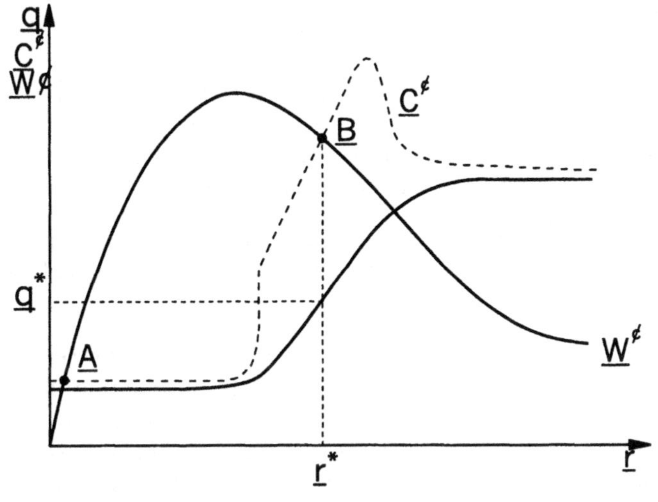

In figure 8.2 we find the double kinked supply curve of figure 8.1 and the dashed marginal cost curve C' corresponding to it. At the lower price limit q_l and the upper price limit q_u, marginal cost is equal to price and the marginal cost curve coincides with the supply curve. In the linear monopolistic range of the supply curve, the marginal cost curve is also linear and has the double slope of the supply curve. The curve of the marginal value of the good or labour-service in production, W', is drawn under the assuption that the firm's selling price of the product is a constant p and that the marginal productivity of the good or labour-service is increasing for smaller quantities and decreasing for larger quantities. In figure 8.2, there are two crossing points of the curves C' and W': A and B. A does not comply with the second order condition (it defines a profit-minimum); only B determines the demander's profit-maximizing situation by setting the price or wage-rate q^* and buying the quantity r^*.

What has been developped here by transforming a Gutenberg double kinked demand curve into a double kinked supply curve, may also be discussed in terms of transforming a Chamberlin demand curve into a supply curve. By this procedure, the famous long term Chamberlin tangent point solution of a sales market (cf. Chamberlin (1965, p. 93)) can be reformulated into a tangent point solution of a buyers' market. This solution presupposes that - as long as a representative demander earns profits - new demanders will enter the market. Supply then is divided among a growing number of demanders, which means that the supply curve relating to a representative demander is shifting to the left. Market entrance will come to an end as soon as the supply curve becomes a tangent to the curve of average value of the good or labour-service in production (not plotted in figure 8.2), because in this situation the profit maximizing price and quantity just give a zero profit to the demander.

8.3 Oligopolistic Imperfect Demand Competition

In a market of oligopolistic imperfect demand competition the first assumption made at the beginning of the previous section changes as follows:

- There are many suppliers and few demanders. Suppliers have a small share in total supply; everyone of the demanders has a considerable share in total demand.

The second assumption about preferences of suppliers for certain demanders, and the third assumption about complete information of demanders and about complete or restricted information of suppliers, do not change. Therefore, our examples for preferences of labour-suppliers as well as our generalization on demanders' investment in buyers' marketing destined to create suppliers' preferences remain applicable in this section.

The assumption of only few demanders with considerable market share means that there is oligopolistic interdependence among the results of their actions. Contrary to the situation discussed in the previous section, a demander's price- or wage-rate setting and his buyer's marketing actions are not negligible, and other demanders will react on these actions. Every demander has reason to consider in his decisions expected reactions of his competitors.

In the following geometric analysis we restrict the concept of few demanders to the number of two, i.e., we concentrate to duopolistic imperfect demand competition. Everyone of the two demanders considers, in his view, a supply function expressing suppliers' comparative preferences. Supply r_1 offered to demander 1 depends positively on the price or wage-rate q_1 he will pay, but negatively also on the price or wage-rate q_2 of demander 2. Supply r_2 offered to demander 2 depends negatively on q_1 and positively on q_2. The two supply functions are as follows:

$$r_1 = a_1 q_1 - b_1 q_2 - c1 \tag{8.1}$$

$$r_2 = -a_2 q_1 + b_2 q_2 - c2 \tag{8.2}$$

$$\tag{8.3}$$

$$a_i, b_i, c_i > 0 \qquad i = 1, 2 \tag{8.4}$$

$$a_1 > a_2 \tag{8.5}$$

$$b_2 > b_1 \tag{8.6}$$

The two inequalities mentioned at the end make sure that total supply rises if one of the prices offered by demanders increases. Constant coefficients imply that demanders' investment in buyers' marketing and, thereby, suppliers' preferences are taken as given. The problem of the following analysis is to determine profit-maximizing price- or wage-rate setting of the demanders. We will discuss two types of duopolistic price equilibrium: the Cournot solution and the Stackelberg solution.

Equation (8.1) in the (r_1, q_1)-diagram is for a constant price q_2 a linear supply function for demander 1 with positive slope and positive ordinate segment. For a rising given price q_2, this linear function shifts parallel in upward direction. In the example of figure 8.3, the linear function is plotted for $q_2 = 0, 10, 20, 30$ and 40.

In order to determine profit-maximizing prices and demand quantities for demander 1 at a given price set by demander 2, we are going to construct isoprofit-curves. Analogously we may derive isoprofit-curves for demander 2. To keep things easy, we assume that both demanders produce solely with the good or labour-service demanded, and that the input of this factor is proportional to output. If y_1 and y_2 are outputs produced by demanders 1 and 2, then

$$y_1 = d_1 r_1 \quad \text{and} \quad y_2 = d_2 r_2, \qquad \text{with } d_1, d_2 > 0 \tag{8.7}$$

are the production functions, and profits G_1 and G_2 are for sales prices p_1 and p_2

$$G_1 = d_1 r_1 p_1 - r_1 q_1 \quad \text{and} \quad G_2 = d_2 r_2 p_2 - r_2 q_2 \tag{8.8}$$

We may rewrite these equations and interprete them for alternative constant profits G_1', G_2':

$$q_1 = -G_1'/r_1 + d_1 p_1 \quad \text{and} \quad q_2 = -G_2'/r_2 + d_2 p_2 \tag{8.9}$$

Fig. 8.3. Supply curves and isoprofit-curves for demander 1

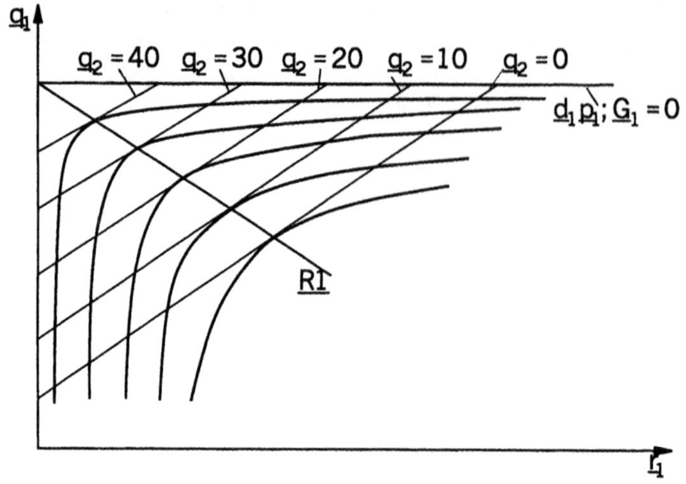

If sales prices p_1 and p_2 are assumed to be given, the second terms in these equtions are constants, and we may plot the equations in (r_i, q_i)-diagrams.

For demander 1, we get an isoprofit-curve by subtracting from the constant d_1p_1, to be drawn horizontally, in vertical direction the hyperbola G_1'/r_1. For $G_1' = 0$, the isoprofit-curve coincides with d_1p_1. In figure 8.3, we have further plotted those isoprofit-curves (for alternative positive values of G_1') which are tangent to the linear supply functions for $q_2 = 0, 10, 20, 30$ and 40. The points of tangency may be connected by a curve R1, which is linear in our example.

The isoprofit-curves and R1 are now transposed from the (r_1, q_1)-diagram of figure 3 into the (q_2, q_1)-diagram of figure 8.4. It can easily be verified that in figure 8.4 an isoprofit-curve begins and ends on the vertical axis of the diagram; its slope changes from positive to negative values in the crossing point with R_1', where the curve is vertical. R_1' is the (in our example: linear) reaction curve of demander 1 to a given price q_2 set by demander 2, because, in terms of his profit G_1', demander 1 cannot do better than set his price q_1 according to R_1'.

For demander 2, we may similarly derive isoprofit-curves. Transposed to figure 8.4, the isoprofit-curves will begin and end on the horizontal axis, and R_2' will connect points where the isoprofit-curves are horizontal. R_2' is the reaction curve of demander 2, because he cannot do better than react to a given price q_1 by setting q_2 according to R_2'.

In figure 8.5, we have plottet isoprofit-curves and reaction curves of both demanders. H is the crossing point of the reaction curves R_1' and R_2'. If demander 1 takes q_2 and demander 2 takes q_1 as given, the price setting of both

Fig. 8.4. Isoprofit-curves and reaction curve for demander 1

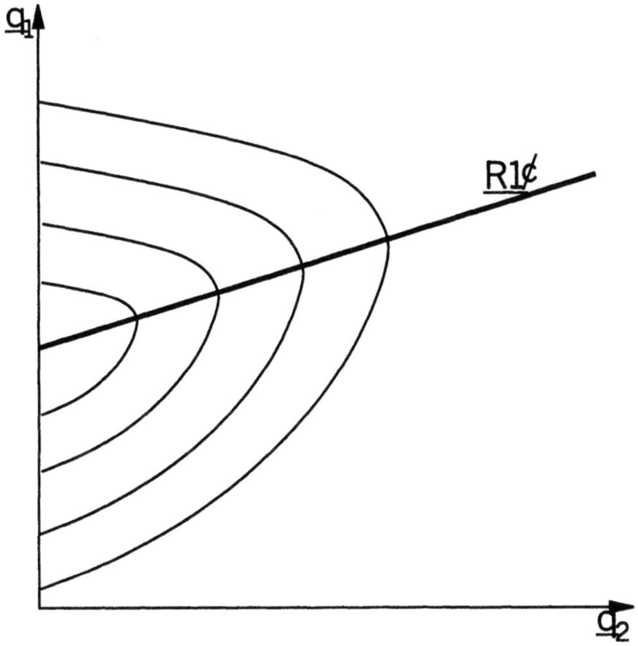

demanders is consistent in the sense that the expected price setting of both competitors is equal to the actual price setting. This solution corresponds to the concept of Cournot (1838, chapter 7). He was the first one to discuss the solution for oligopolistic suppliers' competition on a homogenous market, where the price of all suppliers must be the same, and where the object of their decisions are profit-maximizing supply quantities. For oligopolistic suppliers on a heterogenous market with locational preferences of demanders for certain suppliers, it were Launhardt (1885) and Hotelling (1929), who found profit-maximizing price-setting Cournot solutions. What we offer here by point H in figure 8.5 is the Cournot price-setting solution in an oligopolistic demanders' heterogenous market, where heterogenity means that preferences of suppliers for certain demanders are the result of demanders' buyer marketing activities.

The Cournot solution of taking as given the competitors' actions has been subject to criticism - with respect to all of the just mentioned oligopoly models. It neglects oligopolistic interdependence, i.e., a duopolist does not learn that his competitor will react. One approach to overcome this shortcoming was suggested by von Stackelberg (1951, chapter IV.3): If one of the duopolists is aware of the problem, he will not act on his own reaction curve but will choose his own profit-maximizing action on the other duopolist's

Fig. 8.5. Determination of Cournot and Stackelberg equilibria

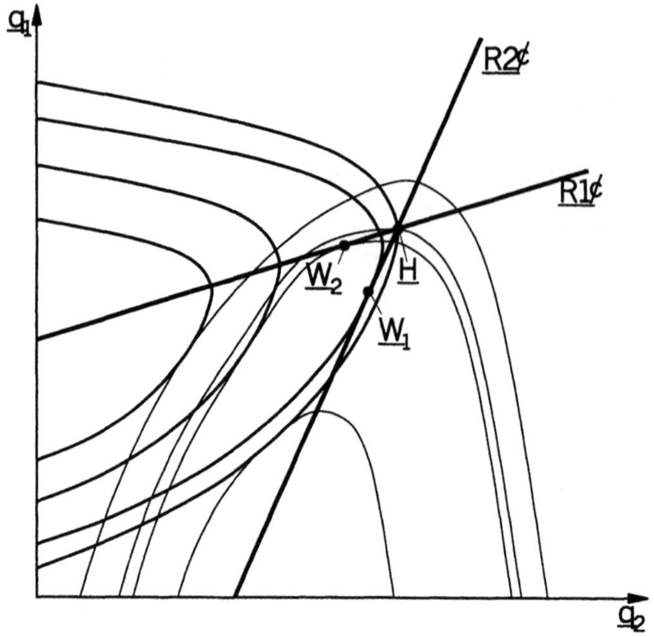

reaction curve. In the model of two demanders' heterogenous competition discussed here, this means that in figure 8.5 the point W_1 is the equilibrium price solution if demander 1 is the independent and demander 2 is the reacting competitor – because W_1 is the point of tangency of the reaction curve R_2' with the highest attainable isoprofit-curve of demander 1. If, however, demander 2 is independent and demander 1 is reacting, W_2 is the equilibrium price solution.

The Stackelberg solution concept did not convince its author, because both competitors would have the incentive to choose the independence position. The present literature tries to solve this problem by interpreting the situation in terms of a two-stage game where one of both is the first mover. We will not go into this literature but finish by saying that it can be applied to the model of oligopolistic demanders' heterogenous competition discussed in this section.

References

[1] Chamberlin, E. (1965). *The Theory of Monopolistic Competition, a Reorientation of the Theory of Value.* (8th ed.). Cambridge/Mass.

[2] Cournot, A. (1838). *Recherches sur les principes mathématiques de la théorie des richesses.* German edition: Untersuchung über die mathematischen Grundlagen der Theorie des Reichtums. Jena 1924. English edition: Researches into the Mathematical Principles of the Theory of Wealth. New York 1927.

[3] Gutenberg, E. (1979). *Grundlagen der Betriebswirtschaftslehre. Bd. II: Der Absatz* (16th ed.). Berlin etc.

[4] Hotelling, H. (1929). Stability in Competition. *Economic Journal 39*, 41–57. Reprinted in: Boulding, K.E. and G.J. Stigler (eds.): Readings in Price Theory. London 1953, pp. 467-484.

[5] Launhardt, W. (1885). *Mathematische Begründung der Volkswirtschaftslehre.* Leipzig. esp. pp. 157-164.

[6] Robinson, J. (1933). *The Economics of Imperfect Competition.* London.

[7] Schumann, J. (1992). *Grundzuege der Mikrooekonomischen Theorie* (6th ed.). Berlin etc.

[8] von Stackelberg, H. (1951). *Grundlagen der theoretischen Volkswirtschaftslehre* (2nd ed.). Tuebingen-Bern.

9 The Global Homo Oeconomicus
Integrating Economic Theories

Hans Wiesmeth

Abstract. Most often, the Homo Oeconomicus of mainstream economic theories is placed in rather peculiar settings with assumptions and cet. par. conditions imitating specific economic environments. As a consequence, "Homo Oeconomicus" acts flawlessly and rationally within its predefined and well designed setting. But without a more global view it rarely resembles a human being.

Given this background, this paper then considers first an integration of the usually purely local theory of labour unions with the theory of international trade. Recent publications backed by actual developments on the security markets show that institutional characteristics of national labour markets may have surprising consequences for the economies of trading partners. Next, the paper will take up the issue of international environmental concerns. The interactions of unhibited market forces in international trade with market failure associated with environmental effects illustrates the complexity of this area of economics. Both "case studies" demonstrate that a more "global" approach to economic theory allows insight, which cannot be obtained from the theories of international trade and labour unions, and environmental economics alone.

9.1 Introduction

The relationship between economics and neighbouring fields like psychology and theology in particular, and philosophy in general, has not been of much interest to the scientific community in the last decades.[1] Although the problems and questions, which are at the heart of modern economics, originated from these social sciences, although the "Homo Oeconomicus" was born out of these social sciences, economists usually tend to neglect the roots of their science. They thus tend to neglect the role of economics as a truly social science, covering many diverse aspects of human life.

Horst Todt has always been among those comparatively few economists, who tried to point to and to strengthen the ties between economics and other social sciences. Some 25 years ago he already drew the attention of his students to the psychologically important idea of an adjustment of aspiration levels instead of a pure utility maximization, and since then he has been teaching classes on the philosophical and psychological background of eco-

[1] It seems to me that scientists from these "neighbouring" fields are surprisingly more interested in economics than economists e.g. in the law sciences or in the language sciences.

nomics. Horst Todt had thus realized quite early the importance of these interdisciplinary relationships linking economics to the other social sciences.[2]

Nevertheless, the Homo Oeconomicus of mainstream economic theory is always placed in a rather peculiar setting with assumptions and cet. par. conditions imitating specific economic environments, and without much relevant contact to the outside world. In general, its only interest is utility maximization and profit maximization without taking specific notice of aspects like the adjustment of aspiration levels, or problems with processing a huge amount of information, or strategic interactions in the sense of influencing the economic behaviour of other agents in an economic environment.[3]

As a consequence, the Homo Oeconomicus acts flawlessly and rationally within its predefined and well designed setting, but without a more "global view" it rarely resembles a human being. It is, e.g., well known that personal characteristics of individuals participating in an economic bargaining process play a decisive role in this area of economic decision making. Moreover, the complex calculations often required for an equilibrium solution go beyond the problem solving capacity of any human being.[4]

These critical remarks on the links of modern economics to the social sciences in general apply as well to the importance attached to the relationship between different areas of economics itself. Traditionally, the Homo Oeconomicus "lives" in a particular environment of economic decision making, other fields of economics are of no importance. Thus, one considers e.g. the theory of international trade with the Homo Oeconomicus acting in free and unrestricted markets: market forces should be unleashed to further the wealth of nations. On the other hand, the environmentally concerned Homo Oeconomicus is affected by market failure, its activities are restricted by interferences with supply and demand, and guided by Pigou taxes, charges and markets for emission certificates. Alternatively, the theory of labour unions often assumes a monopolistic Homo Oeconomicus, again contrasting the context of free markets, and neglecting possible effects on international competitiveness.

The questions that immediately come to mind with these examples point to the problem of a missing more "global" view of economics, which should integrate economic theories, and which should appropriately link economics to other social sciences. Hence, taking the above examples, the Homo Oeconomicus should be engaged in free trade on the one hand, and environmentally concerned on the other. The Homo Oeconomicus should behave like a monop-

---

[2] In recent years some more economists have devoted their research efforts to these problems. Among them is Nobel prize winner R. Selten with his investigations into the observable economic behaviour of individuals by means of sophisticated "games".

[3] These remarks refer in particular, but not exclusively, to quite a few equilibrium concepts applied in modern game theory.

[4] In many experiments by R. Selten and others it turns out that the observed economic behaviour is far from an immediate maximization of utility or of profit.

olistic labour union on the one hand, but should not forget the international dimensions of a globalized economy. What we thus need is a "Global Homo Oeconomicus", or an integrative approach to economic theory.

This paper therefore considers first an integration of the usually purely local theory of labour unions with the theory of international trade. Institutional characteristics of national labour markets will in some sense be transferred to the trading partners with surprising effects. Next the paper will take up the issue of international environmental concerns. The interactions of uninhibited market forces in international trade with market failure associated with environmental effects will illustrate the complexity of this innovative area of economics. Both "case studies" will demonstrate that a more integrative approach allows additional insight, which cannot be obtained from the theories of international trade and labour unions, resp. environmental economics alone.

9.2 International Trade and National Labour Markets

It is common knowledge that institutional arrangements on national labour markets affect international competitiveness in one way or the other. However, there usually is little theoretical background for a more precise analysis of the expected economic effects. The question therefore is, how do differences in national factor market institutions affect global trade, to what degree are characteristics of the national labour markets in international trade transferred to the other trading partners? This section will help to bring light into this problem, which can be dealt with appropriately neither in the theory of international trade nor in the theory of labour unions alone.

As already indicated, governments usually recognize possible detrimental effects of a restrictive union wage policy on international competitiveness. They do, however, not expect serious consequences for their own country following an increase in trade activities or following a flow of immigrants extending the foreign labour market.

Such surprising conclusions are possible, however, whenever institutional peculiarities of the national labour markets allow a transfer of equilibria to other countries via free trade. A model proposed by Douglas R. Davis demonstrates this possibility in a convincing way. The following analytical investigations are broadly based on Davis (1998).

9.2.1 Rigid and Flexible Wages in International Trade

We consider two countries, flexible-wage America and rigid-wage Europe. The stylized characterization of Europe as an economy in which wages, at least for unskilled labour, are more rigid is due to the assumption of strong labour unions, e.g. The Heckscher-Ohlin model is used to link the two countries in international trade. The focus of the investigations of Davis (1998) is then on the factor markets in fixed-wage Europe and flexible-wage America.

How do institutional characteristics of national labour markets affect wages and employment? Consider the following basic assumptions of a model of free trade between America and Europe (cp. also Davis (1998)): there are two factors of production, skilled and unskilled labour with factor prices r and w. Denote by (H_A, L_A) and (H_E, L_E) endowments of these factors in America and Europe, resp. These factors are used to produce two commodities, X and Y, under constant returns to scale. X is assumed to be relatively more skill intensive than Y, P is the price of X in units of Y. Households are characterized by the homothetic utility function $U(X, Y)$.

Assume now that the minimum wage rate for unskilled labour is fixed to $w = \bar{w}$ in Europe. Equilibrium conditions in a competitive framework then imply for the unit costs

$$c^X(\bar{w}, r) = P \qquad \text{and} \qquad c^Y(\bar{w}, r) = 1.$$

If we first consider autarky in Europe, we arrive at the following equilibrium conditions:

$$c_r^X(\bar{w}, r) * X_E + c_r^Y(\bar{w}, r) * Y_E = H_E,$$
$$\frac{u_X(X_E, Y_E)}{u_Y(X_E, Y_E)} = P.$$

Thus, we obtain four equations for the four variables X_E, Y_E, P and r. The quantities X_E and Y_E are the quantities of X and Y produced and consumed in Europe. As usual with identical homothetic utility functions, there is, by assumption, only one representative household. Denote the equilibrium values by X_E^*, Y_E^*, P^* and r^*.

The fact that there is no equilibrium condition for supply and demand of unskilled labour in Europe is due to the basic assumption of a fixed-wage Europe. Thus, unemployment will arise in Europe if the minimum wage rate $\bar{w}$ is above the equilibrium rate. The more complete argument involves the fundamental theorems of the Heckscher-Ohlin theory (cp. again Davis (1998)): a higher wage rate $\bar{w}$ will yield a higher relative price of Y and, thus, a lower price P^* of X. A reduced relative price P^* will increase the equilibrium factor supply ratio $h^* = H/L$. But due to a flexible wage rate r^* for skill, $H = H_E$, and, therefore, $L < L_E$.

The extent of unemployment U_{AT}^* for unskilled labour in Europe in autarky is then given by:

$$U_{AT}^* = L_E - \left(c_w^X(\bar{w}, r^*) * X_E^* + c_w^Y(\bar{w}, r^*) * Y_E^*\right)$$

Consider now the case of free trade between America and Europe with a fixed wage $\bar{w}$ for unskilled labour in Europe. The above equilibrium conditions apply with X_E, Y_E, L_E and H_E replaced with their corresponding "world" values X_W, Y_W, $L_W = L_A + L_E$, and $H_W = H_A + H_E$. Observe that the equilibrium conditions with respect to unit costs will not change. P^* will therefore only depend on the level of $\bar{w}$. Similarly, h^*, the ratio of employed factor supplies, will remain constant, too.

In order to illustrate the consequences of free trade between a flexible-wage America and a rigid-wage Europe for unemployment in Europe assume for a moment that both countries are of equal size. Thus, in particular $L_W = 2L_E$ and $H_W = 2H_E$. Similarly, $X_W^* = 2X_E^*$ and $Y_W^* = 2Y_E^*$. Thus, in absolute terms unemployment of unskilled labour doubles in this integrated world economy (cp. also Davis (1998)).

For a complete picture, however, we have to consider the equilibrium conditions for America and Europe separately. Besides the implications for unit costs and utility maximization, we obtain:

$$c_w^X(\bar{w}, r) * X_A + c_w^Y(\bar{w}, r) * Y_A = L_A$$
$$c_r^X(\bar{w}, r) * X_A + c_r^Y(\bar{w}, r) * Y_A = H_A$$
$$c_r^X(\bar{w}, r) * X_E + c_r^Y(\bar{w}, r) * Y_E = H_E$$

If the solutions for X_A, X_E, Y_A and Y_E of the complete equilibrium system are strictly positive, i.e., if there is incomplete diversification between America and Europe, then factor price equalization holds for the two countries.[5] American workers enjoy the high European wages without, however, suffering from the unemployment that sustains $\bar{w}$. Again, if America and Europe are of equal size, then unemployment of unskilled labour doubles in Europe in comparison to autarky. Trade forces European workers to bear the burden of high unemployment to maintain the high wage rate both in Europe and America.

Interestingly, if Europe and America are assumed to be completely identical, then trade in the above situation can only arise from the fixed wage rate $\bar{w}$ in Europe. Europe then exports the "high-tech" commodity X, which is relatively more skill-intensive than Y. Moreover, this fact is usually applied to postulate a higher level of education in Europe. Of course, an increase in the share of the skilled population would help to reduce unemployment under the conditions stated above. Vice versa, immigration of unskilled labour to America will again, by the same kind of arguments, increase unemployment in Europe. Davis (1998) presents a more complete discussion of the consequences of south-north migration, thus demonstrating the need for a more global view of the theory of trade unions in the context considered here.

9.2.2 The Keynesian Global Economy

The recent explosion of asset prices on the one hand, and the absence of inflation in the U.S. on the other, even though the U.S. economy is already

[5] Factor intensity reversals, which can disturb this result, are ruled out by assumption.

in its ninth year of recovery, brought forth various explanations. One of these is based on the concept of a "Keynesian global economy" introduced by David I. Fand (1999).

The main line of arguments applied by Fand (1999) refers to substantial idle capacities in Europe, Japan, Southeast Asia and Latin America, which add significantly towards generating an elastic augmented supply for America. As a consequence of this hypothesis of a Keynesian global economy, an increase in American aggregate demand will lead to an increase in the U.S. trade deficit but not necessarily to any rise in U.S. prices as measured by the CPI, the PPI or the ECI. But the absence of inflation in the U.S. tends to "handcuff" the Fed since the chairman finds it difficult to restrict the accelerating growth of money supply in this rather extraordinary situation. Consequently, market professionals are liberated to borrow and leverage their portfolio positions, and equity prices continue to rise.

Although quite convincing, this concept of a Keynesian global economy deserves some comments, which perhaps allow a more thorough understanding of the current economic situation primarily in Europe and the U.S. (cp. also Wiesmeth (1999)).

According to Fand (1999), the aggregate supply curve facing the U.S. from the rest of the world should be almost infinitely elastic. Thus, the aggregate supply curve for Europe, Japan, Southeast Asia and Latin America should be perfectly elastic, too. There should be a Keynesian unemployment in most of these parts of the world. Some empirical facts, however, do not support this theoretical conclusion.

- If there was a typical Keynesian situation in Europe, then there should be one in Germany as well, in particular due to the size of the German economy. Indeed, idle capacities characterize vast parts of the German economy and unemployment of labour has been in the two digit area almost always since the last five or six years. There is no doubt that many economists hold institutional inflexibilities on the labour market and wage rigidities responsible for this persistent unemployment. Nevertheless, many economists would deny the possibility of a typical Keynesian unemployment for Germany. In fact, the government tries to cut public spending in order to reduce the public deficit, which is certainly not the textbook method to handle a Keynesian unemployment.
- Over the last few years, there was no extraordinary increase in German exports. Only since the last few months, German exports seem to rise at a faster pace. In general, there is no clear evidence that the American trade deficit is linked to exceptionally soaring export markets in the rest of the world. In particular, Japanese exports have been down over the last few years due to the financial crisis in East and Southeast Asia. As a consequence, it is not clear at all, to what degree the economic situation in Europe and in other parts of the world contributed towards a perfectly elastic aggregate supply curve for America.

An alternative explanation should accommodate these observations. Such an alternative approach is again based on the model of Davis (1998). This model demonstrates that free trade with Europe will transfer the high European wage rates to America, if factor prize equalization holds. Moreover, modest shifts in import demand from the U.S. will not affect relative prices of the traded commodities. Free trade thus links the goods prices, whereas the extent of trade between America and Europe is not that important.

The model of Davis (1998) is based on minimum wages in Europe. The justification for this assumption, as discussed in the previous section, is that the stronger unions make wage rates in Europe more rigid in comparison to American wages. If one assumes that unions would respond to a decrease in unemployment, resulting from an increase in public spending or any other expansionary fiscal policy, with higher wage rates, then the economic situation is, as mentioned above, not of a typical Keynesian type, at least not, if the governments are aware of these interdependencies and refrain from discrete expansionary policies.

But this seems to be the case in Germany and elsewhere in Europe. As a result, governments in the European Union are hesitating to initiate expansionary fiscal policies. There are, however, continuing efforts to reduce institutional rigidities on the labour markets and wage rigidities in these countries. Thus, Davis' approach seems to model typical institutional characteristics of European and American labour markets. More importantly, however, his approach allows an explanation of the fact that, over the last few years, there has been no upward pressure on the wages, neither in Europe nor in Asia. We therefore arrive at a Keynesian situation in Europe and in Asia, which is not handled in the strict Keynesian way, at least not in Europe.[6]

In a certain sense, the "stable" situation on the European labour markets is transferred to the American labour and commodity markets by free trade and allows thus an explanation of the extraordinary situation on the security markets. This example illustrates once more the need for a more extensive integration of economic theories.

9.3 International Trade and the Environment

Again, it is common knowledge that national environmental policy measures may adversely affect international competitiveness. Therefore, governments usually hesitate to raise environmental standards without binding in-

[6] There have been expansionary fiscal policy measures in Japan to revive the economy. But only until recently they have not shown any significant effect on Japanese exports to the U.S.

ternational agreements,[7] or other attempts to harmonize environmental standards.[8]

In the background of these issues is the still missing integration of two theories: the theory of international trade on the one hand, and environmental economics on the other.[9] Nevertheless, free trade and the protection of the environment are two important issues on the current global agenda. The swift rise of environmental concerns coincides perfectly with the enhanced importance that questions of international trade have now acquired. World trade has been significantly liberalized during the last four decades; average tariffs have fallen from 40% in the 1950s to less than 5% in the 1990s. The lowering of selected tariffs has not meant an end to protectionism, however. A new rationale for protectionism is emerging which argues for the restriction of trade as a means of preserving and protecting the environment. As environmental problems are usually associated with market failure, the "greening" of protectionism and the merging of environmental standards into international trade agreements could fundamentally change the world trading system, and "free" trade.

Thus, there is not much harmony among supporters of free trade and supporters of the environment and it is not yet clear, in which directions trade and environmental policies will develop. Bhagwati (1996) has discussed what he calls the "genuine" problems associated with free trade and the protection of the environment. These genuine problems cover questions of a "level playing field" or "harmonization", as a basis for fair trade, or of "losing one's higher standards" combined with a "race towards the bottom" resulting from international competition and lax environmental standards, and of an "immiserization" following an expected degradation of the environment in international trade:

- Unfair Trade: If a country does something what appears less concerning for the environment, this is considered to be tantamount to the lack of "level playing fields" and therefore amounts to "unfair trade".
- Losing One's Higher Standards: If free trade occurs with countries having lower environmental standards, then the effect will be to lower one's own standard with the possibility of a "race towards the bottom".
- Immiserization: If free trade leads to an expansion of a process that is harmful to the global environment, then the gains from trade might be offset by the damages to the environment.

[7] An excellent example for such an international agreement is the Kyoto-Protocol, in which industrial countries basically agreed to reduce emissions of greenhouse gases according to certain percentage levels.

[8] There are regular attempts to harmonize environmental standards within the European Union.

[9] The literature in the combined area of international trade and environmental economics is, until now, far from abundant. For some recent publications cp. Weber and Wiesmeth (1999).

There are quite a few questions associated with these "genuine" problems: Are different environmental standards necessarily due to different attitudes towards the environment? Does harmonization increase welfare in the participating countries? Does increasing competition due to free trade necessarily induce a race towards the bottom in terms of environmental standards? What is the driving force behind immiserization? Is it possible that too much protection of the environment is the reason for immiserization? Can all trading partners simultanously suffer from lower welfare levels?

These questions refer to the most important areas of conflict between free trade and the protection of the environment. A first answer can only be provided by a thorough investigation of these issues in a formal model integrating the two theories (cp. Weber and Wiesmeth (1999)).

9.3.1 An Attempt to Integrate Free Trade and Environmental Economics

The integration of environmental objectives into economic policy typically introduces strategic interactions due to the public goods character of the environmental commodities, and due to the fact that environmental regulations are usually expected to affect the competitiveness of the national economy.

This model then focusses on the transition from autarky to free trade in terms of the equilibrium structure adjusted for international environmental problems.[10] The model allows a rigorous formulation of the above problems in the context of the basic theory of international trade.

The model considers two countries each of which can produce two commodities by employing two factors of production, labour and environment. The production functions exhibit constant returns to scale with respect to labour input. A higher level of the environmental standard adopted in a country will decrease the output levels associated with a given labour input. Moreover, in each country there is a representative consumer, whose utility is given by a homothetic utility function. As already mentioned, the model deals with international environmental problems, for which pollution in one country directly affects economic conditions in the other country.

More formally, $f_{ij}(e_i, z_{ij}) = \beta_{ij}(1 - e_i)z_{ij}$ with $z_{ij} \leq Z_i$ denotes production of commodity $j = 1, 2$ in country $i = 1, 2$. Country 1 possesses a comparative advantage in the production of commodity 1, i.e.,

$$\frac{\beta_{11}}{\beta_{12}} < \frac{\beta_{21}}{\beta_{22}}$$

[10] "International" environmental problems originate in one country but affect economic conditions in other parts of the world. Weber and Wiesmeth (1999) also consider the case of purely regional environmental problems. In addition to that their paper contains an inquiry into the possibilities and the limits of effecting the foreign environmental policy by application of the common instruments of trade policy.

e_i with $0 \leq e_i \leq 1$ is the level of the environmental standard in country i; Z_i denotes the endowment of country i with respect to the factor "labour".

Agents are identical and characterized by the homothetic utility function

$$u_i\left(x_{i1}, x_{i2}, e^i\right) = x_{i1}^{\alpha_{i1}} * x_{i2}^{\alpha_{i2}} * \left(e^i\right)^{\alpha_{i3}}$$

with $\alpha_{ij} \geq 0$ and $\alpha_{i1} + \alpha_{i2} = 1$ for $i, j = 1, 2$. For $i, j = 1, 2$ the parameter α_{ij} thus denotes the share of total income of consumer i spent on commodity j, whereas α_{i3} is the "propensity" of consumer i towards the protection of the environment. $e^i = 0.5*(e_1+e_2)$, $i = 1, 2$, describes the effect of environmental problems, which are intrinsically international in nature, on utilities.

The two commodities are produced and exchanged in each country according to the rules of a market economy. The choice of an appropriate environmental standard is, however, the task of governmental agencies. They propose the environmental standards in accordance with the welfare of the consumers while taking into account the respective action of the other country. Thus, a Nash equilibrium will result from the interaction of these governmental agencies in the two countries.

9.3.2 Equilibrium Concepts

More exactly, subgame-perfect equilibria of the resulting two-stage games will allow an analysis of the mentioned "genuine" problems. In the first stage of the game the governments choose the environmental standards. Their goal is maximization of the welfare of the representative consumer. In the second stage producers and consumers make their decisions. The idea of the analysis is then to compare subgame-perfect equilibria in autarky and in free trade. Here are the required equilibrium concepts:

An allocation $\left(x_{ij}^A, z_{ij}^A, e_i^A\right)_{i,j=1,2}$ is an autarky equilibrium in country i, if there exist price systems (w_i^A, p_{ij}^A) such that for $i, j = 1, 2$:

- $x_{ij}^A = f_{ij}\left(e_i^A, z_{ij}^A\right)$,
- $z_{i1}^A + z_{i2}^A = Z_i$,
- $\left(z_{i1}^A, z_{i2}^A\right)$ is a profit-maximizing factor allocation in country i,
- $\left(x_{i1}^A, x_{i2}^A\right)$ maximizes utility in country i with respect to the budget $w_i^A * Z_i$,
- e_i^A maximizes $u_i\left(x_{i1}^A, x_{i2}^A, e^i\right)$ with e_j^A, $j \neq i$ given.

An allocation $\left(x_{ij}^T, z_{ij}^T, e_i^T\right)_{i,j=1,2}$ is a free trade equilibrium in country i, if there exist price systems such that for $i, j = 1, 2$:

- $x_{1j}^T + x_{2j}^T = f_{1j}\left(e_1^T, z_{1j}^T\right) + f_{2j}\left(e_2^T, z_{2j}^T\right)$,
- $z_{i1}^T + z_{i2}^T = Z_i$,
- $\left(z_{i1}^T, z_{i2}^T\right)$ is a profit-maximizing factor allocation in country i,
- $\left(x_{i1}^T, x_{i2}^T\right)$ maximizes utility in country i with respect to the budget $w_i^T * Z_i$,

- e_i^T maximizes $u_i\left(x_{i1}^T, x_{i2}^T, e^i\right)$ with e_j^T, $j \neq i$ given.

Thus, both equilibrium concepts refer to an equilibrium allocation in the goods and factor markets and to the optimal choice of environmental standards by the governmental agencies. In the case of free trade the environmental decisions of the governments are in addition to the state of the environment affected by the amount of the commodities, which are available for import or export. Moreover, the governmental agencies first choose the environmental standards before the firms and the households make their production and consumption decisions. As the governments take the reactions of the individual agents on their own choice of an environmental standard into account, we arrive at a subgame-perfect Nash equilibrium.

The following section contains the investigation of the properties of these subgame-perfect Nash equilibria in view of the "genuine" problems of free trade.

9.3.3 Answers to the "Genuine" Problems

One of the advantages of the model considered here is the fact that all equilibrium solutions can be obtained and analysed explicitly. As usual in the context of subgame-perfect equilibria, the game is solved backwards by maximizing indirect utility in terms of the values of the environmental standards (cp. Weber and Wiesmeth (1999) for more details).

- Unfair Trade: Differing environmental standards are often related to differing propensities to the protection of the environment. In order to admit a "level playing field" for international trade, countries with lower standards should therefore raise their standards in the sense of a "harmonization". Consider the example:

$$\alpha_{11} = 0.3; \quad \alpha_{12} = 0.7; \quad \alpha_{13} = 0.5; \quad \beta_{11} = 1; \quad \beta_{12} = 1; \quad Z_1 = 40;$$
$$\alpha_{21} = 0.3; \quad \alpha_{22} = 0.7; \quad \alpha_{23} = 0.5; \quad \beta_{21} = 1; \quad \beta_{22} = 2; \quad Z_2 = 50.$$

  In equilibrium $e_1^A = e_2^A = 0.2$, but $e_1^T = 0.6$ and $e_2^T \approx 0.667$. Therefore, this example demonstrates that identical propensities toward the protection of the environment, even identical utility functions, can give rise to quite differing standards in equilibrium. In conclusion, different environmental standards need not signal different attitudes towards the protection of the environment, they need not signal "unfair trade".
- Race Towards the Bottom: For the equilibrium values of the environmental standards we obtain:

$$e_i^A = \frac{\alpha_{i3} + \alpha_{i3}\alpha_{j3} - \alpha_{j3}}{\alpha_{13} + \alpha_{13}\alpha_{23} + \alpha_{23}}$$
$$e_i^T = \frac{\alpha_{i3}\left(\alpha_{jj} + \alpha_{j3}\right) - \alpha_{ii}\alpha_{j3}}{\alpha_{11}\alpha_{23} + \alpha_{13}\alpha_{22} + \alpha_{13}\alpha_{23}}$$

for $i \neq j$. Thus, we have $0.5 * (e_1^A + e_2^A) < 0.5 * (e_1^T + e_2^T)$. This result demonstrates that at least one of the environmental standards will be raised in free trade in comparison to autarky. The fear of "losing one's higher standards" is therefore not necessarily justified, and a "race towards the bottom" will not take place.

- Immiserization: Consider the following concrete example, which gives rise to the utility levels v_1^A, v_2^A in autarky and v_1^T, v_2^T in free trade:

$$\alpha_{11} = 0.05; \quad \alpha_{12} = 0.95; \quad \alpha_{13} = 0.5; \quad \beta_{11} = 3; \quad \beta_{12} = 1; \quad Z_1 = 40;$$
$$\alpha_{21} = 0.90; \quad \alpha_{22} = 0.10; \quad \alpha_{23} = 0.5; \quad \beta_{21} = 1; \quad \beta_{22} = 1; \quad Z_2 = 50.$$

We obtain: $v_1^A \approx 17.53, v_1^T \approx 15.00$ and $v_2^A \approx 18.28, v_2^T \approx 17.05$. Interestingly, the reason for this effect of an immiserization has to be found in a too strong reduction in the production of the consumption commodities, and not, as is often argued in environmental groups, in an increasing degradation of the environment due to higher production activities.

An additional remark refers to the increasing demands for "harmonized" environmental standards. Of course, the Nash equilibria represented by the environmental standards (e_1^A, e_2^A) and (e_1^T, e_2^T) are, in general, inefficient. Specifically, in autarky there is "too little" concern about the environment in the sense that there exist values $e_1^* > e_1^A$ and $e_2^* > e_2^A$, such that both countries would be better off by adopting these higher standards. In free trade equilibrium, however, there could be "too much" or "too little" concern about the environment, there could even be the case that there is too much concern in one country and too little in the other one (cp. Weber and Wiesmeth (1999)).

Some international agreements to protect the environment postulate harmonization in the sense of a uniform percentage reduction of emission levels of some hazardous substance. In our framework this would correspond to a uniform percentage increase of the values of the environmental standards. Clearly, for small increases in the environmental standards starting out from autarky equilibrium (e_1^A, e_2^A) this policy will, in the context considered here, lead to an increase in utility for both countries. In free trade equilibrium, however, harmonization in the sense of a uniform percentage adjustment of the equilibrium values will only be sustainable in exceptional situations. This is also an interesting result from this analysis, integrating two different economic theories.

9.4 Concluding Remarks

The above results demonstrate that, in general, the integration of different areas of economics allows additional insight into certain aspects of public interest. In view of these results, a more "global" approach to economic problems, even in the "weak" sense of integrating different theories, seems therefore to be justified.

This holds first of all for the integration of international trade with some aspects of environmental economics. The fundamental results refer to a rigorous analysis of the "genuine" problems of free trade in its relation to environmental pollution. The main conclusions with respect to questions of "unfair trade", "race towards the bottom", and "immiserization" illustrate the advantages of this more integrative approach.

Similarly, although the fact that institutional characteristics of national labour markets may affect international competitiveness is widely known, the degree of these effects is usually underestimated. The investigations in the first part of the paper show that wage rigidities, which characterize the labour market in one country, may contribute to surprising structural results in the countries of the trade partners. There are indications that even the recent development on the stock markets is the consequence of such a peculiar constellation.

In summary, economists should increasingly be aware that economics is a "social" science, which tries to analyze part of the huge variety of social interactions of human beings. This implies that different areas of economic theory should be integrated, and aspects of other social sciences should carefully be taken into account in economic considerations. An isolated Homo Oeconomicus, restricted to aspects of international trade, national labour markets, or environmental economics alone, is therefore not always the right approach to an economic problem.

References

[1] Bhagwati, J. (1996). Trade and the Environment: The False Conflict? in: *The Political Economy of Trade Policy: Papers in Honor of J. Bhagwati.* R. C. Feenstra, G. M. Grossman, D. A. Irwin, eds. pp. 159-190.

[2] Davis, D. (1998). Does European Unemployment Prop up American Wages? National Labor Markets and Global Trade. *American Economic Review 88*(3), 478–494.

[3] Fand, D. (1999). Are We Facing a Stock Market Bubble? Discussion Paper, George Mason University, in: *Financial Structure and Stability*, A. Karmann (ed.), Springer-Verlag, to appear.

[4] Weber, S. and H. Wiesmeth (1999, September). Free Trade and the Environment. Discussion Paper, Technische Universität Dresden.

[5] Wiesmeth, H. (1999). Remarks on: David I. Fand: Are We Facing a Stock Market Bubble? in: *Financial Structure and Stability*, A. Karmann (ed.), Springer-Verlag, to appear.

10 International Trade and Spatial Markets

Trade Policy from a Theory of Spatial Pricing Perspective

Klaus Schöler

10.1 Introduction

In a time marked by enlarged economic regions transcending national borders and continuously growing international trade the question rises anew, if traditional Ricardian theory and Neo-Ricardian approaches to the theory of international trade hold as valid and sufficient explanations of international trade flows. Early doubts by August Lösch, raised in an age of protection and autarchy, despite not having provoked a substantial rethinking among scholars over the past sixty years, they have become ever more appropriate through the emergence of integrated regional markets in Europe and elsewhere around the world. Therefore, it seems worthwhile to take a closer look at Lösch's competing, explicitly spatial approach.

As much as Lösch regards the theory of comparative costs as suitable to explain the interpersonal division of labour, as unsuitable an instrument it is in his opinion to determine international specialization, Losch (1938, 1939). To explain the international division of labour, the theory of comparative costs assumes spaceless national territories, and thus uniform production conditions across each country. These conditions, however, are not at all identical across different regions of a national economy. "Diese Degradierung der Länder zu Punkten erleichtert die Irrlehre von ihrer wirtschaftlichen Einheit", Losch (1944, p. 176). Moreover, transport costs within countries are supposed to be zero and are considered between countries at best. Yet, the location of a production facility within a country may determine greatly its export perspectives. Quite often the total costs of transportation are higher within a country than between countries, whether due to lower charges of naval compared to surface freight-rates, or due to respective proximity to a common border. Finally, the theory of comparative costs proceeds from a uniform national price level, cutting short at the national border. But if this does not apply to the domestic territory, since transportation costs increase the commodity price from the place of production onwards, and consequently there is no uniform domestic price level, this conception cannot apply to international trade either. International trade rather connects domestic and foreign prices at the border. Price increases do not lift one single domestic price level, they spread across economic space changing the respective delivered price at every consumer's location, possibly affecting the foreign country likewise. Now, what does Lösch's proposal, countering the theory of comparative costs, look like? "Staaten sind", according to Losch (1944, p. 178) "... wirtschaftlich gesehen völlig willkürliche Bezugsgebilde. Da bleibt nichts übrig, als die Erzeugung aller Standorte zunächst ohne Rücksicht auf die politischen Grenzen festzustellen, diese Grenzen dann einzuzeichnen und ihre Wirkungen auf die Ausdehnung der Marktgebiete zu berücksichtigen. Dann sind alle Waren, deren Absatzgebiete von den Grenzen durchschnitten werden, Ausfuhrgüter, wenn das Erzeugungszentrum diesseits, und Einfuhrgüter, wenn es jenseits der Grenze liegt."

Apart from the few theoretical contributions combining spatial and international economics listed below, this approach has greatly been lying idle, even though it offers novel insight into international trade. One reason might be the sustained lack of a comprehensive synthesis between these two fields of economic theory. Now as before - this applies by and large - space is not included in the theory of international trade, and spatial economics do not deal with trade across national borders.

This essay seeks to combine those contributions based on the Löschian ideas in a spatial model of an international oligopoly, i.e. with at least one supplier's market area stretching across a national border. In an early paper, Benson and Hartigan (1983) demonstrate that import tariffs may reduce the (profit-maximizing) mill price, even that of the domestic firm. In further papers, these authors also tackle the effects of import quotas (1984) and the distributional incidence of tariffs (1987). An early discussion of welfare effects in the mentioned analytical framework can be found for certain special cases in Porter (1984) as well as, with endogenous revenue and protective tariffs, in Schöler (1990). Heffley and Hatzipanayotou (1991) investigate the impact of tariffs on population distribution and land rents as well as on consumers' mobility. Furthermore, alternative conjectural variations and heterogenous goods are treated by Heffley et al. (1993) in a spatial market model with tariffs. Hass (1996) extends the analysis to alternative models of spatial competition on the one hand, and to endogenous welfare maximizing tariff rates on the other hand. This kind of endogenous welfare maximizing tariff rates, though calculated in a different fashion, is also applied by Schöler (1997). Finally, Hass and Schöler (1999) reach a differentiated welfare-theoretical assessment of export subsidies. Certainly, not all the above-mentioned evidences can be shown here, thus in the present paper we will concentrate on the major lines of analytical reasoning.

The paper is organised as follows: In section 10.2, the assumptions and the basic spatial market model with free trade are illustrated, i.e. in a situation without administrative impediments to trade. Section 10.3 is committed to tariff policy. We investigate exogenous tariffs as well as endogenous tariff rates under three alternative aims: Total protection of domestic firms, public revenue maximization and social welfare maximization. Section 10.4 deals with non-tariff barriers to trade, specifically import quotas and export subsidies. Concludingly, in section 10.5, we discuss some aspects regarding the stability of the market results and hint to remaining open questions.

10.2 Free Trade in a Spatial Market

It is appropriate to formulate some of the assumptions common to the spatial pricing literature in order to keep the model manageable:

- $A1$: Domestic and foreign consumers continuously occupy a homogenous line $\overline{0R}$ at uniform density equal to 1. The locations of the firms are exogenously given at the left and right ends of this line, i.e. at 0 for the domestic firm and at R for the foreign competitor.
  ($A1.1$) The foreign firm exports part of its production to the domestic market, so that it serves the foreign market between its location R and the national border R_G as well as the domestic market between the national border R_G and the market area boundary R_C. The domestic firm delivers to the remaining part of the domestic market, covering $\overline{0R_C}$.
  ($A1.2$) Alternatively, the domestic firm could export part of its production to the foreign country. In this case it serves the domestic market between its location 0 and the national border R_G as well as the foreign market between the national border R_G and the market boundary R_C. The foreign firm then delivers to the remaining part of the foreign market, covering $\overline{R_C R}$. From the domestic perspective, we have imports in case $A1.1$ ($R_C < R_G$) and exports in case $A1.2$ ($R_C > R_G$).

  $0 - - - - - - - - R_C - - - - - - - - R_G - - - - - - - - R$ *imports*

  $0 - - - - - - - - R_G - - - - - - - - R_C - - - - - - - - R$ *exports*

- $A2$: To keep the algebra less cumbersome we assume domestic and foreign individual consumer demand to be identical with respect to utility and expenditure functions, and represented by a linear function ϕ of the respective delivered price $p(r)$:

$$q_I = \phi(p_I), \quad p_I = m_I + r, \quad \phi' < 0, \quad r \in [0,\ R], \tag{10.1}$$

$$q_A = \phi(p_A), \quad p_A = m_A + r, \quad \phi' < 0, \quad r \in [0,\ R]. \tag{10.1a}$$

The delivered prices of the domestic firm $p_I(r)$ and the foreign firm $p_A(r)$ are the sum of the mill prices m_I or m_A, respectively, and the transportation costs between the production and consumption locations r, with r signifying the distance between the two locations. The freight rate per quantity and distance unit for both domestic and foreign transportation is assumed to equal 1. The results for the special case of linear individual consumer demand are provided in the appendix.

- *A3*: Production technology and cost functions are identical in both countries. Hence, the cost functions read:

$$K_I = K_A = K_f, \tag{10.2}$$

with variable costs set to zero.
- *A4*: The firms aim at maximizing their profits under Löschian competition. The consumers aim at maximizing their consumers' surplus and purchase the good from the firm which offers the lowest delivered price.
- A5: The model is confined to the short run analysis, i.e. relocations are neither undertaken nor expected of the competitors.

The existence of a spatial market implies the following conditions:

(a) $m_I < m_A + R$ and $m_A < m_I + R$, respectively: A firm cannot be entirely pushed out of the market via price undercutting by the competitor at the former firm's own location.
(b) $\phi(m_I + R_C) > 0$ and $\phi(m_A + R - R_C) > 0$, respectively: At the competition boundary R_C, the delivered price is not allowed to be higher than or equal to the prohibitive price $\phi^{-1}(0)$.
(c) $R \leq m_I - m_A + 2R_C$: Due to the fact that at the competition boundary the delivered prices of both firms are identical, we get the admissible distance R between the firms' locations, with R_C being less or equal to the monopoly market size.

If at least one of these three conditions is not fulfilled, the market will be divided into one or two spatial monopolies.

Under the assumptions *A*1.1 and *A*2 to *A*5, spatial competition under free trade can be modelled as follows. The domestic firm's profit is given by:

$$\Pi_I = m_I \int_0^{R_C} \phi(m_I + r)dr - K_f. \tag{10.3}$$

The profit-maximizing domestic mill price, as a function of the market area size, reads:

$$m_I^* = \psi_I(R_C). \tag{10.4}$$

Given assumption *A*1.1, the foreign firm serves the foreign market between R_G and R as well as a part of the domestic market $\overline{R_C R_G}$. The profit is given by:

$$\Pi_{A/I} = m_{A1} \int_0^{R-R_G} \phi(m_{A1} + r)dr + m_{A2} \int_{R-R_G}^{R-R_C} \phi(m_{A2} + r)dr - K_f. \tag{10.5}$$

Under free trade and non-discriminatory pricing, the foreign firm sets one single mill price for both the domestic and the foreign market, i.e. $m_{A1} = m_{A2} = m_A$, since the national border does not induce any economic effects. On the other hand, in the presence of tariff or non-tariff trade restrictions, the foreign firm may determine either a common mill price for its foreign and domestic market or separate prices in the sense of spatial price discrimination. If we focus on the profit realized by the foreign firm in the domestic market, we can disregard this issue and rewrite the profit function as follows:

$$\Pi_A = m_A \int_0^{R_G - R_C} \phi(m_A + D + r)dr - K_f, \tag{10.6}$$

with $D = R - R_G$. The profit-maximizing foreign mill price for the domestic market, as a function of the domestic market size, reads:

$$m_A^* = \psi_A(R_G - R_C, D). \tag{10.7}$$

Due to the fact that according to $A4$, the delivered prices of both firms are identical at the competition boundary R_C:

$$\psi_A(R_G - R_C, D) + R_G - R_C = \psi_I(R_C) + R_C, \tag{10.8}$$

this boundary with profit-maximizing foreign and domestic mill prices m_A^*, m_I^* can endogenously be derived as

$$R_C^* = R_C^*(R_G, D). \tag{10.9}$$

Inserting this result (10.9) into the price equations (10.4) and (10.7), the mill prices will read:

$$m_I^* = \psi_I[R_C^*(R_G, D)] \tag{10.10}$$

and

$$m_A^* = \psi_A[R_C^*(R_G, D)]. \tag{10.11}$$

At first glance, it might be surprising that due to the equilibrium condition (10.8), both prices are dependent on the foreign firm's as well as the domestic firm's distance to the national border. Consequently, the firms' profits – apart from the fixed costs – are functions of the transportation costs between the firms' locations and the national border:

$$\Pi_I = \psi_I[R_C^*(R_G, D)] \cdot \Phi\{\psi_I[R_C^*(R_G, D)] + R_C\} - K_f \tag{10.12}$$

and

$$\Pi_A = \psi_A[R_C^*(R_G, D)] \cdot \Phi\{\psi_A[R_C^*(R_G, D)] + D + (R_G - R_C)\} - K_f. \tag{10.13}$$

Within this basic framework, we are now able to discuss the various tariff and non-tariff barriers to international trade.

10.3 Tariff Policy in a Spatial Market

Tariffs accrue as commodities cross national borders, where the imposition of tariffs on imported goods – as opposed to the imposition on exported goods – is the empirically predominant case, which shall be assumed henceforth. This import duty can be distinguished in two different ways, i.e. with respect to the calculation base and with respect to the purpose of the imposition. Tariffs can be calculated either per quantity (specific tariff) or per value (ad valorem tariff). The arguments in favour of tariffs are threefold, with several subordinate motives in each case:

(a) By the imposition of an import tariff, domestic industries can be protected from international competitors. The complete protection rate keeps all foreign goods away from the domestic market. The rate of this protective tariff is optimal, if imports are prevented completely.
(b) By imposing a tariff, the government obtains a revenue. The importance of this revenue depends on whether other sources of revenue (taxes, public debt) are available. The rate of this tariff is optimal, if the tariff revenue of the government is maximized.
(c) Tariffs do not only influence welfare in the tariff-imposing country but also abroad. A domestic welfare maximizing tariff thereby has an effect on welfare in those countries having a trade relationship with the inland, too. In a two-country-world, welfare of the home country and the foreign country add to *world welfare*, which is influenced by a tariff, too. Retaliatory measures (e.g. tariffs imposed by the foreign country) shall not be considered because $A5$ assumes a short period.

The model can easily be modified to include either tariffs on the value of imports or tariffs on the quantity of imports. In the former case, the amount of the tariff, t, is added to the price of the foreign enterprise, changing foreign profits to

$$\Pi_A = m_A \int_0^{R_G - R_C} \phi(m_A + D + t + r)dr - K_f. \tag{10.14}$$

In the latter case, the price increases by a constant factor, $(1 + t)$, which yields

$$\Pi_A = m_A \int_0^{R_G - R_C} \phi((m_A + D)(1 + t) + r)dr - K_f, \tag{10.15}$$

if the value of the freight at the border between the two countries $(m_A + D)$ is taken as reference. The condition for an equilibrium reads

$$\psi_A(R_G - R_C, D, t) + R_G - R_C = \psi_I(R_C) + R_C. \tag{10.16}$$

This condition which now contains the profit maximizing price of the importing firm based on exogenously given market areas and tariffs, $m_A^* = \psi_A(R_G - R_C, D, t)$, causes the mill price of the domestic firm to depend on the tariff rate, too:

$$m_I^* = \psi_I[R_C^*(R_G, D, t)] \tag{10.17}$$

and

$$m_A^* = \psi_A[R_C^*(R_G, D, t)]. \tag{10.18}$$

Not only the classification of tariffs according to their base is important, but also the motivation for imposing a tariff. The following statements are related to this question.

The complete protection tariff rate keeps any foreign goods away from the country. In the spatial model, this means that the national border between the two countries coincides with the border between the market areas: $R_C = R_G$. The equilibrium condition $\psi_A(D, t) = \psi_I(R_G) + R_G$ serves to calculate the lowest tariff rate appropriate to prevent any imports:

$$t_s^* = t_s^*(R_G, D). \tag{10.19}$$

Consequently, this tariff rate only depends on the distances (and thus the transport costs) between the locations of the firms and the border between the two countries. If, on the other hand, the government aims at maximizing the revenue from tariffs (maximum revenue tariff), the tariff rate to be calculated must permit a certain quantity of imports. The tariff revenue generally equals:

$$T = t \cdot \int_0^{R_G - R_C} \phi(m_A + D + r, t)dr \tag{10.20}$$

or, considering the equilibrium condition (16) and the profit maximizing foreign mill price for the domestic country (18)

$$T = t \cdot \Phi\{\psi_A[R_C^*(R_G, D, t)] + D + (R_G - R_C^*(R_G, D, t)), t\}. \tag{10.21}$$

Provided that equation (10.21) is two times differentiable, maximization with respect to t $[dT/dt = \Phi(\cdot) + t \cdot (\frac{\partial \Phi}{\partial \psi_A} \frac{\partial \psi_A}{\partial R_C^*} \frac{\partial R_C^*}{\partial t} - \frac{\partial \Phi}{\partial R_C^*} \frac{\partial R_C^*}{\partial t} + \frac{\partial \Phi}{\partial t}) = 0]$ yields from the first-order condition:

$$t_f^* = t_f^*(R_G, D). \tag{10.22}$$

Again, the endogenous tariff rate depends solely on the transport costs between the locations of the firms and the border between the two countries.

The definition of the policy-relevant domestic welfare level determines the welfare maximizing tariff. One plausible definition would be the sum of the profit of the domestic firm and the consumers' surplus. Following this definition, welfare reads $\Omega_I = \Pi_I + \Lambda_I + \Lambda_{IA}$, where Π_I is the profit of the firm, Λ_I is the consumers' surplus in the market area of the domestic firm and Λ_{IA} symbolizes the consumers' surplus in the domestic market area of the foreign firm. If the foreign firm spends the profit it attains in the home country, Π_A, either for consumption or reinvestment purposes, this amount has to be added to the welfare function. Also, if the tariff revenue, T, leads to reductions of taxes or government expenditures of the same amount in the domestic country, the tariff revenue has to be added as well. The welfare maximizing tariff thus depends on the employed concept of welfare. While Hass (1996, 1997) used the definition $\Omega_I = \Pi_I + \Pi_A + \Lambda_I + \Lambda_{IA}$, Schöler (1997) employed the approach $\Omega_I = \Pi_I + \Lambda_I + \Lambda_{IA} + T$, which is applied in the discussion of the model with linear demand curves in the appendix, too.

Consumers' surplus at point r within the market area of the domestic firm is

$$\lambda(r) = \int_{p_I(r)}^{\phi^{-1}(0)} \phi(m_I + r)dp, \tag{10.23}$$

where $\phi^{-1}(0)$ is the prohibitive price and $p_I(r) = m_I + r$ symbolizes the local price at point r. The total consumers' surplus in this market area is

$$\Lambda_I = \int_0^{R_C} \int_{p_I(r)}^{\phi^{-1}(0)} \phi(m_I + r)dpdr. \tag{10.24}$$

In the same manner, consumers' surplus at a point within the domestic part of the foreign firm can be calculated as

$$\lambda(r) = \int_{p_A(r,t)}^{\phi^{-1}(0)} \phi(m_A + D + r, t)dp, \tag{10.25}$$

where $\phi^{-1}(0)$ is the prohibitive price and $p_A(r,t)$ stands for the price at point r. The total domestic consumers' surplus in the market area of the foreign firm thus reads

$$\Lambda_{IA} = \int_0^{R_G - R_C} \int_{p_A(r)}^{\phi^{-1}(0)} \phi(m_A + D + r, t)dpdr. \tag{10.26}$$

Under consideration of R_C^* and equations (10.17) and (10.18), welfare effects, however they are composed, are a function of the distance between the locations of the firms and the border between the countries:

$$\Omega_I = \Omega_I(R_G, D, t). \tag{10.27}$$

If it is assumed that this welfare function is twice differentiable, its maximum with respect to the tariff rate can be calculated. In accordance with the theory of international trade, the welfare maximizing tariff is referred to as the 'optimal tariff'.

$$t_{\Omega}^{*} = t_{\Omega}^{*}(R_G, D), \tag{10.28}$$

which, just as the other endogenously determined tariff rates, depends on the distance between the firms and the border between the two countries. The results for the optimal tariff and welfare depend, however, on the chosen definition of welfare which is determined by the political and economical environment.

10.4 Non-Tariff Barriers to Trade in a Spatial Market

Apart from tariffs, non-tariff restrictions to trade, such as import quota and export subsidies, are more and more common interventions in international trade. In the former case, the government only allows for a given quantity of imports per unit of time. In a spatial model, this means the limitation of the domestic market area being supplied by the foreign firm (see Hass (1996)). With regard to allocation, an import quota has the same effects as an import tariff or, put differently, for any tariff rate, there exists an import quota having the same spatial and economical effects. There are, however, differences with regard to distribution. More specifically, the government has no revenue if the import quota is not attached to firms by auctions or sales of licences. In the latter case, goods crossing the border become cheaper, which causes the market area of the exporter to be larger (see Hass and Schöler (1999)).

Import quota: If it is assumed that trade policy does not aim at autarky, the import quota Q is strictly positive. It can be expressed in terms of demand:

$$Q = \int_{0}^{R_G - R_C} \phi(m_{A,Q} + D + r)dr. \tag{10.29}$$

If an import quota is effective, the amount of the imports has to be smaller than with free trade. Consequently, the mill price from equation (10.29) must be higher than under free trade:

$$m_{A,Q} = g(Q, D, R_G - R_C) > m_A^{*}. \tag{10.30}$$

The amount of the import quota enters into the equilibrium condition

$$g(Q, D, R_G - R_C) + D + R_G - R_C = \psi_I(R_C) + R_C \tag{10.31}$$

and, by applying the endogenously derived border between the market areas (see equation (10.31)) $R_C^* = R_C^*(R_G, D, Q)$, into the price of the domestic firm:

$$m_I^* = \psi_I(R_C^*(R_G, D, Q)). \tag{10.32}$$

Is there – in analogy to an optimal tariff – an optimal import quota? If licences for imports are not sold, the objective of earning a maximum revenue does not apply to this case. Also, if maximum protection is the aim of the government, the optimal import quota amounts to zero. Only the welfare maximizing import quota is a political option. Assuming that the welfare function, being composed of the elements $\Omega_I = \Pi_I + \Lambda_I + \Lambda_{IA}$ and reading

$$\Omega_I = \Omega_I(R_G, D, Q), \tag{10.33}$$

is twice differentiable, its maximum can be calculated with respect to the import quota. The welfare maximizing quota equals:

$$Q_\Omega^* = Q_\Omega^*(R_G, D). \tag{10.34}$$

Just as the endogenously derived tariff rates, it depends on the distance between the locations of the firms and the border between the two countries. The amount of the welfare maximizing quota and the welfare maximum are determined by the composition of the welfare effects.

Export subsidies: Throughout this paper, it has been assumed that the domestic country is larger than the market area of the domestic firm ($R_G > R_C$), the remaining area being supplied by the foreign firm. In this setting, trade can have only one direction. Within this subsection, the inverse shall be assumed ($A1.2$). Accordingly, the domestic firm not only supplies the entire domestic market, but also a part of the foreign market area ($R_G < R_C$). Furthermore, it shall be assumed that exports are subsidized by the amount of s per unit because the government aims – for what reason ever – at increasing the exports (see Hass and Schöler (1999)). The profit function of the domestic firm becomes

$$\Pi_I = m_{I1} \int_0^{R_G} \phi(m_{I1} + r)dr + (m_{I2} + s) \int_{R_G}^{R_C} \phi(m_{I2} + r)dr - K_f, \tag{10.35}$$

where $S = s \int_{R_G}^{R_C} \phi(m_{I2} + r)dr$ signifies the sum of export subsidies which is paid to the domestic firm. Allowing only for a non-discriminatory pricing policy, there is only one mill price $m_{I1} = m_{I2} = m_I$, depending on the amount of export subsidies:

$$m_I^* = \psi_I(R_G, R_C, s). \tag{10.36}$$

With export subsidies, too, the equilibrium condition

$$\psi_I(R_G, R_C, s) + R_C = \psi_A(R - R_C) + R - R_C \tag{10.37}$$

causes both mill prices to depend on the amount of subsidies:

$$m_I^* = \psi_I(R_G, s, R_C^*(R, R_G, s)) \tag{10.38}$$

and

$$m_A^* = \psi_A(R - R_C^*(R, R_G, s)). \tag{10.39}$$

Provided that the welfare function, being composed of the elements $\Omega_I = \Pi_I + \Lambda_I + \Lambda_{IA} - S$ and reading

$$\Omega_I = \Omega_I(R_G, R, s), \tag{10.40}$$

is twice differentiable, its maximum can be calculated with respect to the amount of export subsidies. The welfare maximizing rate of subsidy is

$$s_\Omega^* = s_\Omega^*(R_G, R), \tag{10.41}$$

with $R = R_G + D$. By now, we discussed trade policies under the precondition that firms are not able to apply discriminatory pricing techniques. If each exporting firm is setting different prices in home country and in the foreign country, respectively, thus applying spatial price discrimination, we shall yield other results.

10.5 Conclusion

The variations of a spatial border-crossing dyopoly as shown above correspond to the ideas proposed by Lösch within his critique of the traditional international trade theory: International trade arises if a border divides a market area. It can be shown that trade-political parameters of optimal welfare (tariffs, import quotas and export subsidies) for given locations can be explained by spatial variables and thus be endogenized. As described in other articles (see Schöler (1997), Hass and Schöler (1999)), under certain conditions within the framework of such models it is possible to practise a trade policy which leads to a higher level of welfare than free trade. Those results support our findings on strategic trade policy, which are derived from models of non-spatial markets (see also Brander and Spencer (1981)). However, it has to be considered that only partial analytical solutions referring to only one market are being found whereas the traditional international trade theory, besides partial analytical results, also offers total analytical results. Furthermore, in deriving the optimal trade policy, especially the parameters t_Ω^*, Q_Ω^* or s_Ω^* for maximum welfare, it has to be taken into account that different solutions may arise depending on the distance variables R_G, D and R, respectively, and/or the assumed type of the demand function of individual consumption $\phi(m + r)$:

(a) For all admissible distances, an internal solution might arise (e.g. for $q = 1 - m - r$ and t_f^*, see Schöler (1997)).
(b) There may be an internal solution for restricted combinations of distances (e.g. for t_Ω^*, see Schöler, (1997)).
(c) Non-internal solutions may arise, e.g. for non-price discrimination and export subsidies (see Hass and Schöler (1999)).
(d) It is possible that there is no valid solution (e.g. only a complex one).

Despite these difficulties it should be noted that with each trade-political activity the design of an optimal trade policy depends on the distances between the producers' locations and the national border. Finally, the results of our model vary with the conjectural variations of the firms (Löschian competition or any other type of competition), their pricing strategy (price discrimination or fob pricing) and the number of participants (two or more). This leads to a higher number of possible solutions of the model which correspond more appropriately to the concrete questions.

Appendix

The trade policy which has been shown for any demand functions should be discussed for the specific consumer individual demand function $\phi(m + r) = 1 - m - r$.

Free trade: The profit function of the domestic firm is

$$\Pi_I = m_I \int_0^{R_C} (1 - m_I - r)dr - K_f \tag{10.A1}$$

and the profit maximizing mill price for the given market area with a boundary at R_C is

$$m_I^* = 0,5 - 0,25R_C. \tag{10.A2}$$

The profit of the foreign firm is

$$\Pi_A = m_A \int_0^{R_G - R_C} (1 - m_A - D - r)dr - K_f \tag{10.A3}$$

and the profit maximizing mill price for the given market area is

$$m_A^* = 0,5 - 0,25R_G + 0,25R_C - 0,5D. \tag{10.A4}$$

The equilibrium condition is

$$m_I^* + R_C = m_A^* + R_G - R_C + D, \tag{10.A5}$$

which leads to

$$R_C^* = \frac{2D + 3R_G}{6}. \tag{10.A6}$$

If we use (10.A6) in the price equations (10.A2) and (10.A4), we get:

$$m_I^* = \frac{12 - 2D - 3R_G}{24} \tag{10.A7}$$

and

$$m_A^* = \frac{12 - 10D - 3R_G}{24}. \tag{10.A8}$$

Exogenous tariffs: Under the assumption of a tariff per quantity, the profit function of the importer reads as follows:

$$\Pi_A = m_A \int_0^{R_G - R_C} (1 - m_A - D - t - r)dr - K_f, \tag{10.A9}$$

and the profit maximizing mill price in the market area $R_G - R_C$ is

$$m_A^* = 0,5 - 0,25R_G + 0,25R_C - 0,5D - 0.5t. \tag{10.A10}$$

The application of the equilibrium condition $m_I^* + R_C = m_A^* + R_G - R_C + D + t$ in the case of import tariffs results in a market boundary of

$$R_C^* = \frac{2D + 3R_G + 2t}{6} \tag{10.A11}$$

with $\partial R/\partial t = 1/3$. Using (10.A11) the equilibrium mill prices are:

$$m_I^* = \frac{12 - 2D - 3R_G - 2t}{24} \tag{10.A12}$$

and

$$m_A^* = \frac{12 - 10D - 3R_G - 10t}{24} \tag{10.A13}$$

with the partial derivatives $\partial m_I^*/\partial t = -1/12$ and $\partial m_A^*/\partial t = -5/12$.

Endogenous tariffs: The lowest protective tariff preventing imports is due to $R_C = R_G$:

$$t_s^* = 1,5R_G - D. \tag{10.A14}$$

The optimal finance tariff results from

$$\max_{t_f} T(t_f) = \int_0^{R_G - R_C^*} t_f(1 - m_A^* - D - t_f - r)dr \tag{10.A15}$$

with

$$t_f^* = 2/5 + 2R_G/5 - 2D/3 - \sqrt{c_f}/30, \tag{10.A16}$$

in which

$$c_f = 279R_G^2 - 12R_G(10D + 21) + 4(25D^2 - 30D + 36).$$

The partial derivatives are $\partial t_f^*/\partial D < 0$ and $\partial t_f^*/\partial R_G \lesseqgtr 0$. Applying the optimal finance tariff, the equilibrium mill prices are

$$m_I^* = 7/15 - 19R_G/120 - D/36 + \sqrt{c_f}/360 \tag{10.A17}$$

and

$$m_A^* = 1/3 - 7R_G/24 - 5D/36 + \sqrt{c_f}/72 \tag{10.A18}$$

with

$$R_C^* = 2/15 + 19R_G/30 + D/9 - \sqrt{c_f}/90.$$

The optimal tariff may be determined by using the welfare function $\Omega_I = \Pi_I + \Lambda_I + \Lambda_{IA} + T$. The equations of the consumers' surplus of the market area $\overline{0R_C^*}$ are

$$\Lambda_I = \int_0^{R_C^*} [(1 - m_I^* - r)^2/2]dr \tag{10.A19}$$

and for the market area $R_G - R_C^*$

$$\Lambda_{IA} = \int_0^{R_G - R_C^*} [(1 - m_A^* - D - t - r)^2/2]dr. \tag{10.A20}$$

The profit of the domestic firm is

$$\Pi_I = m_I^* \int_0^{R_C^*} (1 - m_I^* - r)dr - K_f \tag{10.A21}$$

and the tariff revenue is

$$T = \int_0^{R_G - R_C^*} t(1 - m_A^* - D - t - r)dr. \tag{10.A22}$$

The optimal tariff results from

$$\max_{t_\Omega} \Omega(t_\Omega) = \Lambda_I(t_\Omega) + \Lambda_A(t_\Omega) + \Pi_I(t_\Omega) + T(t_\Omega) \qquad (10.A23)$$

with

$$t^*_\Omega = 20/49 + 16R_G/49 - 29D/49 - \sqrt{c_\Omega}/98, \qquad (10.A24)$$

in which

$$c_\Omega = 1600D^2 - 32D(67R_G + 47) + 1465R_G^2 + 1384R_G - 752.$$

For the optimal tariff $R_G \in [R_{G_1}\ R_{G_2})$ is valid. For $R_G < R_{G_1}$ there is no real solution, and for $R_G \geq R_{G_2}$ the non-negativity condition does not hold. The partial derivatives are $\partial t^*_\Omega/\partial D < 0$ and $\partial t^*_\Omega/\partial R_G \lesseqgtr 0$. By using the optimal tariffs, the equilibrium mill prices are as follows:

$$m^*_I = 137/294 - 179R_G/1179 - 5D/147 + \sqrt{c_\Omega}/264 \qquad (10.A25)$$

and

$$m^*_A = 97/294 - 307R_G/1176 - 25D/147 + 5\sqrt{c_\Omega}/1176 \qquad (10.A26)$$

with

$$R^*_C = 20/147 + 179R_G/294 + 20D/147 - \sqrt{c_\Omega}/294.$$

Import quotas: For the given demand function the import quota equals

$$Q = \int_0^{R_G - R_C} (1 - m_A - D - r)dr, \qquad (10.A27)$$

which leads to a foreign mill price at a level of

$$m_{A,Q} = \frac{R_c^2 - 2R_C(D + R_G - 1) + 2DR_G + R_G^2 - 2R_G + 2Q}{2(R_C - R_G)}. \qquad (10.A28)$$

Together with the mill price of the domestic firm $m^*_i = 0,5 - 0,25R_C$ we can now determine the equilibrium condition $m_{A,Q} + D + R_G - R_C = m^*_I + R_C$ from which the market boundary may be derived:

$$R^*_C = 0,1(-\sqrt{c_Q} + 7R_G + 2) \quad mit \quad c_Q = (3R_G - 2)^2 + 80Q. \qquad (10.A29)$$

Now the mill prices are

$$m^*_I = 0,025(18 - 7R_G + \sqrt{c_Q}) \qquad (10.A30)$$

and

$$m_{A,Q} = 0,025[-7\sqrt{c_Q} + 9R_G - 2(20D - 17)]. \quad (10.A31)$$

The welfare function

$$\begin{aligned} \Omega_I = & \int_0^{R_C^*} (0,5(1 - m_I^* - r)^2 + m_I^*(1 - m_I^* - r))dr - K_f \\ & + \int_0^{R_G - R_C} 0,5(1 - m_{A,Q} - D - r)^2 dr \end{aligned} \quad (10.A32)$$

serves to calculate a welfare optimal import quota at the level of

$$\begin{aligned} Q_\Omega^* = & [211R_G^2 - 713R_G + 556 - \sqrt{(553R_G^2 - 1064R_G + 592)} \\ & \cdot |7R_G - 13|]/4356. \end{aligned} \quad (10.A33)$$

Export subsidies: The profit function of the domestic firm in the case of export subsidies reads:

$$\Pi_I = m_I \int_0^{R_G} (1 - m_I - r)dr + (m_I + s) \int_{R_G}^{R_C} (1 - m_I - r)dr - K_f \quad (10.A34)$$

and the corresponding profit maximizing mill price is:

$$m_I^* = -\frac{R_C^2 + 2R_C(s - 1) - 2sR_G}{4R_C}. \quad (10.A35)$$

Together with the mill price of the foreign firm $m_A^* = (2 + R_C - R)/4$, it is possible to determine the equilibrium condition $m_A^* + R - R_C = m_I^* + R_C$ from which the market boundary

$$R_C^* = (1/12)(\sqrt{c_s} + 3R + 2s) \quad mit \quad c_s = (3R_G - 2s)^2 - 48R_G s \quad (10.A36)$$

may be derived. The mill prices are:

$$m_I^* = -(1/48)[7\sqrt{c_s} - 15R + 2(7s - 12)] \quad (10.A37)$$

and

$$m_A^* = -(1/48)(\sqrt{c_s} - 9R + 2s + 24). \quad (10.A38)$$

The welfare function

$$\begin{aligned} \Omega_I = & \int_0^{R_G} (0,5(1 - m_I^* - r)^2 + m_I^*(1 - m_I^* - r))dr - K_f \\ & + (m_I^* + s) \int_{R_G}^{R_C} (1 - m_I^* - r)dr - s \int_{R_G}^{R_C} (1 - m_I^* - r)dr \end{aligned} \quad (10.A39)$$

does not lead to a general solution for the welfare optimal rate of export subsidy. If, however, we assume R_G to be 0,5 and R to be 1, the welfare optimal rate of subsidy would be $s^*_\Omega = 0,5094$.

References

[1] Benson, B. L. and J. Hartigan (1983). Tariffs Which Lower Price in the Restricting Country: An Analysis of Spatial Markets. *Journal of International Economics 15*, 117-133.
[2] Benson, B. L. and J. Hartigan (1984). Tariffs and Quotas in a Spatial Duopoly. *Southern Economic Journal 50*, 965–978.
[3] Benson, B. L. and J. Hartigan (1987). Tariffs and Location Specific Income Redistribution. *Regional Science and Urban Economics 17*, 223–243.
[4] Brander, J. A. and B. Spencer (1981). Tariffs and Extraction of Foreign Monopoly Rents Under Potential Entry. *Canadian Journal of Economics 16*, 371-389.
[5] Hass, D. (1996). *Internationaler Handel in einem räumlichen Oligopolmarkt.* München.
[6] Hass, D. (1997). Optimale Zölle in einem internationalen Dyopol. *Jahrbuch für Regionalwissenschaft 18*, 21–35.
[7] Hass, D. and K. Schöler (1999). Exportsubventionen im internationalen räumlichen Oligopol. *Jahrbücher für Nationalökonomie und Statistik 218*, 45–62.
[8] Heffley, D. and P. Hatzipanayotou (1991). Tariff Protection in an Open Spatial Economy. *Journal of Regional Science 31*, 1–15.
[9] Heffley, D., P. Hatzipanayotou, and P. Mourdoukoutas (1993). Tariffs, Price Conjectures and Welfare in an Open Spatial Economy. *Papers in Regional Science 72*, 87–100.
[10] Lösch, A. (1938). Wo gilt die Theorie der komparativen Kosten? *Weltwirtschaftliches Archiv 38*, 45.
[11] Lösch, A. (1939). Eine neue Theorie des internationalen Handels. *Weltwirtschaftliches Archiv 40*, 308.
[12] Lösch, A. (1944). *Die räumliche Ordnung der Wirtschaft* (2nd ed.). Jena.
[13] Porter, R. (1984). Tariff Policies in a Small Open Spatial Economy. *Canadian Journal of Economics 17*, 270–282.
[14] Schöler, K. (1990). Zollwirkungen in einem räumlichen Oligopol. *Zeitschrift für Wirtschafts- und Sozialwissenschaften 110*, 393–411.
[15] Schöler, K. (1997). Tariffs, Factor Prices, and Welfare in a Spatial Oligopoly. *Annals of Regional Science 31*, 353–367.

11 Trans–European Effects of "Trans–European Networks"

Results from a Spatial CGE Analysis

Johannes Bröcker*

11.1 Transnational Infrastructure Policy in Europe

With the Maastricht Treaty, which became effective in November 1993, cf. Eutrecht (1997), the European Union (EU) for the first time took over a responsibility in providing infrastructure networks for transport, telecommunication and energy. A new title XII (now XV) has been introduced into the treaty, with Article 129b (now 154) assigning the obligation to the union level to contribute to the establishment of trans-European networks in the three areas. Emphasis is put on the interconnection and interoperability of national networks and on access to the networks. The networks shall also support the cohesion objective by linking islands, landlocked and peripheral regions with the central regions of the community.

The union shall, according to the new regulations, set up guidelines for the development of the networks, and in particular shall identify so-called "projects of common interest", which are eligible for support through feasibility studies, loan guarantees and interest subsidies by EU institutions such as the European Investment Bank, and by the Cohesion Fund. This Fund is a special fund of the EU budget supporting infrastructure and environmental projects in the four poorest countries of the Union (Ireland, Portugal, Spain, and Greece). Furthermore, the Union shall develop the necessary norms and standards guaranteeing interoperability of national systems for each mode as well as interoperability between modes. For the Community area itself an expert group appointed by the European Council December 1993 in Brussels (the CHRISTOPHERSEN-Group) suggested a list of projects of common interest. Based on this report a decision has then been made by the European Council in Essen, December 1994, about 14 high priority projects and 21 further important projects (see figure 11.1 for the road projects in this list). The cost estimate of the high priority projects is more than 300 bn Euro. In between (1999) 3 projects are finished and the others are either under construction or in a mature planning phase. Up to now, Union institutions were involved in 30% of the financing, cf. Ten (1997).

* Financial support by the Deutsche Forschungsgemeinschaft for the project "Wie wirken sich neue Verkehrstechnologien und die Entwicklung Transeuropäischer Netze auf die Europäische Standortverteilung aus?" is gratefully acknowledged. The author thanks Frank Richter for excellent computer work.

Fig. 11.1. TEN-tr priority projects within the EU

Parallel with these activities also a dialogue with the countries of central and eastern Europe was launched aiming at an extension of the network to the east. It started at the European Conference of Ministers of Transport 1995 in Crete. A set of transport corridors were suggested, and a final decision was then made by the 3rd Pan-European Transport Conference in Helsinki, June 1997. The conference declaration defined 9 combined rail/road corridors and the Danube inland water way as the 10th transport corridor in central and eastern Europe (see figure 11.2).

Fig. 11.2. Helsinki-Corridors

A third activity closely connected with the two before mentioned processes, the so-called TINA (Transport Infrastructure Needs Assessment) started in September 1995, when the European Transport Council and the ministers of transport of the ten countries in central and eastern Europe, which are now candidates for EU membership, decided to coordinate the transport network planning for these countries and the EU. A TINA secretariat is now installed in Vienna coordinating the assessment process. The Pan-European corridors are the backbone of the network, which is going to be specified in detail and to be extended by local links in the TINA process. The costs for the projects specified by now are estimated to be around 90 bn Euro. The EU is going to cofinance 1 bn per year in the framework of the so-called ISPA fund (Instrument for Structural Policies for Pre-Accession), starting in 2000. As it turned out that there are transport needs in the candidate countries not fitting into the corridor concept, 4 so-called PETrAs (Pan-European Transport Areas) have been added to the corridors in the TINA master plan, cf. European Commission and TINA Secretariat (1999).

There is a consensus among economists and political practitioners that increased trade and moving of people in an enlarged and more deeply integrated EU requires a well developed network for the flow of goods, services, people, information and energy, and that emphasis has to be put on border crossing links and interoperability between countries as well as between modes of transport in particular. Economists raise some doubts, however, whether this implies the necessity to assign responsibilities for infrastructure provision to the highest EU level of administration, cf. Junkernheinrich (1997), Laaser (1997), Wink (1997). Allocative principles from the theory of local public finance require that the subsets of people who decide about provision of a public good, who pay for it and who reap the utility generated by it should coincide as far as possible.

Ideally, one would like to delineate for each public good the smallest set for which this coincidence can be fulfilled. This is the best guarantee that marginal benefits and costs of a project do not deviate. Of course, no special institution can be installed for each type of public good, however. The practical solution is the subsidiarity principle assigning the responsibility to the lowest possible level of administration. Whether one has to change to a higher level (from the nation to the EU level, for example) has to be made dependent upon the degree of regional externalities. If an infrastructure investment generates significant welfare gains in another country without an obligation of that country to contribute to the cost, the national administration would have an incentive to under-invest. Even this, however, does not necessarily call for centralization. If the number of institutions (national governments, say) involved is small, they should, according to the COASE theorem, be able to detect the potential gains from cooperation. Two neighbor countries considering to establish a cross border link, for example, would evaluate their respective costs and benefits and would have a strong incentive to find a bargain making them both better off, if the project is profitable for both countries taken together.

Only if a larger number of potential partners is involved, they run into a dilemma of collective action. With sufficiently high network externalities the individual incentive to contribute to a network improvement is too small, even though the net benefit may be high from a social point of view. This is a valid argument in favor of centralized action for establishing norms and standards guaranteeing interoperability. Transport policy on the EU level was also successful in breaking up national monopolies and enforcing deregulation. The separation of rail networks from operation and the access of new operators to the network, which is realized now in many (though not all) EU countries has been made possible by EU transport policy. Here the EU bodies acted as a leverage of newcomers as well as customers against vested national interests. Hence, an efficiency enhancing role of the EU institutions in the areas of interoperability and of deregulation is obvious.

Serious doubts must be raised, however, regarding centralized EU responsibilities in the provision of transport infrastructure links itself. The issue is an empirical one: is it true that the international links of the masterplan generate welfare gains widely spreading over Europe, such that externalities are sufficiently large to justify centralization? Or is it true that gains mainly accrue to the regions themselves, where the links are going to be built? It is hard to justify a new centralized infrastructure provision policy, if the latter holds true. The following aims at giving a quantitative answer, based on an exercise in spatial computable general equilibrium analysis.

The next section critically reviews standard methods for evaluating welfare effects of transport investments and suggests computable general equilibrium analysis as the method of choice for our problem. Section 11.3 explains the structure of the model in a non-formal manner. The formal details are published in Bröcker (1998b), where the same type of model is applied to estimating welfare effects of economic integration. Section 11.4 explains the welfare measurement based on the equilibrium model and detects close formal similarities between our approach and the so-called potential approach traditionally favoured in regional science. Section 11.5 shows how the system is empirically implemented, section 11.6 presents comparative static simulations, and a final section draws conclusions.

11.2 Evaluation Methods

The standard cost-benefit approach measures the benefit generated from using a new or an improved link by the consumers' surplus which, by the way, has been invented by a transport engineer, Dupuit. For a quantification one typically estimates a demand function for flows along the link to be studied, specifying the flow as a function of the generalised cost (time cost plus out-of-pocket costs). The benefit is the area left of the demand curve between the generalised costs before and after the investment. If the link did not exist before the investment, a prohibitively high generalised cost has to represent the before-investment situation. This approach has a sound microeconomic foundation, but it does not help to answer our question about the regional distribution. We do not know anything about where households eventually benefiting from the investment are located.

The German assessment procedure requires a regional allocation of benefits because, due to regional policy reasons, an extra plus is assigned to investments favouring lagging regions. The method prescribed by the official German assessment manual (cf. Bundesminister für Verkehr (1993)) is simple but strange: regional benefits are calculated as a fixed proportion of regional investments. Hence, a fast train crossing a region without stop nevertheless generates a benefit there. Yet, no benefits are assigned to regions not touched by the train, even if the new link greatly reduces the costs for trips originating or ending in these regions. This approach is obviously inadequate.

Another method widely used in the literature is the economic potential approach, rooted in the social physics tradition in regional science. According to this approach, the regional impact of a new link is measured by the change of economic potential, which is an indicator of accessibility. The typical indicator is

$$P_r = \sum_s S_s f(g_{sr}). \tag{11.1}$$

S_r is measures the market size in region r, g_{sr} is the transport distance from s to r, and f is a strictly monotonic decreasing function attributing lower weights to more distant markets. A new link reduces distances and, hence, increases the potential P_s. A well made example of this approach is Vickerman et al. (1999), see also Rietveld and Bruinsma (1998) for an extensive survey and application of this method.

Assessing the regional distribution of benefits by the potential approach is clearly preferable over the procedure mentioned before. Nevertheless, the problem is that there is no obvious way how to translate changes in the potential index to economically meaningful quantities like real income or money-metric welfare measures like HICKSian variation. The potential indicator is an ad-hoc index without microeconomic foundation and, therefore, assigning an economic meaning to this indicator must be ad-hoc as well.

The up to date alternative to the before mentioned approach is to set up a multiregional computable general equilibrium, in which transport costs explicitly appear as an impediment to interregional trade. This is what we are going to do in this paper. It confines to the regional welfare effects resulting from the use of the new links for commodity trade. Effects from the construction phase, from financing and maintenance are not considered. Use of the links for other than trade purposes, such as commuting, tourism, leisure trips et cetera are not considered either. We model a static equilibrium for a closed economy covering the whole world, subdivided into a large number of regions interacting through commodity trade. Europe (from Atlantic to Ural) is subdivided into 800 regions; the rest of world is aggregated to five broad areas. Trade between regions is costly, with costs depending on transport distances through a given transport network as well as on national trade impediments. Welfare implications of new transport links are quantified by simulating effects of transport distance reductions.

11.3 A Spatial CGE Analysis

In each region of our system there is a representative household and a production sector; no public sector, no taxes and public consumption. As the model gives a one-period shot, there is no investment demand either. All demand is consumption demand of the household, consuming two types of goods, a local good produced by firms of the same region, and a bundle of tradable goods. There is a large number of varieties of tradables, each of which is produced by only one single producer in the world. Firms in a specific region produce a larger or smaller subset of these varieties, the size of which is endogenously determined. Households are price takers and maximise a two-level nested utility. In the upper nest they choose between local goods and tradables, in the lower they choose between varieties of tradables, which enter symmetrically into their preferences. The upper nest is COBB-DOUGLAS, the lower is CES.

Households own a fixed stock of a single factor. They get their income by selling the factor service to the firms of the region where they live. Allowing for just a single factor is not restrictive in our setting, because we do not introduce factor intensity variations over sectors. One may regard the single factor as a composition of many factors.

Firms use three types of inputs: the just mentioned factor service, tradable goods and local goods. Being price takers on the input side, they combine these inputs according to a two level nested constant returns production function. On the upper level they choose between factor services, tradables and local goods, on the lower they choose between tradable varieties. The upper nest is COBB-DOUGLAS. The lower is CES; it is identical with the lower nest in households' preferences. Putting it differently, firms and households use the same CES-composite of tradables for consumption and production, respectively, and they pay the same price, which is the minimal cost per unit of a composite tradable (called q_r for region r).

By combining the inputs, firms generate a single homogeneous intermediate good, costing p_r per unit in region r. It serves a double purpose: (1) It is transformed one-to-one into a local homogeneous good, sold under perfect competition. Hence, the local good has the price p_r. (2) It is transformed into tradable varieties. Producing a variety requires a fixed input amount per variety plus an amount proportional to output. On the tradables' market firms act under CHAMBERLINian monopolistic competition. They price the goods with a mark-up over marginal costs according to the AMOROSO-ROBINSON-relation. The number of varieties is determined such that the mark-up just covers the fixed costs; free entry drives profits down to zero. This type of modelling differentiated markets is due to Dixit and Stiglitz (1977) and after pioneering work of Krugman (1991, 1993, 1994) it is widely used in new economic geography. It can be shown that, due to the constant price elasticity of demand prevailing in our model, this formalism implies that

1. output per variety is constant,
2. the price of a tradable equals the unit cost of the intermediate p_r, and
3. the number (or measure) of tradables produced in a region equals the real regional tradables output.[1]

Finally, we have to introduce interregional transaction costs which are crucial for modelling the effects of reduced transport distances. Transaction costs do not only cover transport costs in the narrow sense, but also travel costs resulting from establishing business contacts, supplying services related to the traded commodities et cetera, as far as these costs can be assumed to be linear in the trade flows. Transaction costs have to be paid for using up resources. For the sake of simplicity, the only resource used are composite tradables from the destination region. Other specifications are possible (use of factor service and local goods, for example) but have a negligible impact on the results.

We assume transaction costs to be a certain percentage of the trade value, the percentage being an increasing — yet in general not linear — function of road travel time. Furthermore, an extra cost is added for international flows. This cost represents the impediments to international trade resulting from different languages, cultural distance and institutional differences between countries. There is ample evidence about the importance of such impediments (see Helliwell (1998) for a recent survey). Calibrating our model we observed an excessive overestimation of international trade flows without inserting these cost components.

Being more precise, let τ_{rs} denote the mark-up factor for transaction cost, such that $p_r \tau_{rs}$ is the local price (including transport cost) in region s for a commodity delivered from r to s, if p_r is the mill-price in region r. For τ_{rs} we choose the flexible form

$$\tau_{rs} = \exp\left(\zeta g_{rs}^{\omega}\right) \delta_{kl}. \qquad (11.2)$$

g_{rs} is road travel time along the shortest route from r to s, ζ and ω are parameters. The parameter ω, which is expected to be positive and less than one, allows for reproducing the observation that the percentage price increase per unit of distance is decreasing in distance. δ_{kl} is the mark-up factor representing international trade impediments between countries k and l, when regions r and s are located in different countries k and l, respectively.

11.4 Measuring Welfare Effects of New Road Links

Welfare effects of new road links are obtained from a comparative static simulation. The equilibrium is calculated for the "old" world without the

[1] "Equality" in 2. and 3. means equality up to arbitrary multipliers depending on the choice of units.

respective link and for the "new" world with the link. Welfare change is measured by the HICKSian equivalent variation, which is the hypothetical income change under constant prices rendering the same utility change as the road link under study. The regional relative equivalent variation is the ratio of the equivalent variation to regional GDP. It can be shown that the relative equivalent variation in region r equals the relative change of the inverse terms of trade p_r/q_r times the ratio of tradables to GDP, cf. Bröcker (1998a, p. 101, equation (11)).

From a methodological point of view it is interesting to observe that the relative change of the terms of trade is closely related to the relative change of economic potential as defined in equation (11.1). The formula for q_r in our model is (see Bröcker, 1998a, p. 103, equation (13))

$$q_r = \psi \left[\sum_s S_s p_s^{-\sigma} \tau_{rs}^{1-\sigma} \right]^{\frac{1}{1-\sigma}} . \tag{11.3}$$

The relative change of q_r equals the relative change of the term in brackets times $1/(1-\sigma)$.[2] Obviously, the term in brackets is a supply potential looking like (11.1), modified by weighting supply S_s by the price term $p_s^{-\sigma}$. That means higher weights are attached to the supply from regions with lower prices.

Similarly, for p_r one obtains from equations (19) and (20) in Bröcker (1998a, p. 105)

$$p_r = \left[\sum_s D_s (\pi_s \tau_{rs})^{-\sigma} \right]^{\frac{1}{\sigma}} , \tag{11.4}$$

with D_s denoting demand for tradables in s. Demand is weighted by $\pi_s^{-\sigma}$, π_s being itself a modified potential

$$\pi_s = \left[\sum_r S_r (p_r \tau_{rs})^{-\sigma} \right]^{\frac{1}{\sigma}} .$$

The relative change of p_r equals the relative change of the term in brackets in (11.4) times $1/\sigma$. Obviously, the term in brackets in (11.4) is a demand potential, modified by weighting demand D_s by $\pi_s^{-\sigma}$. That means higher weights are attached to demand in regions with lower supply potentials. Empirically, the weights in (11.3) and (11.4) vary only little over regions, because

[2] We assume $\sigma > 1$, because else the suppliers' optimization problem is ill defined. In fact, from calibration we obtain a σ much higher than one. Hence, $\sigma/(1-\sigma) < 0$, such that the price for tradables q_r is the lower, the higher the supply potential. Yet it is worth mentioning that formula (11.3) also makes sense for $\sigma < 1$. In this case the term in brackets mutates from a potential to a weighted average distance, and q_r is the lower, the lower is this distance to the market.

our estimate of σ is large. Hence, the modified potentials and non-modified potentials do not differ much.

Summarising this we find that the relative welfare change is a weighted sum of the relative change of the demand potential and the relative change of the supply potential. This yields a rationale for using percentage changes of simple potentials like (11.1) for distributing welfare gains among regions. It should be noted, however, that in the formula (11.1) the "masses" S_s are held fixed, while the masses (and their weights) change endogenously in the general equilibrium welfare measure. The change of potentials with fixed masses can be regarded as the direct effect of cost reductions, while the changes of masses (and weights) are the indirect general equilibrium feedbacks.

11.5 Calibration

Calibrating the model means to assign numbers to the parameters and exogenous variables, namely:

1. the road distances g_{rs},
2. the share parameters in the COBB-DOUGLAS utility and production functions,
3. the regional factor stock and its level of productivity,
4. the parameters ζ and ω of the transaction cost function, and
5. the elasticity of substitution in the aggregator for tradables.

We deal with them briefly in turn.

(1) The road distance g_{rs} is the shortest time distance through a road network with about 3600 links and 6300 non-directed arcs. Average speeds are assigned to motorways (80 km/h) and fast roads (65 km/h) and ordinary roads (50 km/h). Ferry times include expected waiting times. Waiting times at controlled borders are also taken into account.

(2) Share parameters are rough guesses, made after having a look at German national accounts. There is considerable uncertainty with respect to the share of local goods in production input and consumption. Our guess is a ratio 3:2 for local to tradable goods. Sensitivity analysis shows that this ratio has a certain impact on levels, but virtually non on the spatial distribution of welfare effects.

(3) The model does not distinguish between the stock of a factor in a region and its level of productivity. Doubling the stock is the same as doubling its productivity. Hence, the parameter to be calibrated is the factor stock multiplied by ist level of productivity. Given all other parameters, these parameters are simply calibrated such that observed regional GDPs in purchasing-power-parities and regional GDPs in the equilibrium solution coincide.

(4) The parameters ζ and ω of the transaction cost function determine the spatial pattern of trade flows and, therefore, are essential for the spatial pattern of welfare gains. The calibration is based on the fact that the

equilibrium solution of the model generates a gravity form of trade flows

$$t_{rs} = \frac{S_r(p_r\tau_{rs})^{-\sigma}}{\sum_r S_r(p_r\tau_{rs})^{-\sigma}} D_s.$$

t_{rs} is the trade flow from r to s, S_r and D_s are supply and demand of tradables in r and s, respectively, all measured in value terms. Gathering terms with index r and s in A_r and B_s, respectively, and inserting (11.2) for τ_{rs} yields

$$t_{rs} = A_r B_s \exp(-\sigma\zeta g_{rs}^{\omega})\delta_{kl}^{-\sigma}.$$

Controlling for effects of source and destination regions (represented by A_r and B_s, respectively) and international trade impediments (represented by δ_{kl}) by appropriate dummies, we could estimate ω and the composite parameter $\sigma\zeta$ by non-linearly regressing trade flows on distance.

Unfortunately, we do not have observations on trade flows between regions. Hence, we assume the same equations to hold also for flows between countries, which can be well observed. In this context, the log of δ_{kl} is regarded as a linear function of a set of dummies explaining trade impediments. Then the regression for trade from country k to l reads

$$t_{kl} = \exp(a_k + b_l - \sigma\zeta g_{kl}^{\omega} + \pi z_{kl}) + v_{kl}.$$

with $a_k = \log A_k$ and $b_l = \log B_l$. z_{kl} is a vector of dummies for country pair (k, l), π is the associated parameter vector. v_{kl} is the error term. Regarding z_{kl}, we tried dummies for existence/non-existence of a common border (CB), existence/non-existence of a common language (LA), a dummy taking on a value of one if the respective flow crosses the former iron curtain (IC) and zero otherwise, and a few more dummies.

It turns out that the estimates for $\sigma\zeta$ and ω are stable. A typical result is given in table 11.1, obtained from 1995 trade between 37 European countries. The estimate is based on the assumption that the errors are independent and have a variance proportional to the conditional expectation of the trade flows (see Bröcker and Rohweder (1990) for details). The values of the standard errors are White's (1980) heteroskedastic-consistent estimates. All parameter

Table 11.1. Regression results, international trade

	ω	$\sigma\zeta$	IC	LA
Coefficient	0.582	0.036	-0.659	0.696
Standard error	0.056	0.014	0.067	0.072

estimates are as expected. The former iron curtain roughly halves, a common language roughly doubles trade, ceteris paribus. Both effects are highly significant. The distance impact is highly significant with the expected sign as well. The parameter ω is significantly larger than zero and significantly smaller than one, as required.

(5) The regression yields an estimate of the compound $\sigma\zeta$, not of σ and ζ separately. How to calibrate σ? We use two pieces of information, empirical observations on monopolisitic price mark-ups and evidence about the share of transport cost in the value of traded goods. The monopolistic competition approach implies that $\sigma/(\sigma-1)$ is the price mark-up, i.e. the ratio of average to marginal costs. Recent OECD estimates, cf. Martins et al. (1996), render mark-ups in the order of 1.2, averaged over industries. There are strong variations over sectors, of course, but minor ones over countries. This estimate corresponds to a σ-estimate around 6.

There is another independent piece of information, however, letting this estimate of σ appear rather low. If the estimate $\widehat{\sigma\zeta}$ is held constant, $\hat{\zeta}$ and, hence, transaction costs are inversely related to $\hat{\sigma}$. Using (11.2) and $\hat{\zeta} = 0.036/\hat{\sigma}$ we can calculate the share of transaction costs in the value of tradables as a function of $\hat{\sigma}$:

$$\text{Transaction cost share} = \frac{\sum_{rs} \hat{t}_{rs} \exp\left(\frac{0.036}{\hat{\sigma}} g_{rs}^{\omega}\right)}{\sum_{rs} \hat{t}_{rs}} - 1.$$

It is plottet in figure 11.3. $\hat{t}_{rs}$ is the calibrated trade flow, which only depends on estimates of ω and the compound parameter $\sigma\zeta$, not on σ separately.

Fig. 11.3. Transaction cost share

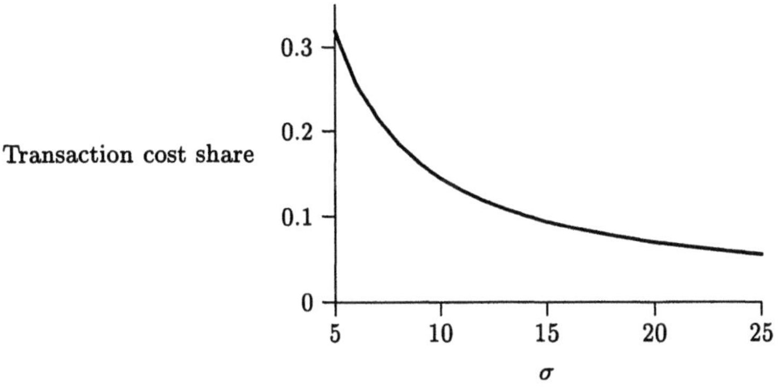

Following the literature, this ratio should be smaller than 0.1 (see Weber (1987) for a survey), implying a σ larger than 13. The following simulations are calculated with $\sigma = 16$. Lower estimates imply implausibly high transport costs and, hence, implausibly high welfare gains generated by transport distance reductions. Sensitivity studies show that varying σ, while holding

$\sigma\zeta$ and ω constant, has a negligible impact on the spatial distribution of the welfare effects, whereas it has a considerable impact on the level of effects. Note that holding $\sigma\zeta$ and ω constant while varying σ implies that an increasing σ is compensated by a decreasing ζ and vice versa. This is responsible for an approximate inverse proportional relation between levels of welfare effects and the parameter σ (see Bröcker (1998b) for results of the sensitivity analysis).

11.6 Results

For answering our main question regarding the degree of network externalities, we have studied 30 road link projects, which are either among the 14 priority projects of the Essen council or part of the Helsinki-corridors. As reported above, the Helsinki conference left the detailed specification of the structures to be built along the corridors open. The details are now going to be specified in the TINA process. Without referring to the details of the current state of the planning process, we made the general assumption that motorways are built along all corridors, as far as they do not yet exist. All specified links cross one international border. They are shown in figure 11.4.

Fig. 11.4. Cross-border road links

Table 11.2 summarizes the distribution of welfare gains for the 30 links. Welfare gains are equivalent variations, measured on the regional level. The table shows for each link the share of the two connected countries in the total welfare generated by the respective links. The sum of these two shares is shown in the last column, and the table is ordered by this last value. Hence, the least trans-European links are on top and the most trans-European ones

on the bottom of the table. For three links regional effects are plotted in figures 11.5 to 11.7. The first (Dublin–Belfast) is absolutely not trans-European, the second (Berlin–Warszawa) has a medium position, the last (Maribor–Zagreb) is "very trans-European".

Fig. 11.5. Dublin–Belfast: regional welfare effects, percent of GDP

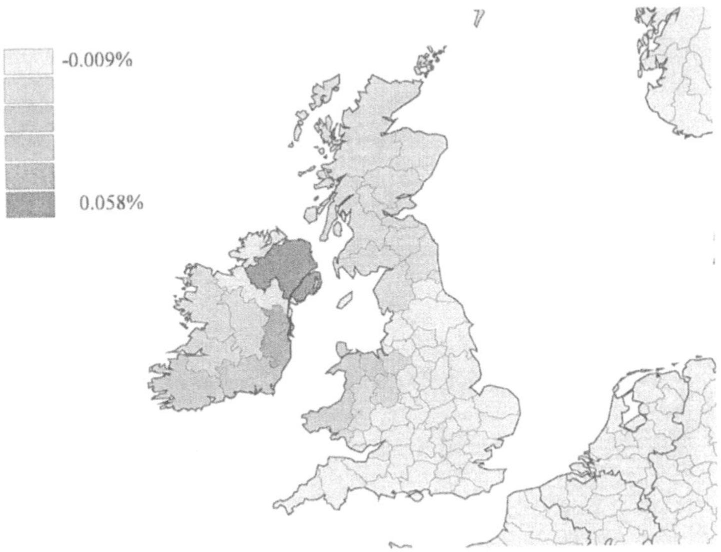

It might seem strange that, for the first three links in the table, more than 100% accrues to the two countries, which are connected by the respective link. This is because new links also generate welfare losses in regions losing markets due to re-orientation of trade flows towards those regions which become better accessible after the new links have been installed.

Coming back to our main question about the degree of international externalities, the results are mixed. 10 out of 30 links generate less than one fifth of their gains in countries other than those directly connected by the links. That means the two countries directly affected obtain the bulk of the benefit. It is therefore difficult to justify why a higher level institution should be involved in planning and financing. They are not "trans-European". The extreme case is the Dublin-Belfast link which even harms countries other than the two ones directly involved. There are links at the other extreme end, however, with the two connected countries reaping one third or less of the total gain. The fixed link over the Fehmarnbelt is a good example. It connects Germany and Denmark, but welfare gains spread widely over the Scandinavian peninsula. In these cases coordination failures between the

Fig. 11.6. Berlin–Warszawa: regional welfare effects, percent of GDP

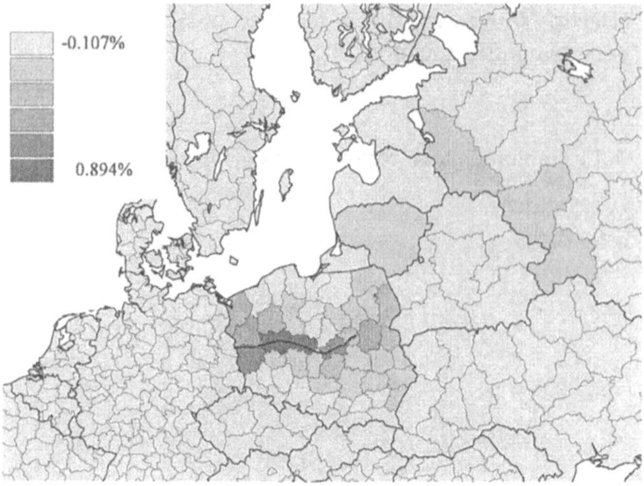

Fig. 11.7. Maribor–Zagreb: regional welfare effects, percent of GDP

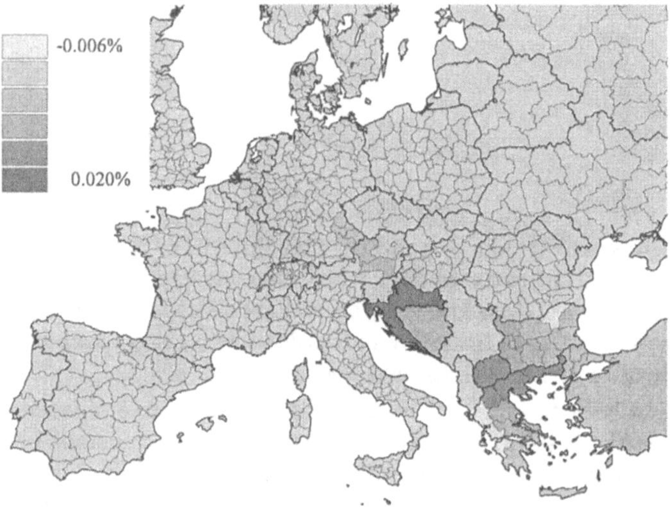

Table 11.2. Share of connected countries in the welfare effects of cross-border links

link	country	%	country	%	Σ
Dublin – Belfast	Ireland	54.9	United Kingdom	66.9	121.8
Stockholm – Oslo	Sweden	71.4	Norway	34.3	105.7
Dresden – Praha	Germany	1.6	Czech Republic	99.5	101.1
Nice – Cuneo	France	57.1	Italy	38.9	96.0
Sofija – Therssaloniki	Bulgaria	73.3	Greece	15.2	88.5
Kraków – L'viv	Poland	79.4	Ukraine	8.5	87.9
Arad – Sofija	Romania	74.0	Bulgaria	13.8	87.8
Nürnberg – Praha	Germany	38.2	Czech Republic	48.8	87.0
Helsinki – St. Peterburg	Finland	58.3	Russia	25.5	83.8
Lyon – Torino	France	42.0	Italy	39.3	81.3
Göteborg – Oslo	Sweden	7.1	Norway	61.2	68.3
Budapest – Užgorod	Hungary	61.2	Ukraine	6.7	67.9
Lisboa – Valladolid	Portugal	48.7	Spain	18.2	66.9
Budapest – Arad	Hungary	39.2	Romania	26.6	65.8
Berlin – Warszawa	Germany	14.8	Poland	45.4	60.2
Trieste – Ljubljana	Italy	38.5	Slovenia	17.0	55.5
Dresden – Wrocław	Germany	28.2	Poland	23.6	51.8
Ljubljana – Siófok	Slovenia	15.8	Hungary	35.4	51.2
Katowice – Zilina	Poland	40.0	Slovak Republic	7.8	47.8
Öresund link	Danmark	8.5	Sweden	39.1	47.6
Warszawa – Kaunas	Poland	36.1	Lithuania	10.1	46.2
Skopje – Thessaloniki	Macedonia	0.6	Greece	43.1	43.7
Gdańsk – Kaliningrad	Poland	2.1	Russia	33.8	35.9
Bratislava – Győr	Slovak Republic	0.3	Hungary	34.4	34.7
Tallinn – Riga	Estonia	19.8	Latvia	12.9	32.7
Warszawa – Minsk	Poland	0.5	Belarus	17.1	27.6
Fehmarnbelt link	Germany	14.9	Danmark	10.2	25.1
Budapest – Beograd	Hungary	18.9	Yugoslavia	0.3	19.2
Ljubljana – Zagreb	Slovenia	4.2	Croatia	11.9	16.1
Maribor – Zagreb	Slovenia	-0.3	Croatia	11.2	10.9

countries positively affected could be compensated by responsibilities of EU institutions.

Before drawing too far reaching conclusions about the desirability of central action one has to keep in mind, however, that only a subset of utilities generated by new transport links is incorporated in the model. A large share of private car traffic on motorways in densely populated areas is local traffic, generating welfare gains only in regions close to the new road. Including these gains would render local shares in welfare larger than the ones estimated in our model. On the other hand, environmental damages of new roads are completely neglected in our study. They are, except for greenhouse gas emissions due to induced traffic, also to a large extent local in character, implying — other things equal — a smaller share of local gains in total gains. It is likely, however, that the former effect exceeds the latter, i.e. the local share is likely to be underestimated in our figures.

11.7 Summary

This paper tried to quantify the distribution of welfare gains from new border crossing road links in Europe by means of a spatial computable general equilibrium model. It has been shown in particular, to what extent the gains also accrue to countries not directly touched by the new links. Without a significant amount of such network externalities a shift of responsibilities in infrastructure policy towards the EU level, which is in fact going on since the Maastricht Treaty, is not justified. Results are mixed. One third of 30 international links under study generate less than one fifth of their respective welfare gains in countries other than those two directly connected by the link. They do not merit to be called "trans-European". Others, however, have really a trans-European character. Two thirds of their effects benefit countries other than those directly touched by the link.

References

[1] TEN-T Progress Report. (1997, July). www.europa.eu.int/en/comm/dg07/-tentpp9807/index.htm.

[2] (1997, November 10). Treaty Establishing the European Community. Official Journal of the European Communities C 340.

[3] Bröcker, J. (1998a). How Would an EU–Membership of the Visegrád Countries Affect Europe's Economic Geography? *Annals of Regional Science 32*, 91–114. Erratum 34:?–?, 2000.

[4] Bröcker, J. (1998b, November 10). Spatial Effects of New Transport Links: Preliminary Results from a Spatial Computable General Equilibrium Analysis. Diskussionsbeiträge aus dem Institut für Wirtschaft und Verkehr, Technische Universität Dresden, Nr. 4/98.

[5] Bröcker, J. and H. Rohweder (1990). Barriers to International Trade: Methods of Measurement and Empirical Evidence. *The Annals of Regional Science 4*, 289–305.

[6] Bundesminister für Verkehr (1993). Gesamtwirtschaftliche Bewertung von Verkehrswegeinvestitionen. Schriftenreihe des BMV, Heft 72, Bonn.

[7] Dixit, A. and J. Stiglitz (1977). Monopolisitic Competition and Optimal Product Diversity. *American Economic Review 67*, 297–308.

[8] European Commission and TINA Secretariat (1999, June). TINA draft final report. CD.

[9] Helliwell, J. F. (1998). *How Much Do National Borders Matter?* Washington, D.C.: Brookings Institution Press.

[10] Junkernheinrich, M. (1997). Europäische Infrastrukturpolitik — Neue Aufgaben im Spannungsfeld von Ausgleichs- und Wachstumszielen. In H. Karl (Ed.), *Transeuropäische Netze — Die infrastrukturpolitischen Aufgaben der EU*, pp. 17–30. Bonn: Europa Union Verlag.

[11] Krugman, P. (1991). *Geography and Trade.* London: MIT Press and Leuven University Press.

[12] Krugman, P. (1993). On the Number and Location of Cities. *European Economic Review 37*, 293–298.

[13] Krugman, P. (1994). Complex Landscapes in Economic Geography. *American Economic Association Papers and Proceedings 84*, 412–416.

[14] Laaser, C.-F. (1997). Infrastrukturpolitik der Europäischen Union — Ein Widerspruch zum Subsidiaritätsprinzip? In H. Karl (Ed.), *Transeuropäische Netze — Die infrastrukturpolitischen Aufgaben der EU*, pp. 31–58. Bonn: Europa Union Verlag.

[15] Martins, J. O., S. Scarpetta, and D. Pilat (1996). Mark–up Ratios in Manufacturing Industries: Estimates for 14 OECD Countries. OECD Working Papers, Vol. IV, Economic Department Working Papers. No. 162, Paris.

[16] Rietveld, P. and F. Bruinsma (1998). *Is Transport Infrastructure Effective? Transport Infrastructure and Accessibility: Impacts on the Space Economy.* Advances in Spatial Science. Berlin: Springer.

[17] Vickerman, R., K. Spiekermann, and M. Wegener (1999). Accessibility and Economic Development in Europe. *Regional Studies 33*, 1 - 15.

[18] Weber, J. (1987). *Logistikkostenrechnung.* Berlin: Springer.

[19] White, H. (1980). A Heteroskedastic–Consistent Covariance Matrix Estimator and a Direct Test of Heteroskedasticity. *Econometrica 48*, 817–838.

[20] Wink, R. (1997). Aufbau Transnationaler Verkehrsnetze — Eine institutionelle Überforderung der Europäischen Union? In H. Karl (Ed.), *Transeuropäische Netze — Die infrastrukturpolitischen Aufgaben der EU*, pp. 59–83. Bonn: Europa Union Verlag.

12 Asset Disposition and Economic Development

John-ren Chen

12.1 Introduction

Although John Maynard Keynes as well as James Tobin have stressed the importance of the asset disposition effect, the importance of this effect is still not recognized by many economists. In this paper I will investigate the consequences of the asset dispositon effect for economic development. In poor countries land ownership is still one of the most important assets, and land reforms as a 'radical' change of the land ownership structure are therefore a straightforward possibility to influence the asset disposition behaviour. Land reform in a capitalist country is carried out in the form of the constraint of the highest rent, redistribution of land to tenants and small farmers, and restriction of landholding to peasants and farmers. A land reform is expected to raise agricultural productivity in developing countries where a unfavorable structure of landholding is supposed to exist, though empirical observations do not support this expectation in all cases. In general, land is usually prized as a precious asset and many people accumulate land ownership since it gives them high social prestige, control over rural population and an especially high reward as an income yielding asset. The profitability of land as an asset results not only from the rent but more importantly from the increasing asset price, since the supply of land in a country is, in general, given. Any increase in demand for land will result in an increasing land price. A redistribution of land included by land reform in a developing country is expected to give more incentives to peasants who become land owners after the land reform. However, land reform has rarely been successful, especially in countries where reforms were attempted as a once for all measure, they were usually reversed through the market. Mexico, Egypt and India are good examples of this phenomenon, cf. Rao (1988), Bagchi (1982). In South Korea and Taiwan the land reform was implemented in the post World War II period; a ceiling of three hectares was imposed and the market in land was virtually abolished. In Taiwan the maximal rent of the agricultural land is set at no more than 37.5% of the main agricultural products.

In this paper we are going to show that the land reform in a capitalist land can raise the growth rate and encourage economic development if the land reform incorporates a restriction of the land ownership and abolishes the market in land. We argue that the constraint of the maximum rent for agricultural land and the abolishment of the market in land reduces the profitability of land as an asset. This will encourage investment (i. e. building of industrial capital) and therefore economic growth. We call this influence of land reform the asset disposition effect. We shall show that this effect is the main effect of the land reform on economic growth and development. Fisher, Keynes and Tobin (1955, 1965), among others, have drawn the fruitful analytical distinction between decision on the income disposition and on the asset or wealth disposition. The latter is related to the problem in what forms savers hold their savings, while the first set of decision determines how much is saved rather than consumed. The interactions of these two kinds of behavior in determining the rate of interest was much discussed in economic literature. Tobin has concerned himself with the respective roles of both kinds of decision and their relevance for economic growth. In this paper the wealth disposition will be considered explicitly in our model with land and industrial capital as two types of assets for portfolio decisions. To show the meaning of the wealth disposition effect of a land reform on economic development we will consider only the effect of the restriction on the property right of land holding introduced by the land reform. We shall show that because of the wealth disposition effect land reform can be expected to influence economic development positively, even if land reform does not increase the agricultural productivity directly.

Most models of economic development are models with reproducible capital as only asset which can be used as store of value. In such a model there is no place for significant portfolio choices. As long as saving continues it necessarily takes the form of real investment, i.e. accumulation of capital. In monetary models of economic development there are at least two types of assets as store of value, namely real capital and money. They offer therefore place for significant portfolio choices. As long as saving continues it may take the form of real investment or money. The significance of disposition of wealth for economic growth was shown by Tobin (1955, 1965) in both of his pioneering papers on monetary theory growth. In this paper we shall study a nonmonetary model of economic development with two types of assets. This offers the possibility of analyzing the influences of portfolio selection on economic development. The two types of assets considered in our model are reproducible capital and land, both of which can be used as productive factor as well as store of value. For portfolio decisions the rate of return on the asset and the risk about it are the main arguments for ranking the preference of the decision maker. If both types of asset involve the same risk, the rate of return on both assets will be the same for the optimal portfolio decision. By the rate of return on an asset we mean the yield of the asset as well as the gain or loss in the value of asset.

In comparison with the reproducible capital land is an asset with less risk of accident loss. Because of its non reproducible character there is a long-run trend of increasing land price in general. Therefore land is an attractive asset, especially in an agricultural economy. We shall show in this paper that saving will not have any effect on economic growth and economic development, if the land is chosen dominantly as a store of value. In this case the price of land will increase, and so the value of land without a rise of real wealth. In such an economy the existence of a low level equilibrium trap seems to be a natural result. A land reform to restrict the transaction of land may influence its rate of return negatively, even though the yield of land will not differ as a result of the land reform, since the price of land cannot increase as before. In this case, reproducible capital will increase as saving takes place.

The paper is organized as follows: In the next section we construct a simple dynamic macroeconomic model with two kinds of asset. In section 12.3 we analyze the model in the short-run and in section 12.4 in the long-run. In the last section we consider the application of the analytical results for economic development.

12.2 The Model

The model can be described by the following functions:

(A) Production function:

$$Q = F(K, M) \tag{12.1}$$

or in intensity form

$$q = f(k, m) \tag{12.1a}$$

$$x = g(h) \tag{12.1b}$$

with $q = Q/L$; $k = K/L$; $m = M/L$; $x = Q/M$; $h = K/M$

Q: output (net output after making good the depreciation of capital)
K: capital input;
M: labor input in unit of working time (in efficiency units)
L: employment;
q: output per worker
k: capital input per worker;
m: working time per worker (in efficient unit)
x: output per working time;
h: capital input per working time

(B) Wealth (in units of output):

$$V = PB + K \tag{12.2}$$

with V: wealth (in terms of output)
P: price of land (in terms of output)
B: amount of land in a country (an economy)

(C) Growth of wealth:

$$\dot{V} = \dot{P}B + \dot{K} \tag{12.3}$$

where $\dot{V} \equiv dV/dt$ means growth of wealth, and similar $\dot{P} \equiv dP/dt$ and $\dot{K} \equiv dK/dt$.

(D) Disposable income:

$$Y = Q + \dot{P}B \tag{12.4}$$

where Y stands for disposable income (in terms of output)

(E) Consumption function:

$$C = (1 - s)Y \qquad \text{with} \quad 1 > s > 0 \tag{12.5}$$

where C is consumption and s marginal propensity to save

(F) Growth of wealth and saving:

$$\dot{V} = S = sY \tag{12.6}$$

where S stands for Savings

(G) Growth of labor (population):

$$\hat{L} = n \qquad \text{where} \quad \hat{L} \equiv \dot{L}/L \tag{12.7}$$

(H) Equilibrium in the output market:

$$Q = C + \dot{K} \tag{12.8}$$

(I) Portfolio decision:

$$\dot{K} = b\dot{V} \qquad \text{with} \quad 1 \geq b \geq 0 \tag{12.9}$$

$$b = b(k, P) \qquad \text{with} \quad b_k < 0,\ b_P > 0 \tag{12.10}$$

$$\dot{P}B = (1 - b)\dot{V} \tag{12.11}$$

(J) The efficient manhours:

$$m = u(y, K) \tag{12.12}$$

with $u_y < 0,\ u_{yy} < 0,\ u_K > 0,\ u_{KK} < 0$

$$u_1 = \frac{yu_y}{u} < 0 \qquad \text{and} \qquad u_2 = \frac{Ku_K}{u}$$

where $y = Y/L$ is percapita disposable income, $u_y < 0$ may be called manhours reducing effect of increasing per capita disposable income; while $u_K > 0$ could be called the learning by doing effect of technical progress. The production function is assumed to be neoclassical (see Burmeister and Dobell (1970)), and fulfills the Inada conditions. It is to be noted that the labor input in our production function is the amount of hours worked in an economy, i.e. the product of employment and the manhours per worker. Therefore the labor input in our model can be increased either by increasing labor (population) or by increasing manhours per worker. Two arguments can be given for this specification of the production function:

First, during the long run of economic development the manhours are not constant, but decrease as the per capita income grows. Therefore, by using employment as labor input in the production function, the effect of economic growth on the working hours per worker as well as the effects of the decreasing number of manhours per worker on economic development cannot be taken into account.

Second, the controversy, whether the marginal product of agricultural labor in a labor surplus economy is zero or substantially above zero, can be avoided by our specification. Sen (1966) made a clear distinction between the marginal productivity of a worker and the marginal productivity of manhours. He showed that the marginal productivity of labor could be zero even though the marginal productivity of working time is substantially above zero. In our model we assume that the marginal productivity of manhours is substantially above zero. The marginal productivity of a labor can be zero, if the growth rate of labor is equal to the decreasing rate of manhours, i.e. if $n = -\hat{m}$[1]. Since the production function (12.1) is assumed to be linear homogenous, the production function in intensity form (12.1a) is also linear homogenous. In general the production function in intensity form (12.1a) has the same characteristics as the original production function (12.1). In addition, we can show that (12.1b) gives another intensity form of production (12.1):

$$F_K = f_k = g_h \qquad \text{and} \qquad F_M = f_k = g - g'h,$$

where $F_K \equiv \partial F/\partial K$ is the marginal productivity of capital, etc.

Function (12.2) is a definition equation for wealth. The two types of assets, land and the reproducible capital in our paper, are considered in this definition. Wealth is quoted in units of output.

Function (12.3) is a derivative of function (12.2) with respect to time. As it can be seen in (12.3) land is assumed to be constant, while reproducible capital can be increased by investment. For simplification of analysis

[1] This assertion means that both $dQ/dL = 0$ and $F_M > 0$ can occur in our model. It can be shown as follows: we differentiate (1) total: $dQ = F_K dK + F_M dM$. Using $dK = 0$ and $dM = mdL + Ldm$ we have $dQ = F_M(Ldm + mdL)$ then $dQ/dL = F_M(Ldm/dL + m) = 0$, if $Ldm/dL + m = 0$, or equivalently $dL/L = -dm/m$, i. e. $\hat{L} = -\hat{m}$, since $F_M > 0$ is assumed for the neoclassical production function

the reproducible capital is assumed to have permanent duration of life. In reality the productivity of land can be improved by measures such as a land conservation program. Therefore the assumption of land as given is only a approximation to reality. If the productivity of land is improved the input of land should be considered in efficiency units in the production function. The cost for improvement of the land productivity is equivalent to the investment. The improvement in the productivity of land will increase the yield of land and can therefore influence the price of land. In our model we assume that the productivity of land is given. This may not coincide with reality, but we believe that the price increase of land is mainly due to the increased demand for land. In addition, the assumption of constant productivity of land allows us to demonstrate the effects of land reform on the economic development and economic growth with respect to the disposition of wealth in a very simple way.

In function (12.4) the disposable income is defined as the sum of the produced income and the reward of wealth, i.e. the sum of reward for the reproducible capital (the yield of capital) and for land which is equal to the sum of the yield and the increase of value of land. Since capital is the output of earlier periods and has the price of unity, there is no increase of value for capital. In the sense of the neoclassical theory of income distribution, the yield of capital and land is paid by the output, i.e. they are included in the produced income (output). Therefore the disposable income is defined as in the monetary growth model of Tobin (1955, 1965) namely the sum of yields for factors and the increase of value of land. Since land is a fixed factor in our model, it is not considered in the production function explicitly.

Function (12.5) is a linear consumption function with disposable income as the only determining variable. Function (12.6) defines the wealth accumulation effect of saving, i.e. net saving means a growth of wealth. The growth rate of labor is assumed to be exogenous as in (12.7).

Equation (12.8) shows that output is in equilibrium when the quantity of output produced (on the left hand side) is equal to the quantity demanded (on the right hand side). As can be seen on the right hand side of (12.8) there are two sources of demand for output, i.e. consumption and investment.

Equations (12.9) and (12.11) describe the portfolio decision. We show in these equations that capital and land are the two types of assets. Saving is invested either in land or in capital or in both of it. These simple portfolio selection equations are used to demonstrate the effect of a land reform in a very simple way. We assume that before the land reform land is the dominate type of asset for portfolio decision, i.e. $b = 0$. In this case capital will not be chosen as a store of value. After the land reform capital becomes the only type of asset for portfolio decision. The reality is much more complicated. In an econometric model a more sophisticated specification of the portfolio selection functions is necessary.

Function (12.12) shows that the efficient working time per worker is a function of disposable income per capita and capital input. The working time per worker is assumed to depend negatively on disposable income per capita. This relationship can be explained with the traditional utility maximizing behavior of the consumer in microeconomics. The demand for free time increases with disposable income per capita, assuming that free time is not an inferior good. The positive dependence of working time per worker on capital stock can be justified with technical progress in the form of learning by doing in the sense of Arrow (1962).

12.3 The Short-Run Analysis

In the short run the capital stock and the labor force are given. The short run equilibrium (solution) of our model is characterized by full employment of labor and full utilization of the capital stock.

Proposition 1.

- *Case 1:*

$$\dot{P} = \frac{sQ}{(1-s)B} \quad \text{and} \quad C = Q \quad \text{if} \quad b = 0$$

- *Case 2:*

$$Y = Q \quad , \quad K = S \quad \text{and} \quad P = 0 \quad \text{if} \quad b = 1$$

Remarks:

1. The proof of this proposition can be sent on requirement.
2. According to case 1 of this proposition the land price will increase proportionally with the saving. Output is used only for consumption, since saving is invested only in land. In this case the demand for land increases proportionally with saving. Since the supply of land in a country is given, the price of land must increase as the demand increases. The value of land rises so as that total saving is absorbed. No output will be used for accumulating industrial capital. This adjustment process of the land price due to saving can be described as following: Every land owner is a potential supplier of land, but only those who have to sell their land to finance consumption are active suppliers in the land market. The active supply in the land market depends in general negatively on the output. In times of declining output more people must sell their land to finance consumption and the demand for land is lower. The rise in the price of land will therefore be moderate. In times of high output the active supply on the land market will be low and the demand will be high because of high savings. The land price will increase to a level high enough to clear

the land market. The value of land transactions is in this case ($b = 0$) always equal to the saving of the economy. Since the reason for the new land supply is to finance consumption, which cannot be realized by the usual income, the value of land transaction will be consumed.

3. Case 2 of this proposition shows some properties of the short- run equilibrium if only industrial capital is used as a store of wealth. These properties are similar to the Solow model (1956) in which the capital stock is the sole object used as a store of wealth. The land price does not increase in this case, because the demand for land does not increase during the period of economic growth.
4. As one can see both cases of this proposition describe the short-run properties of our model in two extreme cases. The reality can be described by $1 > b > 0$. If land is the most attractive object used as a store of wealth in an economy, then b may lie close to 0. Otherwise b may be almost equal to 1.

12.4 The Long-Run Development

In the long-run, the industrial capital as well as the population (labor force) are no longer given. The population growth is assumed to be exogenous with a given growth rate n. The industrial capital can be increased by investment which is not only influenced by saving (income disposition) but also by portfolio decisions on saving disposition (wealth disposition). To prove the long-run properties of the model we can easily show:

(a) $q = f(k, m)$ is linear homogenous;

(b) The growth of working time per worker:

$$\hat{m} = \frac{1}{1 - u_1} \left(u_1 \hat{x} + u_2 bsa \frac{g(h)}{h} \right) \tag{12.13}$$

where $a = (1 - (1 - b)\, s)^{-1}$

(c)

$$\hat{k} = \hat{K} - n = \frac{bsag(h)}{h} - n \tag{12.14}$$

(d) The growth rate of per capita output

$$\hat{q} = \frac{1}{1 - u_1} \left(u_2 \hat{K} + \hat{x} \right) = \frac{1}{1 - u_1} \left(u_2 \hat{K} + r\hat{h} \right) \tag{12.15}$$

where r is the capital share of output, $1 > r > 0$

(e) The fundamental differential equation of the model is

$$\dot{h} = bsaZ_1 g(h) - Z_2 nh \tag{12.16}$$

where $Z = [1 - (1 - r)u_1]^{-1} > 0$ and $1 > Z > 0$
r is the capital share of output
$Z_1 = (1 - u_1 - u_2)Z > 0; \quad Z_2 = (1 - u_1)Z > 0$

Remarks:

1. Since $u_1 < 0$ and $1 > r > 0$ thus $Z, \quad Z_2 > 0$
   As $1 > u_2 > 0$, thus $1 > Z > 0, \quad Z_1 > 0$ and $Z_2 > Z_1$
2. $g' > 0$ and $g'' < 0$ according to the neoclassical production function.

Theorem 1.

1. *The fundamental differential equation*

$$\dot{h} = bZ_1 sag(h) - Z_2 nh \tag{12.17}$$

   with $Z_2 > Z_1 > 0$ and $b > 0$, has a unique stable stationary solution for $1 \geq b > 0$
2. *The capital input (in units of working time) decreases with a a rate nZ, if $b = 0$.*

Fig. 12.1.

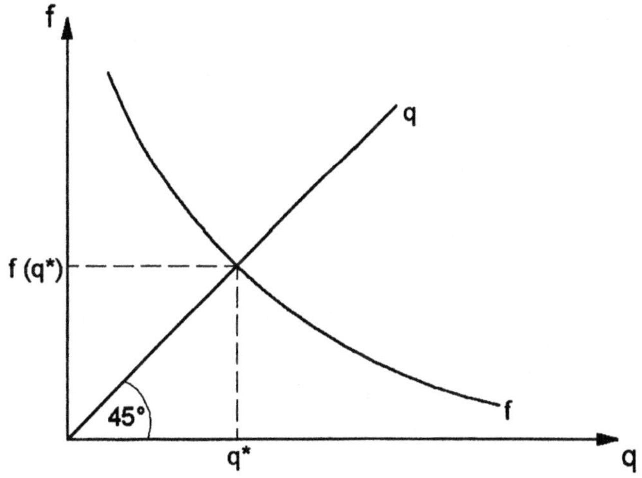

Proof.

1. See Burmeister and Dobell (1970, pp. 25-26)
   A phase-diagram is shown in figure 12.1 for $1 \geq b > 0$.

2. The fundamental differential equation for $b = 0$ becomes

$$\dot{h} = -nZ_2 h \qquad \text{or} \qquad \hat{h} = -nZ_2 < 0$$

3. To show that h^* is asymptotically stable in the region $h > 0$ we define $D = h - h^*$ and $A(D) = D^2$
Then $A(D) \geq 0$ and $A(D) = 0$ if and only if $D = 0$

$$\begin{aligned}
\dot{D} &= 2D\dot{h} = 2D\left[bZ_1 sag(h) - nZ_2 h\right] \\
&= 2D\left[Z_1 basg(h^* + D) - Z_2 n(h^* + D)\right] \\
&\geq 2D\left[Z_1 basg(h^*) + DZ_1 basg'(h^*) - Z_2 nD - Z2nh^*\right] \\
&= 2D^2\left[Z_1 basg'(h*) - nZ_2\right] \\
&= 2D^2\left[\frac{Z_2 nhg'(h^*)}{g(h^*)} - nZ_2\right] \qquad \left(\text{since} \quad Z_1 bsa = \frac{Z_2 nh^*}{g(h^*)}\right) \\
&= \frac{-2D^2 Z_2 n}{g(h^*)}\left(g(h^*) - h^* g'(h^*)\right) < 0 \quad \text{unless} \quad D = 0
\end{aligned}$$

since $g(h^*) - h^* g'(h^*) = F_M(K^*, M^*) > 0$
The marginal productivity of labor with respect to working time is assumed to be always positive in a neoclassical production function. Thus, by Lyapunov's theorem the equilibrium $h = h^*$ is stable. QED.

Now we can investigate the properties of the long-run development. Two cases can be classified:

- Case 1: stagnant economy: $b = 0$.
In this case land is the only repository of savings. The development of the economy can be described by the following differential equation:

$$\dot{h} = -nZ_2 h \tag{12.18}$$

- Case 2: growing economy: $b > 0$.
The development of the economy can be described by the fundamental differential equation (12.17). The growing economy has a stable long-run development path (see theorem 3).

Theorem 2. *The long-run development of the stagnant economy can be characterized by the following properties:*

$$\begin{aligned}
&h = -nZ_2 < 0 \\
&x = -rnZ_2 < 0 \\
&\hat{x} > \hat{h} \\
&\hat{m} = -rnZu_1 > 0 \\
&\hat{k} = -n < 0 \\
&\hat{q} = -rnZ < 0 \qquad \textit{and} \\
&\hat{Q} = n(1-r)Z > 0 \qquad \textit{if} \quad b = 0
\end{aligned}$$

with $Z = [1-(1-r)u_1]^{-1} > 0$ *and* $Z_2 = (1-u_1)Z > 0$

Remarks:

1. These properties of long-run development are the characteristics of a 'low level equilibrium trap' in Leibenstein's sense.
2. In this case the capital input per worker decreases, since output is used fully for consumption and labor force grows with a constant rate n. The saving of the economy is absorbed completely in increment of land.
3. As the disposable income per capita decreases, the working time per worker increases. This and the population growth together cause a growth of output. But the growth rate of output is less than that of population therefore the output per capita contracts in the long-run.

Theorem 3. *The long-run development of the growing economy can be characterized by the following properties:*

$$\begin{aligned}
\hat{h}(h^*) &= 0 \\
\hat{x} &= 0 \\
\hat{K}^* &= (1-u_1)Zn > 0 \qquad \textit{with} \quad Z = (1-u_1-u_2)^{-1} > 0 \\
\hat{k} &= u_2 Zn > 0 \\
\hat{q} &= \hat{k} + (1-r)n > 0 \\
\hat{m} &= \hat{k} \\
\hat{y} &= \hat{q} \qquad \textit{and} \\
\hat{Q} &= r\hat{K}^* + (1-r)(\hat{m}+n) > 0, \qquad \textit{if} \quad b > 0
\end{aligned}$$

Remarks:

1. The steady state is characterized by constant capital input per efficient working time of labor and constant output per efficient working time of labor.
2. The capital input per labor force grows in steady state development, since $(1-u_1)Zn > n$. The learning by doing technical progress specified in the model is responsible for this development.
3. These properties of a growing economy characterize a favorable case of economic development.
4. The growth rate does not depend either on the marginal propensity to save or on the share of saving invested, but depends positively on the growth rate of population and on the elasticity of working time per worker with respect to per capita disposable income and capital stock.

12.5 The Wealth Disposition Effect of Land Reform and Economic Development

Land as an asset is distinguished by its low risk and high rentability, since a piece of ground cannot be lost or is seldom destroyed by a natural catastrophe. Thus in comparison to other assets land is characterized by its low risk. Because the land in a country is generally given, the land price will increase as the demand for land grows. Moreover, land is an indispensable factor for agricultural production. The reward for the use of land in agricultural production (i.e. rent) grows in general as the demand for food expands. Because of these reasons land is seen as an attractive object for portfolio decisions not only in developing countries.

A land reform will reduce in general the attractivity of land as an object of portfolio decisions. A land reform used as a once for all measure will increase the risk of landholding. The land reform as implemented in South Korea and Taiwan, which introduces a legal maximal land rent, incorporated with restrictions on the property right of land ownership as well as a ceiling of landholdings by individual, will reduce the attractivity of land as an object of portfolio decision. Therefore the wealth disposition effect of a land reform can be described as increasing the share of savings invested, or, equivalently, decreasing the share of wealth in form of landholdings. The influences of the wealth disposition factor of a land reform on economic development can be classified in two cases:

The first case: the share of saving invested in industrial capital increases after the land reform from initially $b = 0$ to $b > 0$ The influences of the wealth disposition effect of land reform on economic development can be shown easily by comparison of the assertions in the theorem 4 and 5. As one can see, the influences of a land reform on economic development in this case are revolutionary. The economy will change from a low level equilibrium trap to a steady path with growing per capita income.

The second case: the share of saving invested in industrial capital is initially $b > 0$ The influences of the wealth disposition effect of the land reform on economic development are in this case not so revolutionary as in the first case. However, as we shall show in the following, these influences are almost always positive. In the following propositions in this section we consider the case where the share of saving invested in industrial capital increases after the land reform from initially $b > 0$.

Theorem 4. *The capital input per efficient unit of working time in steady state is higher, the higher the share of saving is used for accumulating industrial capital.*

Proof. We differentiate (12.16) with $\dot{h} = 0$ total with respect to h and b:

$$\frac{\partial h^*}{\partial b} = a^2 s(1-s) Z_1 g(h^*) \left[n Z_2 - absZ_1 g'(h*) \right]^{-1} \tag{12.19}$$

In steady state:

$$nZ_2 h^* - absZ_1 g(h^*) = nZ_2 - \frac{absZ_1 g(h^*)}{h^*} = 0$$

$$nZ_2 - bZ_1 sa \frac{g(h^*)}{h^*} < nZ_2 - bZ_1 sag'(h^*) \tag{12.20}$$

since $g(h^*)/h^* > g'(h^*)$ according to the decreasing marginal output. The sign of (19) depends solely on the sign of $(nZ_2 - absZ_1 g'(h^*))$.

According to (20) we find $nZ_2 - absZ_1 g'(h^*) > 0$. Thus we proved $\partial h^*/\partial b > 0$. QED.

Since the output per unit of efficient working time is a positive function of capital input with respect to efficient working time (see (12.1b)) we can prove the following corollary which means that output per unit of efficient working time is higher the higher is the share of saving invested.

Corollary 1.

$$\frac{\partial x^*}{\partial b} = g'(h^*) \frac{\partial h^*}{\partial b} < 0$$

Now we show the results of a comparative dynamic analysis. The star near the symbols means steady-state values of the variables, respectively.

Theorem 5. *The influence of the wealth disposition effect of a land reform on per capita output, total output, capital stock and capital input per worker on the path of steady state are positive, if the efficient working time per worker is not reduced 'dramatically' by the land reform.*

Proof. Assuming that

$$-\frac{\partial m^*}{\partial b} < \frac{m^*}{x^*} \frac{\partial x^*}{\partial b}$$

i.e. the efficient working time per worker does not reduce dramatically, then:

1.

$$\frac{\partial q_t^*}{\partial b} = x^* \frac{\partial m_t^*}{\partial b} + m^* \frac{\partial x_t^*}{\partial b} > 0$$

2.

$$\frac{\partial Q_t^*}{\partial b} = L \frac{\partial q_t^*}{\partial b} > 0$$

3. From

$$K_t = \int_0^t I_r^* \, dr = \int_0^t bsaY_r \, dr$$

$$\frac{\partial K_t^*}{\partial b} = \frac{\partial I_t^*}{\partial b} = sa(1 - abs)Q_t^* + abs\frac{\partial Q_t^*}{\partial b} > 0$$

4.

$$\frac{\partial k_t^*}{\partial b} = \frac{1}{L}\frac{\partial K_t^*}{\partial b} > 0$$

QED.

Theorem 6. *There exists a share of saving invested in industrial capital b^*, which maximizes the disposable income per capita on a steady state path.*

$$1 > b^* > 0 \quad \textit{if} \quad \frac{sq^*}{1-s} > \frac{\partial q_t^*}{\partial b} > sq^*$$

Proof. To find the value of b for the maximum of y we differentiate the following equation: $y = aq$ with $a = [1 - (1-b)s]^{-1}$ with respect to b. This is the short–run equilibrium for y. The first order condition for a local maximum is

$$\frac{dy^*}{db} = a\frac{\partial q^*}{\partial b} sa^2 q^* = 0$$

The second order condition is fulfilled, since

$$\frac{d^2y^*}{db^2} = a\frac{d^2q^*}{db^2} - 2a^2\frac{dq^*}{db} - 2a^3s^3q^* < 0$$

for $d^2q^*/db^2 < 0$; decreasing marginal productivity of capital

The solution of the first order condition gives:

$$a^* = \frac{\frac{dq^*}{db}}{sq^*} \qquad \text{or} \qquad b^* = \frac{1}{s}\left(\frac{sq^*}{\frac{dq^*}{db}} + s - 1\right)$$

If $0 < b^* < 1$, then

$$\frac{1}{1-s} > a^* > 1 \qquad \text{or} \qquad \frac{1}{1-s} > \frac{\frac{dq^*}{db}}{sq^*} > 1$$

or equivalently

$$\frac{sq^*}{1-s} > \frac{dq^*}{db} > sq^*$$

QED.

12.6 The Land Rent and the Portfolio Selection

We showed in the last sections the influences of the wealth disposition effect on economic development. The share of saving invested in industrial capital was treated as a parameter in our model up to now. For practical economic policy it is not possible to determine this parameter in a capitalist economy. Since the share of saving invested in industrial capital is determined by portfolio decision, we study in the following measures of economic policy to influence it. In an economy with two assets the portfolio equilibrium exists, if

$$\dot{P} + R = g'(h^*) + R \tag{12.21}$$

where $\dot{P}$ ... the growth of land price
$g'(h^*)$ ... the reward for capital
R ... the land rent
A ... a risk premium for holding capital

The equilibrium in the asset market can theoretically be classified in the following three cases :

1. $b \leq 0$: in this case land is the sole asset held in the economy.
2. $1 > b > 0$: in this case both, land and capital, are held in the economy.
3. $b \geq 1$: in this case capital is the only asset held in the economy

Fig. 12.2.

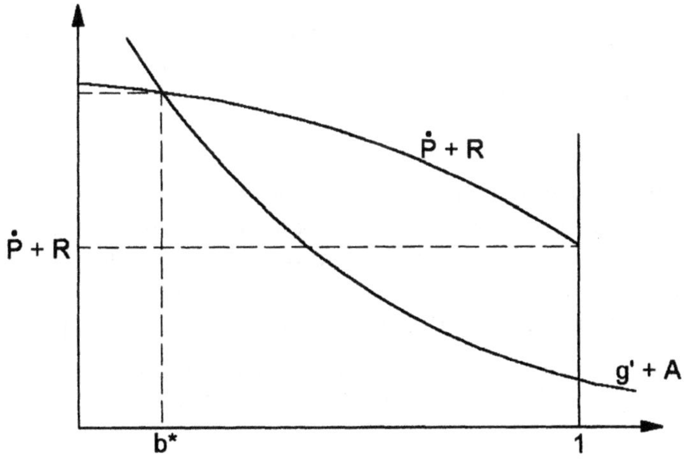

The portfolio equilibrium can be described in the figure 12.2. The marginal product of capital is a convex function in b because $o < f$ the decreasing marginal product of capital. In figure 12.2 the risk premium of holding capital is assumed to be independent of b. The curve for reward of landholding is a concave function in b with

$$\dot{P} = \frac{s}{1-s}\frac{Q}{B} \quad \text{if} \quad b = 0 \qquad \text{and} \qquad \dot{P} = 0 \quad \text{if} \quad b = 1$$

Since $\dot{P} = (1-b)sa(Q/B)$, if $1 > b > 0$

$$\frac{d\left((1-b)a\right)}{db} = -a - (1-b)sa^2 < 0$$
$$\frac{d^2\left((1-b)a\right)}{db^2} = sa^2 + sa^2 + 2(1-b)s^2a^3 > 0$$

The maximal growth of land price lies at $b = 0$ [2]. At the point $b = 1$ the land price remains constant. In figure 12.2 exists a unique equilibrium. Several equilibriums cannot generally be excluded[3].

A reduction of land rent will lower the curve $P + R$ and increase therefore the share of saving invested in capital. An increase of capital reward or risk premium for capital holding will push the $f' + A$ upward and realize a new portfolio equilibrium with a higher share of saving invested in capital.

It seems to be possible to study the portfolio behavior of an economy empirically. The findings of empirical analysis on the portfolio selection of the economy could give important information to manipulate the land rent and other control variables to influence the wealth disposition decisions.

12.7 Concluding Remarks

In this paper we have studied the effects of land reform in a capitalist developing economy. Land is not only an important factor for the production of agricultural products, but also an important asset in an economy. A redistribution of land induced by a land reform is expected to raise output in a developing country. However, land reforms have rarely been successful, especially in countries where reforms were attempted as a once for all measure. A successful land reform which stimulates economic development cannot be achieved by a once for all redistribution of land. In many cases a land reform was carried out not only as a redistribution of land but also as a restriction of the property rights such as a ceiling of landholding and limitation of the maximum land rent. In this form a land reform will reduce theprofitability of

[2] A portfolio equilibrium is shown by a intersection of the two curves in figure 12.2. If the curve $f' + A$ lies always above the curve $P + R$ then $b = 1$ and converserly $b = 0$.

[3] This is the case, if $sa > (1/Q)(Q/b)$.

land and influence the portfolio decision in the economy. This effect of land reform is called in this paper the wealth disposition effect of a land reform.

In this paper a simple growth model is constructed to study the influences of the wealth disposition effect of land reform on economic development. The model is characterized by taking into consideration the interaction of the income disposition and wealth disposition behavior. Two sorts of asset are considered in our model. The wealth disposition effect of a land reform is represented by a parameter, the share of saving invested in capital.

Our main proposition in the short-run: The output is used only for consumption if land is used as the sole asset for storing wealth, i.e. if the share of saving invested in capital is zero. In this case the saving of the economy is totally absorbed by the increase in the price of land. If the capital is used as a store of wealth our model is similar to the Solow model.

In the long-run a land reform in the sense mentioned above will increase the capital input per working time and the output per working time on the steady state path. The influences of the wealth disposition effect induced by a land reform on the economic development are positive throughout. The long-run development of the economy can be classified according to the share of saving invested in capital in two cases: the long-run development is characterized by a level equilibrium trap if the share of saving invested in capital is zero. The development will be characterized by a long-run steady state path with expanding output per capita if the share of saving invested in capital is greater than zero.

References

[1] Allen, R. (1968). *Macro-Economic Theory.* Macmillan.

[2] Arrow (1962). The Economic Implication of Learning by Doing. *Review of Economic Studies*, pp. 155–173.

[3] Bagchi, A. (1982). *The Political Economy of Underdevelopment.* Cambridge University Press.

[4] Bardhan, P. (1970). *Economic Growth, Development and Foreign Trade: A Study in Pure Theory.* Wiley.

[5] Berry, R. and W. Cline (1979). *Agrarian Structure and Productivity in Developing Countries.* Johns Hopkins Univ. Press.

[6] Burmeister, E. and A. Dobell (1970). *Mathematical Theories of Economic Growth.* Macmillan.

[7] Chen, J.-r. (1994). The Effects of Land Reform on the Rice Sector and Economic Development in Taiwan. *World Development 22*(11), 1759–1770.

[8] Rao, S. (1988). Agriculture and Economic Development. in: *The New Palgrave*, Eatwell, J. (ed.).

[9] Sen, A. (1966). Peasants and Dualism With or Without Surplus Labor. *Journal of Political Economy*, 425–450.

[10] Solow, R. (1956). A Contribution to the Theory of Economic Growth. *Quarterly Journal of Economics*, 65–9.

[11] Tobin, J. (12). Money and Economic Growth. *Econometrica*, 671–684.

[12] Tobin, J. (1955). A Dynamic Aggregate Model. *Journal of Political Economy*, 103–115.
[13] Warrier, D. (1969). *Land Reform in Principle and Practice.* Cambridge University Press.

13 Policy Mixes in a Monetary Union

Michael Carlberg

13.1 Introduction

The monetary union is an open economy with perfect capital mobility. It consists of two identical countries, say Germany and France. The targets of macroeconomic policy are price stability in the union and full employment in each of the union countries. The instruments of macroeconomic policy are monetary policy by the European Central Bank, fiscal policies by national governments, and wage restraint by national trade unions. The big questions are: What is the appropriate policy mix? And should policy actions be coordinated? A special feature of this paper is the numerical estimation of policy multipliers. The paper is organized as follows: the model, simple policies, mix of monetary and fiscal policy, mix of monetary policy and wage restraint, conclusion.

As a starting point take the classic papers by Fleming (1962) and Mundell (1968). They discuss monetary and fiscal policy in an open economy characterized by perfect capital mobility. The exchange rate can either be flexible or fixed. They consider both the small open economy and the world economy made up of two large countries. The seminal papers by Levin (1983) as well as by Rose and Sauernheimer (1983) are natural extensions of the papers by Fleming and Mundell. They deal with stabilization policy in a jointly floating currency area. It turns out, however, that the joint float produces results for the individual countries within the currency area and for the area as a whole that in some cases differ sharply from those in the Fleming and Mundell papers. The important book by Hansen et al. (1992) is devoted to the economics of the European Community. As far as the macroeconomics of monetary union is concerned, the main topics are policy coordination, exchange rate expectations, and slow prices.

13.2 The Model

The analysis is carried out within the following framework. The monetary union is an open economy with perfect capital mobility. The world interest rate is given exogenously $r^* = \text{const}$. Under perfect capital mobility, the union interest rate equals the world interest rate $r = r^*$. As a consequence, the union interest rate is invariant, too. The exchange rate between the monetary union and the rest of the world is flexible.

The monetary union consists of two countries, say Germany and France. German goods and French goods are imperfect substitutes. P_1 denotes the price of German goods, and P_2 the price of French goods. In the short run, money wages and prices are rigid. For ease of exposition let be $P_1 = P_2 = 1$. In addition we assume that union countries are the same size and have the same behavioural functions.

Now have a closer look at the market for German goods. The behavioural functions underlying the analysis are:

$$C_1 = \bar{C}_1 + cY_1 \tag{13.1}$$

$$I_1 = \text{const} \tag{13.2}$$

$$G_1 = \text{const} \tag{13.3}$$

$$X_{12} = \bar{X}_{12} + mY_2 \tag{13.4}$$

$$X_{13} = \bar{X}_{13} + he \tag{13.5}$$

$$Q_1 = \bar{Q}_1 + qY_1 \tag{13.6}$$

Equation (13.1) is the consumption function. It states that German consumption is an increasing function of German income. Here C_1 stands for German consumption, $\bar{C}_1$ is the autonomous part of it, Y_1 is German income, and c is the marginal consumption rate of Germany, with $0 < c < 1$. Equation (13.2) has it that German firms decide on German investment. According to equation (13.3), the German government fixes its purchases of goods and services.

Equations (13.4) and (13.5) are the export functions. Equation (13.4) states that German exports to France are an increasing function of French income. X_{12} symbolises German exports to France, $\bar{X}_{12}$ is the autonomous part of it, Y_2 is French income, and m is the marginal import rate of France relative to Germany, with $m > 0$. Equation (13.5) has it that German exports to non-union countries are an increasing function of the union exchange rate. X_{13} designates German exports to non-union countries, and $\bar{X}_{13}$ is the autonomous part of it. e is the exchange rate of the union (e.g. the price of the dollar in terms of the euro). And h is the sensitivity of German exports to the union exchange rate, with $h > 0$. So the message of equation (13.5) is that a depreciation of the euro raises German exports to non-union countries. Equation (13.6) is the import function. German imports are an increasing function of German income. Q_1 is German imports from France and from non-union countries, $\bar{Q}_1$ is the autonomous part of it, and q is the marginal import rate of Germany, with $q > 0$.

German output is determined by the demand for German goods $Y_1 = C_1 + I_1 + G_1 + X_{12} + X_{13} - Q_1$. Taking account of the behavioural functions, we arrive at the goods market equation of Germany:

$$Y_1 = A_1 + cY_1 + mY_2 + he - qY_1 \tag{13.7}$$

Here $A_1 = \bar{C}_1 + I_1 + G_1 + \bar{X}_{12} + \bar{X}_{13} - \bar{Q}_1$ is the autonomous demand for German goods.

Next have a closer look at the market for French goods. The behavioural functions are as follows:

$$C_2 = \bar{C}_2 + cY_2 \tag{13.8}$$
$$I_2 = \text{const} \tag{13.9}$$
$$G_2 = \text{const} \tag{13.10}$$
$$X_{21} = \bar{X}_{21} + mY_1 \tag{13.11}$$
$$X_{23} = \bar{X}_{23} + he \tag{13.12}$$
$$Q_2 = \bar{Q}_2 + qY_2 \tag{13.13}$$

Equation (13.8) is the consumption function. It states that French consumption is an increasing function of French income. Here C_2 denotes French consumption, $\bar{C}_2$ is the autonomous part of it, and c is the marginal consumption rate of France, with $0 < c < 1$. Equation (13.9) has it that French firms decide on French investment. According to equation (13.10), the French government fixes its purchases of goods and services.

Equations (13.11) and (13.12) are the export functions. Equation (13.11) states that French exports to Germany are an increasing function of German income. X_{21} stands for French exports to Germany, $\bar{X}_{21}$ is the autonomous part of it, and m is the marginal import rate of Germany relative to France, with $m > 0$. Equation (13.12) has it that French exports to non-union countries are an increasing function of the union exchange rate. X_{23} symbolises French exports to non-union countries, and $\bar{X}_{23}$ is the autonomous part of it. e is the exchange rate of the union. And h is the sensitivity of French exports to the union exchange rate, with $h > 0$. The message of equation (13.12) is that a depreciation of the euro raises French exports to non-union countries. Equation (13.13) is the import function. French imports are an increasing function of French income. Q_2 is French imports from Germany and from non-union countries, $\bar{Q}_2$ is the autonomous part of it, and q is the marginal import rate of France, with $q > 0$.

French output is driven by the demand for French goods $Y_2 = C_2 + I_2 + G_2 + X_{21} + X_{23} - Q_2$. Upon substituting the behavioural functions we reach the goods market equation of France:

$$Y_2 = A_2 + cY_2 + mY_1 + he - qY_2 \tag{13.14}$$

In this context $A_2 = \bar{C}_2 + I_2 + G_2 + \bar{X}_{21} + \bar{X}_{23} - \bar{Q}_2$ is the autonomous demand for French goods.

Finally have a closer look at the money market of the union. The underlying behavioural functions are:

$$L_1 = kY_1 \tag{13.15}$$
$$L_2 = kY_2 \tag{13.16}$$
$$M = \text{const} \tag{13.17}$$

Equation (13.15) is the money demand function of Germany. It states that German money demand is proportionate to German income. Here L_1 denotes German money demand, and k is the sensitivity of German money demand to German income, with $k > 0$. Likewise equation (13.16) is the money demand function of France. Accordingly, French money demand is proportionate to French income. L_2 stands for French money demand, and k is the sensitivity of French money demand to French income. Equation (13.17) has it that the European Central Bank fixes the money supply of the union. The money demand of the union equals the money supply of the union $L_1 + L_2 = M$. This together with the behavioural functions yields the money market equation of the union:

$$kY_1 + kY_2 = M \tag{13.18}$$

On this foundation, the model can be represented by a system of three equations:

$$Y_1 = A_1 + cY_1 + mY_2 + he - qY_1 \tag{13.19}$$

$$Y_2 = A_2 + cY_2 + mY_1 + he - qY_2 \tag{13.20}$$

$$M = kY_1 + kY_2 \tag{13.21}$$

Equation (13.19) is the goods market equation of Germany, equation (13.20) is the goods market equation of France, and equation (13.21) is the money market equation of the union. The exogenous variables are the autonomous demand for German goods A_1, the autonomous demand for French goods A_2, and the money supply of the union M. The endogenous variables are German income Y_1, French income Y_2, and the exchange rate of the union e.

13.3 Simple Policies

To begin with, solve the model for union income $Y_1 + Y_2$. From the money market equation of the union follows immediately:

$$Y_1 + Y_2 = \frac{M}{k} \tag{13.22}$$

This is the equilibrium level of union income. Obviously, an increase in the demand for German goods has no effect on union income. The same applies to an increase in the demand for French goods. An increase in union money supply causes a proportionate increase in union income. For instance, a 1 percent increase in union money supply produces a 1 percent increase in union income.

Now solve the model for German and French income, respectively. The goods market equations can be written as:

$$(1 - c + q)Y_1 = A_1 + mY_2 + he \tag{13.23}$$

$$(1 - c + q)Y_2 = A_2 + mY_1 + he \tag{13.24}$$

Then take the difference between equations (13.23) and (13.24) to find out:

$$Y_1 - Y_2 = \frac{A_1 - A_2}{1 - c + m + q} \tag{13.25}$$

Further eliminate Y_2 in equation (13.25) by means of equation (13.22) and solve for Y_1:

$$Y_1 = \frac{M}{2k} + \frac{A_1 - A_2}{2(1 - c + m + q)} \tag{13.26}$$

As a basic result, this is the equilibrium level of German income. Finally feed equation (13.26) back into equation (13.22) and solve for Y_2:

$$Y_1 = \frac{M}{2k} - \frac{A_1 - A_2}{2(1 - c + m + q)} \tag{13.27}$$

This is the equilibrium level of French income. $c < 1$ implies $1-c+m+q > 0$.

First consider fiscal policy in Germany. Suppose the German government buys more German goods than before. In terms of the model, G_1 and hence A_1 go up. As a consequence, German income rises whereas French income falls. Strictly speaking, the rise in German income is equal in amount to the fall in French income, so union income does not change. That means, fiscal policy in Germany is effective in Germany. However, fiscal policy in Germany has a negative externality on France.

To illustrate this, take a numerical example with $c = 0.72$, $m = 0.16$, and $q = 0.24$. In other words, the marginal import rate of Germany is $q = 0.24$. The marginal import rate of Germany relative to France is $m = 0.16$. And the marginal import rate of Germany relative to non-union countries is $q - m = 0.08$. Likewise the marginal import rate of France is $q = 0.24$. The marginal import rate of France relative to Germany is $m = 0.16$. And the marginal import rate of France relative to non-union countries is $q - m = 0.08$.

Given these parameter values, the fiscal policy multipliers are $dY_1/dG_1 = 0.735$ and $dY_2/dG_1 = -0.735$. As a result, an increase in German government purchases of 100 produces an increase in German income of 74 and a decline in French income of equally 74. By this standard, the domestic effect of fiscal policy is rather small. On the other hand, the negative externality of fiscal policy is quite large.

Second consider monetary policy by the European Central Bank. An increase in union money supply raises both German income and French income, to the same extent respectively. To illustrate this, take a numerical example with $k = 0.25$. Then the monetary policy multipliers are $dY_1/dM = dY_2/dM = 2$. As a result, an increase in union money supply of 100 causes an increase in German income of 200, an increase in French income of equally 200, and an increase in union income of 400. If we have $A_1 = A_2$, then we get

$Y_1 = Y_2$. Under this initial condition, a 1 percent increase in union money supply produces a 1 percent increase in German income, a 1 percent increase in French income, and a 1 percent increase in union income. By this standard, the monetary policy multipliers are very large.

Next solve the model for the exchange rate of the union. Take the sum of equations (13.23) and (13.24) to verify:

$$(1 - c - m + q)(Y_1 + Y_2) = A_1 + A_2 + 2he \tag{13.28}$$

Then get rid of $Y_1 + Y - 2$ with the help of equation (13.22) and solve for e:

$$e = \frac{(1 - c - m - q)M - k(A_1 + A_2)}{2hk} \tag{13.29}$$

As a result, this is the equilibrium level of the union exchange rate. Because of $c < 1$ and $m < q$ we have $1 - c - m + q > 0$. An increase in the demand for German goods lowers the union exchange rate. That is, it causes an appreciation of the euro. The same holds for an increase in the demand for French goods. Conversely, an increase in union money supply raises the union exchange rate. That is, it causes a depreciation of the euro.

For the remainder of this section we discuss the process of adjustment in greater detail. First consider an increase in German government purchases. The primary effect is an increase in German income. The secondary effect is an appreciation of the euro. Half of the appreciation falls on Germany, the other half falling on France. This in turn reduces both German exports and French exports to non-union countries, respectively. For that reason, both German income and French income decline. The net effect is that German income goes up. On the other hand, French income goes down. And what is more, union income does not change.

Second consider the transmission mechanism of monetary policy. An increase in union money supply causes a depreciation of the euro. This in turn raises both German exports and French exports to non-union countries, respectively. As a consequence, German income and French income go up.

13.4 Mix of Monetary and Fiscal Policy

In this section we consider two targets of macroeconomic policy:

- full employment and price stability in Germany,
- full employment and price stability in France.

On the other hand, we consider three instruments of macroeconomic policy:

- monetary policy in the union,
- fiscal policy in Germany,

- fiscal policy in France.

This section is based on the numerical examples given in section 13.3. Let the parameter values still be $c = 0.72$, $m = 0.16$, and $q = 0.24$. Then the fiscal policy multipliers are $dY_1/dG_1 = 0.735$ and $dY_1/dG_1 = 0. - 735$. And the monetary policy multipliers are $dY_1/dM = dY_2/dM = 2$. Let full-employment output of Germany be $\bar{Y}_1 = 1000$ and let full-employment output of France be the same $\bar{Y}_2 = 1000$. It proves useful to distinguish three cases:

- unemployment in Germany and France,
- inflation in Germany and France,
- unemployment in Germany, inflation in France.

Unemployment in Germany and France

At the beginning let actual output of Germany be $Y_1 = 880$ and let actual output of France be $Y_2 = 920$. That is to say, there is unemployment in both Germany and France. More precisely, unemployment in Germany exceeds that in France. First consider isolated fiscal policy in Germany. The target of the German government is full employment in Germany. What is needed is an increase in German government purchases of 163. This policy measure raises German output from 880 to 1000, given the multiplier of 0.735. On the other hand, it lowers French output from 920 to 800. As a severe side effect, unemployment in France goes up.

Second consider isolated fiscal policy in France. The target of the French government is full employment in France. What is needed here is an increase in French government purchases of 109. This policy action raises French output from 920 to 1000. However, it lowers German output from 880 to 800. Unfortunately, unemployment in Germany goes up. Third consider coordinated fiscal policy in Germany and France. The targets of the German and French governments are full employment in both Germany and France. Obviously there is no way to reach this goal.

Fourth consider isolated monetary policy in the union. The natural target of the European Central Bank, in the initial state, is full employment in France. What is needed is an increase in union money supply of 40. This policy measure raises French output from 920 to 1000 and German output from 880 to 960, given the multipliers of 2. As a favourable side effect, unemployment in Germany goes down. But there still is some unemployment left.

An alternative target of the European Central Bank is full employment in Germany. What is needed, in this case, is an increase in union money supply of 60. This policy action raises German output from 880 to 1000 and French output from 920 to 1040. As an adverse side effect, this causes inflation in France (there is overemployment in France, which drives up money wages and prices). So the European Central Bank will prefer full employment in France to full employment in Germany.

Fifth consider a mix of monetary and fiscal policy. The targets of the policy mix are full employment in both Germany and France. Let us proceed in two logical steps. What is needed in step one is an increase in union income of 200. What is needed, therefore, is an increase in union money supply of 50. This policy measure raises German output from 880 to 980 and French output from 920 to 1020. Then what is needed in step two is an increase in German government purchases of 27. This policy action raises German output from 980 to 1000. At the same time it lowers French output from 1020 to 1000. In this way the policy mix achieves full employment in both Germany and France.

Incidentally there is another policy mix: An increase in union money supply of 50 and a reduction in French government purchases of 27. This policy mix raises German output from 880 to 1000 and French output from 920 to 1000.

As an important result, fiscal policy in Germany and France generally cannot establish full employment in Germany and France. The reason for this is that fiscal policy in Germany and France cannot increase union income. And what is more, monetary policy in the union generally cannot establish full employment in Germany and France either. The reason for this is that monetary policy in the union cannot treat Germany and France differently. What is needed, therefore, is a mix of monetary and fiscal policy. The job of monetary policy is to increase union income. And the job of fiscal policy is to treat Germany and France differently. In this sense, macroeconomic policy should be coordinated between the European Central Bank, the German government, and the French government.

Inflation in Germany and France

At the start let German output be 1060 and let French output be 1040. That means, there is inflation in both Germany and France. Strictly speaking, inflation in Germany is higher than that in France. First consider isolated fiscal policy in Germany. The target of the German government is full employment and price stability in Germany. What is needed is a reduction in German government purchases of 82. This policy measure lowers German output from 1060 to 1000. On the other hand, it raises French output from 1040 to 1100. As a severe side effect, inflation in France goes up.

Second consider isolated fiscal policy in France. The target of the French government is full employment and price stability in France. What is needed here is a reduction in French government purchases of 54. This policy action lowers French output from 1040 to 1000. However, it raises German output from 1060 to 1100. Unfortunately, inflation in Germany goes up.

Third consider isolated monetary policy. The target of the European Central Bank is price stability in both Germany and France. What is needed is a reduction in union money supply of 30 (assuming for the time being that money wages are downwards rigid). This policy measure lowers German output from 1060 to 1000 and French output from 1040 to 980. As an adverse side effect, unemployment occurs in France.

Fourth consider a mix of monetary and fiscal policy. The targets of the policy mix are full employment and price stability in Germany as well as in France. Let us again proceed in two steps. What is needed in step one is a reduction in union output of 100. What is needed, therefore, is a reduction in union money supply of 25. This policy action lowers German output from 1060 to 1010 and French output from 1040 to 990. Then what is needed in step two is a reduction in German government purchases of 14. This policy measure lowers German output from 1010 to 1000. Similarly it raises French output from 990 to 1000. In this way the policy mix establishes full employment and price stability in Germany as well as France.

As an important result, fiscal policy in Germany and France generally cannot establish price stability in Germany and France. On the other hand, monetary policy in the union can indeed establish price stability in Germany and France. But it can only do so by giving rise to unemployment. What is needed, therefore, is a mix of monetary and fiscal policy.

Unemployment in Germany, Inflation in France

Initially let German output be 940 and let French output be 1040. First consider isolated fiscal policy in Germany. The target of the German government is full employment and price stability in Germany. What is needed is an increase in German government purchases of 82. This policy action raises German output from 940 to 1000. On the other hand, it lowers French output from 1040 to 980. As a side effect, the French economy switches from inflation to unemployment.

Second consider isolated fiscal policy in France. The target of the French government is full employment and price stability in France. What is needed here is a reduction in French government purchases of 54. This policy measure lowers French output from 1040 to 1000. The other way round, it raises German output from 940 to 980. As a favourable side effect, unemployment in Germany goes down. But there still is some unemployment left.

Third consider isolated monetary policy in the union. The target of the European Central Bank is price stability in both Germany and France. What is needed is a reduction in union money supply of 20. This policy action lowers French output from 1040 to 1000 and German output from 940 to 900. As an adverse side effect, unemployment in Germany goes up.

Fourth consider a mix of monetary and fiscal policy. The targets of the policy mix are full employment and price stability in Germany as well as in France. Let us once more proceed in two steps. What is needed in step one is an increase in union output of 20. What is needed, therefore, is an increase in union money supply of 5. This policy measure raises German output from 940 to 950 and French output from 1040 to 1050. Then what is needed in step two is an increase in German government purchases of 68. This policy action raises German output from 950 to 1000. Conversely, it lowers French output from 1050 to 1000.

As an important result, fiscal policy in Germany and France generally cannot establish full employment and price stability in Germany and France. And what is more, monetary policy in the union generally cannot establish full employment and price stability in Germany and France either. What is needed, therefore, is a mix of monetary and fiscal policy. In this sense, macroeconomic policy should be coordinated between the European Central Bank, the German government, and the French government.

13.5 Mix of Monetary Policy and Wage Restraint

In this section we consider two targets of macroeconomic policy:

- full employment and price stability in Germany,
- full employment and price stability in France

On the other hand, we consider three instruments of macroeconomic policy:

- monetary policy in the union,
- wage restraint in Germany,
- wage restraint in France.

To illustrate this we take a stylised numerical example, making the following assumptions. A 1 percent increase in union money supply causes a 1 percent increase in German output and a 1 percent increase in French output. A 1 percent reduction in German money wages causes a 1 percent decline in the price of German goods and a 1 percent increase in German output. However, it has no effect on French output. Likewise, a 1 percent reduction in French money wages causes a 1 percent decline in the price of French goods and a 1 percent increase in French output. But it has no effect on German output. It proves useful to study two distinct cases:

- unemployment in Germany and France,
- inflation in Germany and France.

Unemployment in Germany and France

Initially let the output gap in Germany be 12 percent. That is, a 12 percent increase in German output is required to achieve full employment in Germany. Similarly let the output gap in France be 8 percent. So we have unemployment in both Germany and France. More exactly, unemployment in Germany exceeds that in France.

First consider monetary policy in the union. The target of the European Central Bank, in this situation, is to bring the French output gap down to zero. What is needed, then, is an 8 percent increase in union money supply. As a favourable side effect, this policy measure brings the German output gap down from 12 percent to 4 percent.

Second consider wage restraint in Germany and France. The target of the German trade union is to bring the German output gap down to zero. What is needed, here, is a 12 percent reduction in German money wages. The target of the French trade union is to bring the French output gap down to zero. What is needed, correspondingly, is an 8 percent reduction in French money wages.

Third consider a mix of monetary policy and wage restraint. The targets of the policy mix are to bring the German output gap as well as the French output gap down to zero. What is needed, therefore, is an increase in union money supply of 8 percent and a reduction in German money wages of 4 percent. Given the stickiness of money wages in the real world, the policy mix seems to be the best solution.

As an important result, monetary policy in the union generally cannot establish full employment in Germany and France. On the other hand, wage restraint in Germany and France can indeed establish full employment in Germany and France. What is superior, however, is a mix of monetary policy and wage restraint. In this sense, macroeconomic policy should be coordinated between the European Central Bank, the German trade union, and the French trade union.

Inflation in Germany and France

Initially let the inflationary gap in Germany be 6 percent. That is, a 6 percent reduction in German output is required to achieve price stability in Germany. Similarly let the inflationary gap in France be 4 percent. So we have inflation in both Germany and France. Properly speaking, inflation in Germany is higher than that in France.

First consider monetary policy in the union. The target of the European Central Bank, in this situation, is to bring the inflationary gap in Germany down to zero. What is needed, then, is a 6 percent reduction in union money supply. As an adverse side effect, this policy action gives rise to an output gap in France of 2 percent.

Second consider a mix of monetary policy and wage restraint. The targets of the policy mix are to bring the inflationary gaps in Germany and France down to zero. What is needed, here, is a 6 percent reduction in union money supply and a 2 percent reduction in French money wages.

13.6 Conclusion

Fiscal policy. An increase in German government purchases causes an appreciation of the euro. This in turn lowers both German and French exports. The net effect is that German income goes up. On the other hand, French income goes down. And what is more, union income does not change. In this sense, fiscal policy in Germany is effective in Germany. However, fiscal policy in Germany has a negative externality on France. In the numerical example, an increase in German government purchases of 100 produces an increase in German income of 74 and a decline in French income of equally 74. That means, the domestic effect of fiscal policy is rather small. But the negative externality of fiscal policy is quite large.

Monetary policy. An increase in union money supply causes a depreciation of the euro. This in turn raises both German and French exports. As a consequence, German and French income go up, to the same extent respectively. In this sense, monetary policy in the union is effective in Germany and France. In the numerical example, an increase in union money supply of 100 produces an increase in German income of 200 and an increase in French income of equally 200. More generally, a 1 percent increase in union money supply produces a 1 percent increase in German income and a 1 percent increase in French income. That is to say, the monetary policy multiplier is very large.

Monetary and fiscal policy. There are two targets of macroeconomic policy:

- full employment and price stability in Germany
- full employment and price stability in France

And there are three instruments of macroeconomic policy:

- monetary policy in the union
- fiscal policy in Germany
- fiscal policy in France

Consider for instance unemployment in Germany and France. As an important result, fiscal policy in Germany and France generally cannot establish full employment in Germany and France. And what is more, monetary policy in the union generally cannot establish full employment in Germany and France either. What is needed, therefore, is a mix of monetary and fiscal policy. In this sense, macroeconomic policy should be coordinated between the European Central Bank, the German government, and the French government. To illustrate this, take a numerical example. Assume that full-employment output of Germany is 1000 and that full-employment output of France is equally 1000. At the beginning, let actual output of Germany be 880 and let actual output of France be 920. What is needed, then, is an increase in union money supply of 50 and an increase in German government purchases of 27.

References

[1] Begg, D., J. von Hagen, C. Wyplosz, and K. Zimmermann (1998). *EMU: Prospects and Challenges for the Euro.* Cambridge.

[2] Buti, M. and A. S. (eds.) (1998). *Economic Policy in EMU.* Oxford.

[3] Calmfors et.al., L. (1997). *EMU - A Swedish Perspective.* Dordrecht.

[4] Carlberg, M. (1999). *European Monetary Union.* Heidelberg, New York.

[5] De Grauwe, P. (1997). *The Economics of Monetary Integration.* Oxford.

[6] Dornbusch, R., C. Favero, and F. Giavazzi (1998). Immediate Challenges for the European Central Bank. in: *EMU*, D. Begg et.al. (eds.), Cambridge.

[7] Eichengreen, B. (1998). *European Monetary Unification.* Cambridge.

[8] Fleming, J. (1962). Domestic Financial Policies Under Fixed and Floating Exchange Rates. *IMF Staff Papers 9*, 369–380.

[9] Gros, D. a. N. T. (1998). *European Monetary Integration.* London.

[10] Hansen, J.D., H. Heinrich, and J. Nielsen (1992). *An Economic Analysis of the EC.* London.

[11] Kenen, P. (1995). *Economic and Monetary Union in Europe.* Cambridge.

[12] Levin, J. (1983). A Model of Stabilization Policy in a Jointly Floating Currency Area. in: *Economic Interdependence and Flexible Exchange Rates*, J. S. Bhandari and B. H. Putnam (eds.), Cambridge.

[13] Masson, P., T. Krueger, and B. T. (eds.) (1997). *EMU and the International Monetary System.* Washington.

[14] Mundell, R. (1968). *International Economics.* New York.

[15] OECD (1999). *EMU: Facts, Challenges and Policies.* Paris.

[16] Rose, K. and K. Sauernheimer (1983). Zur Theorie eines Mischwechselkurssystems. in: *Wirtschaftspolitik in weltoffener Wirtschaft*, M. Feldsieper, R. Groß, Hg., Berlin, 15 - 28.

14 High Order Strategic Thinking

The Subscriber's Dilemma in an Experimental Stock Issuing and the Keynesian Beauty Contest

Alexander Karmann and Marco Lehmann-Waffenschmidt *

14.1 Introduction

In recent years public stock issuings by (new) stock companies, i.e. initial public offerings (IPOs), have attracted steadily rising attention on financial markets worldwide. In Germany, for instance, the number of IPOs on the so-called New Market is supposed to increase from 168 in 1999 up to more than 200 in 2000. A salient characteristic of initial public offerings, at least in Germany, is a significant total excess demand, or let us say oversubscription, at the end of the subscription period. Particularly prominent cases in Germany showing this phenomenon were the going public of the "Deutsche Telekom" in 1996, of "Infineon", the semiconductor daughter of Siemens, in spring 2000, and "T-Online", the internet daughter of the Deutsche Telekom, also in spring 2000.

The massive oversubscription in each of these three cases caused a strict rationing of subscription orders in the final repartitioning procedure. Each time this rationing was perceived as being harsh by the public and, particularly, by those subscribers who had come off badly in the repartitioning procedure. This was even aggravated by the fact that, as it commonly had been expected, from the first moment on in each of these three cases the respective share's price on the stock market exceeded the subscription price by far. Not to have got a look in when the shares were repartitioned, thus, was the same as to have foregone a quasi-safe profit.

Obviously, there arises a lot of generally interesting questions around the actual procedure of initial public offerings. For instance, how is the issuing, or subscription, price (span) determined, who gets how many shares in the repartitioning process after the subscription has been closed, or, how will the share price be on the first market date in relation to the issuing price? To be sure, all of these questions are relevant to a private investor, too. Nevertheless, there is still another question which is of eminent practical interest for every private investor subscribing a newly issued share, namely how many shares

* The authors are grateful to Dr. Horst Bienert, Landesbank Baden-Württemberg, Stuttgart, for essential advice in conceptualising the experimental designs. Thanks for helpful comments and criticisms are also due to participants of seminars and workshops at the Universities of Mannheim, Trento, Saarbrücken and Leipzig, and to the participants of the GEW-Workshop in Meißen 1998.

one should order if an oversubscription and consequently a rationing has to be expected.

If the repartitioning procedure follows a purely proportional rationing scheme where all subscribers are treated equally this question naturally amounts to the problem what each subscriber expects what the other subscribers will do during the subscription period. Actually, this leads into the center of high order strategic thinking. For a rational investor the idea that he should try to guess how many shares the other subscribers will order, surely cannot be the endpoint of his reasoning. Going one step further, he has to take into account that the other subscribers also calculate rationally and, consequently, in particular will consider the same calculation as he did. Thus, in a next step, a rational subscriber will try to guess what the average subscriber believes what the average subscriber will do. But even this is not the end of the story since there is no natural bound for rational subscribers to stop their iteration of re-adapted guesses. Thus, fully rational subscribers inevitably run into a dilemma which we subsequently will call the "subscriber's dilemma".

It is the roots and the nature of this general type of iteration process of re-adapted guesses, called "high order strategic thinking" in the present study, which we are going to deal with. For our analysis we will employ the experimental method. We are particularly interested in the question whether subjects do perform steps of high order strategic thinking at all if they have the opportunity to do so. If the answer is yes, the natural question will be how many steps are performed.

14.2 The Subscriber's Dilemma on the Stock Exchange and Other Examples of a Keynesian Beauty Contest

Generally speaking, a subject has reason to exercise *strategic thinking* if there is an intelligent, rationally planning and acting counterpart - be it single or multiple - who in principle is capable of anticipating and counteracting the subject's potential actions by making the same, and possibly even more and even better, observations and reasoning than the subject himself. If it is common knowledge that all subjects involved are fully rational, every subject who wants to be successful at the end runs into a potentially infinite regress of

- *first* guessing *the others' decisions and deciding with regard to that* = strategic thinking of <u>**order one**</u>,
- *second* guessing the **others' guesses about one's own guess about** *the others' decisions and deciding with regard to that* = strategic thinking of <u>**order two**</u>,
- *third* guessing the ***others' guesses about one's own guess about the*** **others' guesses about one's own guess about** *the others' decisions and deciding with regard to that* = strategic thinking of <u>**order three**</u>,

and so on.[1]

Let us look again at the subscriber's dilemma on the stock market against this general background. A subscriber clearly cannot expect to receive his desired number of shares under a proportional repartitioning scheme if he orders the desired number, and the total amount of issued shares is less than the total number of ordered shares, i.e. if he exercises strategic thinking of *order zero*. So, in a second approximation he has to guess how many shares the other subscribers are going to order and accordingly he has to overstate his intrinsically desired number of shares (strategic thinking of *order one*). (Of course, things become significantly easier for the subscriber if the issuing consortium publishes the changing actual states of the oversubscription rate.) Unfortunately, this is also by no means an adequate plan for a rational subscriber to finally receive his desired number of shares because the other subscribers also will come to the same conclusion. Consequently, a rational subscriber has to calculate his subscription order in a *third approximation* guess according to the newly expected oversubscription rate (strategic thinking of *order two*). But neither this third approximation guess will work properly for the subscriber, but necessarily leads to a *fourth approximation* guess, *and so on.* Finally, each subscriber gets his repartitioned number of shares which equals the number of ordered shares times the "repartitioning rate", i.e. times the reciprocal of the "oversubscription rate" (= total number of ordered shares divided by the total number of issued shares).

There is at least one further situation in real economic life which is of the subscriber's dilemma type. It is the "Mengentender" procedure on the European money market by which banks get an important part of their liquidity from the European Central Bank (ECB) in a two-week rhythm. The procedure is simple: the ECB first fixes the interest rate, and then the banks subscribe for their desired liquidity. Finally, the ECB exercises a proportional repartitioning procedure. Evidently, the banks face the subscriber's dilemma as the subscribing investors did before. As the empirical evidence shows, the total oversubscription by banks in the "Mengentender" procedure has been significantly high during the year 1999 and the repartitioning rate consequently has been low until the beginning of the year 2000 (see Figure 14.1).

The iterative re-adaptation process of guesses in the subscriber's dilemma in essence is the same as the problem of speculators facing rising stock markets, but not knowing when the latest moment has come to sell the shares before everybody sells and the share prices are going to crash. John Maynard Keynes called this kind of a collective decision dilemma a "beauty contest"

[1] Obviously, this process of expectation building of increasingly higher order has a strong reflexive, or self-referential, flavour in that in every step the decision-maker looks at his own decision behaviour again through an additional level of guessing the others' behaviour.

Fig. 14.1. The evolution of "Mengentender" oversubscription in the European money market from 25.8.1999 – 10.5.2000

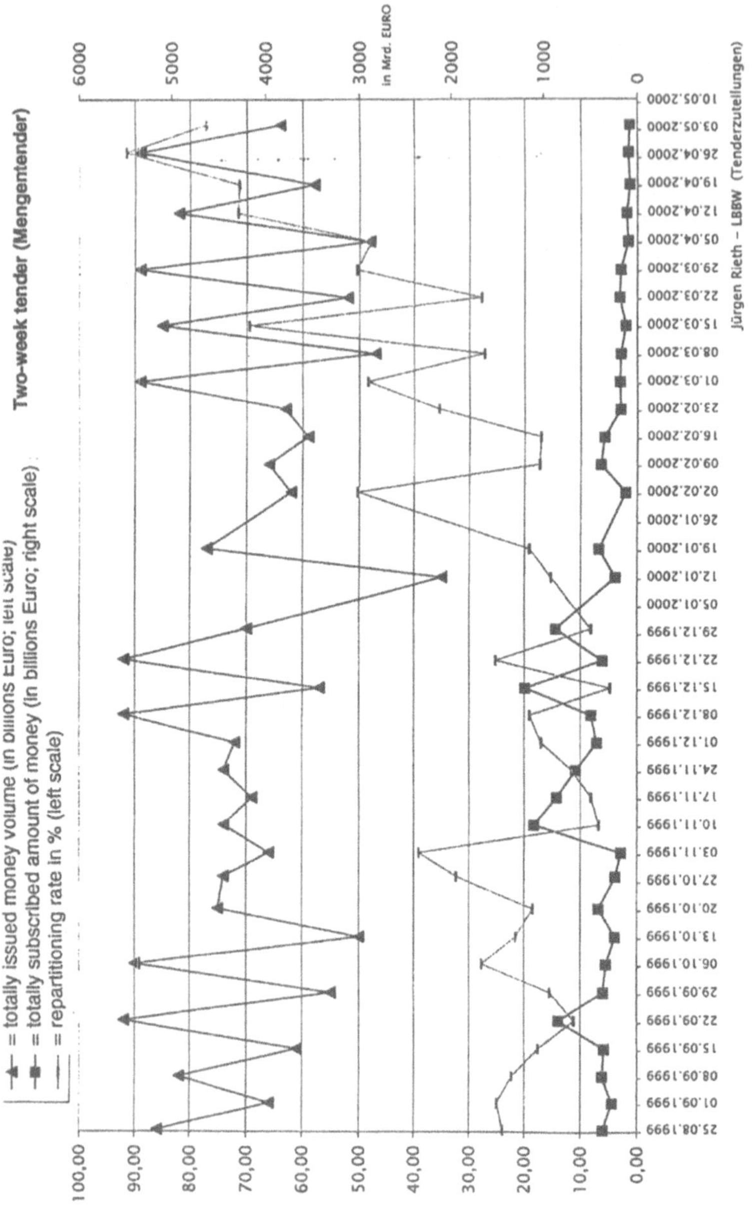

(cf. Nagel 1999).[2] Thereby, Keynes referred to competitions in US American newspapers which were popular in the early 20th century. There the readers should guess which six portrait photographs out of a group of portrait photographs would be guessed as the most beautiful ones by most readers (see e.g. Nagel/Selten (1998), R. Nagel (1999)). Evidently, it is not useful to choose the photos which are one's own personal favourites *(stategic thinking of order zero),* but at least to choose those six which one considers to be the most beautiful ones in the eyes of average taste *(strategic thinking of order one).* But as before, one has to re-iterate this meta-guessing further and further, thus potentially running into an infinite regression.

To be sure, this re-iterated expectation formation procedure in a beauty contest in general need not necessarily lead to a really infinite sequence of new decisions, or choices in this case. We will come back to this in section 14.2 below. However, there are also cases conceivable where there is indeed a never-ending alternating inversion of decisions when passing through the higher orders of iteratively re-adapted guesses. [3]

In recent years a question became popular in experimental economics which at the first moment looks like a brain-teaser, but, in fact, could be considered a prototype example of a beauty contest (see e.g. Nagel, R. (1995), Nagel, R.; Selten, R. (1998), Nagel, R.; Bosch-Domènech, A.; and Satorra, A. (1999), Nagel, R. (1999)). The subjects in the experiment were asked which decimal number between 0 and 100 (the boundaries are included) would equal 2/3 of the arithmetic average of the numbers said by all subjects in the experiment who have to answer the same question. The winner was the one whose number was closest to the true value. If all subjects would answer fully rationally they would say 'zero' of course, and would all be winners. Actually,

[2] Note that today the term "beauty contest" is used by stock exchange professionals in a different sense. For them it means the competition of banks and brokers for getting the lucrative position of being a member of the consortium managing the going public of a new stock company.

[3] A fictional example supporting this is given by the movie "Juggernaut" (Great Britain, 1974, directed by R. Lester). A blackmailer has hidden bombs in an ocean-liner. At sea a bomb disposal-expert manages it to reduce the problem of deactivating the bombs to the 0/1-decision either to cut through a blue, or a yellow wire in cach bomb. A mistake, however, would be fatal. It then turns out that the blackmailer and the bomb disposal-expert have been colleagues and old friends. To use every chance, the bomb disposal-expert phones to the blackmailer since he is the only person who can give any information facilitating the 0/1-decision. After the conversation the bomb disposal-expert has to decide two things in order to draw the right conclusion: first, whether or not the blackmailer wanted to cheat him, and second, if he wanted to cheat him, how many reflection steps he had performed. Fortunately, the bomb disposal-expert finds the right answer: the blackmailer lied and performed no reflection step. Consequently, the wire has to be cut through which was not recommended by the blackmailer. Note that the conjecture that the blackmailer performed only one more reflection step would have caused an inversion of this decision.

this is the necessary conclusion from the following chain of calculations that a fully rational subject exercises knowing that everybody knows that everybody takes the calculations of all others into account which in turn considers the calculation by all others, and so on. Nagel et alii (1999) call this type of reasoning "iterated best reply".

1. *First order calculation step = strategic thinking of order zero:* If all said numbers are equally distributed in the unit interval $[0, 100]$, then 2/3 of 50, i.e. 33 1/3, is the correct answer. (By this we neglect the rather unreasonable idea to choose 66 as 2/3 of 100 as a first order calculation step.)
2. *Second order calculation step = strategic thinking of order one*: The above answer would only be valid if subjects did not calculate their answers, but chose their answers stochastically. However, since a rational subject has to take into account that subjects have reason to calculate their answers in the next step he will say 2/3 of 33 1/3, i.e. 22 approximately.
3. *Third order calculation step = strategic thinking of order two*: Indeed, there is absolutely no reason for a rational subject knowing that the other subjects are also rational to stop the calculation here. 2/3 of 22 approximately equals 14, and this is the rational answer in the third order calculation step.
4. *Calculation of infinite order = perfect strategic thinking:* Continuing in this way a subject ends at "0". Indeed, "0" is the only Nash equilibrium of this game.

But is the theoretical Nash equilibrium also observable in reality? In fact, the experimental evidence of a series of experiments which were conducted, or reported, by R. Nagel and R. Selten (1998), partly even on a grand scale base using the readerships of large daily papers, have shown the following stylized picture: The frequency distributions of numbers told by the subjects in the experiments particularly show peaks at the prominent values discussed above. Even though not all experiments had an identical design (they varied with the base space $[0, 1]$, $[0, 100]$, $[1, 100]$ or all integer numbers between zero and 100, with the boundaries included or excluded, and so on), the empirical evidence of the frequency distribution of choices showed a rather similar picture. In the Selten/Nagel experiment in the journal "Spektrum der Wissenschaft" the winning answer was close to 0,14. In other words, this means that the third order calculation step, or the *strategic thinking of order two,* was successful from the purely behavioural standpoint.

Note, however, that this conclusion is not a causal explanation of the way how to win the number choosing game, for instance by simply arguing that the participants would exercise strategic thinking of order one so that strategic thinking of order two automatically would win. Since a great number of heterogeneous participants is involved the subject pool splits up into several subgroups with different choice behaviour. For instance, from the comments by the subjects it is known that there is a group of fully rational subjects knowing that "0" is the theoretical solution. But a subgroup of this group deliberatly chooses a number greater than "0" since its members do not consider the other subjects to be fully rational. Moreover, Nagel et alii (1999) have found the stylized fact from a series of newspaper experiments by several authors that subjects do perform two, or three, "reasoning steps" and then "jump into infinity", i.e. choose the equilibrium value "0". In our terms, subjects move to *perfect strategic thinking from strategic thinking of order one, or two,* i.e. after they have exercised *a second, or third order calculation step.*

To be sure, the Selten/Nagel beauty contest[4] differs from the subscriber's dilemma in several respects (cf. section 14.4 below for more details). However, according to Keynes' original intention in our eyes the subscriber's dilemma deserves the title "beauty contest" as well. In order to make a difference, however, we will call the subscriber's dilemma a "dilemma of the Keynesian beauty contest" type.

Like the Selten/Nagel beauty contest game of number choosing the subscriber's dilemma well suits for an experimental investigation. In section 14.4 we will present an experiment together with the experimental evidence for the subscriber's dilemma from a series of computerized experiments.

In the next section, however, we will examine first in which way the problem of stategic thinking also plays a role in predicting.

14.3 The Infinite Cycle of High Order Strategic Thinking in Social Predicting: The Morgenstern Paradox

If strategic thinking is characteristic for human life then the problem of high order strategic thinking must be of the same age as mankind.[5] Economic scientific analyzing of high order strategic thinking in fact reaches far back, at least as far as to Cournot who in 1838 published his theory of the strategic behaviour of oligopolists. Thus, it seems only consequent that the first systematic investigation into the topic in modern economics is to be credited to one of the two creators of modern game theory, Oskar Morgenstern. In a famous monograph O. Morgenstern (1928, see also Morgenstern 1935) examined strategic thinking in the specific context of the question for the possibility of correct "social predictions". Social predictions get known to the public, and thus also to the decision-makers whose behaviour is going

[4] We are well aware of the fact that number choosing beauty contest experiments have also been conducted by other authors, but for practical reasons we will say "Selten/Nagel (number choosing game) beauty contest" throughout this study.

[5] The reader can find more on this topic in Section 14.3 below where we will illuminate the question for the evolutionary and anthropological roots of high order strategic thinking.

to be predicted, and consequently are subject to altering effects. This means that for the forecaster his task amounts to a problem of high order strategic thinking.

Morgenstern, however, comes to a fairly pessimistic conclusion with respect to the possibility of correct social predictions. His main argument is, in a nutshell, that the re-iterations of re-adapted forecasts inevitably must run into an infinite regression. In other words, the problem of forecasting correctly in social predictions is indetermined, and consequently unsolvable in principle. Morgenstern illustrated his verdict by the following parable (1928, p. 98):

> "When pursued by his adversary Professor Moriarty, Sherlock Holmes takes a train from London to Dover which stops at an intermediate stop. There he gets out because he has seen Moriarty at the station in London and conjectures that Moriarty would take a faster train to Dover in order to await him there. In fact, Holmes' anticipation turns out to be correct. But what if Moriarty would have still been more intelligent and would have foreseen Holmes' anticipation? Then, clearly, he also would have taken the train stopping at the intermediate stop and would have got out there. However, this in turn could have been anticipated by Holmes, and, consequently, he would have stayed in the train until Dover. Again, this could have been foreseen by Moriarty, and so on. Evidently, the consequence of this infinite chain of conjectured reactions and re-reactions must be a complete paralysis of activity."

Later on, Morgenstern's verdict has been called the "Morgenstern paradox" (e.g. Tietzel, 1981, 1985, the reader can also find a worth reading general survey on the topic of self-altering predictions in Rothschild, 1969). Not earlier than in 1954, this fundamental verdict was seriously doubted. Grunberg and Modigliani (1954) forwarded the argument that the "Morgenstern process", i.e. the iterated re-adaption of predictions, needs not take place at all. Instead, under suitable and not very restricting assumptions a rational forecaster can well settle the problem of correctly predicting a social event by transforming it equivalently into a fixed-point problem which turns out to be solvable using a suitable fixed-point theorem. Actually, this argument turned out to be resistent to attacks in the subsequent discussion (Grunberg/Modigliani 1963). Lehmann-Waffenschmidt (1985, 1990) showed that Morgenstern's impossibility claim is not necessarily valid even if a fixed point exists but cannot be calculated by the forecaster for whatever reason. This argument runs along the line that the Morgenstern process may well be stable, locally or globally, and then the re-iteration of predictions may finally lead to a correct prediction under suitable conditions, i.e. to a fixed point of an adequately chosen self-mapping of a suitable chosen Euclidean subspace.

Another line of argumentation against the general validity of Morgenstern's impossibility claim is simply given by the fact that the high order strategic thinking problem essentially requires at least two opposite parties trying to mutually anticipate, or falsificate, the other side's beliefs. But this is usually not the case with a group whose members either have no reason, or have too high transaction costs, to collude against the forecaster.

A final attack against Morgenstern's impossibility claim makes use of the bounded rationality argument (Lehmann-Waffenschmidt, 1990, section 3.2). Real actors are in no way fully rational so that an infinite regression of iterated re-adaptations of predictions does not occur in reality. Thus, actors are supposed to exercise only a few steps of the Morgenstern process, or in our words a "strategic thinking of low order", so that a "pragmatic solution" becomes possible (Lehmann-Waffenschmidt, 1990, section 3.2). We note that this argument is in complete accordance with the evidence in the Selten/Nagel beauty contest experiments where the winner performed strategic thinking of order two.

14.4 High Order Strategic Thinking Revisited from the Perspective of Anthropology and Evolutionary Biology

Looking more closely at the phenomenon of high order strategic thinking one might come to the question what its roots are from the viewpoint of evolutionary biology. The British psychologist and anthropologist Robin Dunbar (1996) gives an instructive account of the biological and anthropological roots of high order strategic thinking which he calls "theory of mind". If a subject exercises strategic thinking of order k in a strategic interaction Dunbar says the subjects "has a theory of mind with intensionality of order k". (Note Dunbar‘s spelling "s" instead of "t" to separate the technicus terminus "intensionality" from the colloquial term "intention".)

Empirical evidence shows that small children under the age of four years do not have a theory of mind, i.e. they even do not have consciousness of themselves as cognitive and constructive units. Their perception of the world is direct and unreflected in the sense that they cannot imagine that another subject might have a different perception of the same objects, or that one could manipulate another‘s perception by lying or telling fictitious stories. Thus, like autistic persons small children have an intensionality status of *order zero.* Between the third and the fourth year a child develops a theory of mind. An adult human of average intelligence has the capacity of a theory of mind of *order four.* Higher orders, however, make things increasingly intricate. An order-eight situation already causes major problems even to people of above average intelligence.

An interesting question concerning the evolutionary aspect is whether other species also have the capability of a high order theory of mind, with intensionality status of order greater than zero. Systematic observations and experiments with primates and other ape species strongly indicate that at least chimpanzees and other primates are capable of a high order theory of mind. Also other ape species show a behaviour which makes existence of a theory of mind of intensionality order greater than zero plausible. Usually such experiments, or field observations, deal with cheating activities of primates in the context of social hierarchy. A prototype situation is that of a low-rank male which either strives for "forbidden" food or females. If a high-rank male surprises an "insubordinate" low-rank male during a forbidden activity then the latter usually tries to transmit signals giving the impression that he would not be interested at all in the matter at stake. In a famous experiment of this type a high-rank male surprised a low-rank male and pretended to be convinced by the indifference signals of the low-rank male. But after he had left the place he hid behind a remote tree to observe what the low-rank male would do afterwards. Undoubtedly, this can be interpreted as intensionality of *order four* of the high-rank male: "I believe (1) that the low-rank believes (2) that he could deceive me so that I shall think (3) he would not be interested to take the food (4)".

To be honest, however, any such observations can alternatively also be explained without any reference to a "theory of mind". It suffices to recur to a simple conditional reinforcement learning by trial and error which leads the subject to the observed behaviour without any causal or strategic understanding of the counterpart's intentions. Nevertheless, the experimental evidence reported by biologists and ethologists appears to broadly corroborate the existence of a "theory of mind" for primates. Moreover, the question whether primates do have a "theory of mind", or not, undoubtedly is an interesting one because an exact answer to this question would make the border between human and non-human life better understandable.

Let us have a final look at the theory of mind from the perspective of biological evolution. The question why a species' capability of having a "theory of mind" apparently has been rewarded by biological evolution apparently is self-explanatory. Actually, it is just the capability of strategic thinking which provides a creature with the ability to manipulate and cheat its counterpart in order to gain an advantage. Though admittedly simplifying things the popular remark "homo sapiens sapiens is a primate who is able to cheat" thus becomes understandable.

14.5 An Experimental Investigation of the Subscriber's Dilemma on the Stock Market

We have indicated before that the subscriber's dilemma on the stock market lends itself in a natural way to an experimental investigation. In a pilot experiment at a summer school seminar of the Studienstiftung des deutschen Volkes in La Villa, Tirole, and in a series of computerized experiments at the Fakultät Wirtschaftswissenschaften of the Technische Universität Dresden we have observed the behaviour of subjects in the laboratory who faced the subscribers' dilemma in different design variants. However, all design variants started from the following *basic design*.

The issuing price is fixed and does not matter any further in the whole experiment. Each of the n subjects (n is usually between 12 and 15) intends to get finally a well-determined amount of shares after the repartition procedure, let us say 100. This is implemented by a payoff function which rewards the subject by a benefit $r > 0$ for any share he receives by the repartitioning up to 100 shares. From the 101st share on the payoff function punishes the subject for any further share by $s > 0$. The economic intuition of this assumption is the idea that investors usually have a well-determined intrinsic demand for the shares of a certain stock issuing company. This is due to an investor's personal attitudes and conditions like liquidity constraints, short-run expectations for the share price together with his risk attitude, and other long-run portfolio considerations.

Thus, we exclusively concentrate on the quantitative aspect of IPOs. This means that we neglect all aspects of the issuing price formation and, particularly, of any speculative calculations by the subscribers with respect to the share price on the first market date, or later. Actually, for our purposes it seems to be reasonable to consider the issuing price an exogenous parameter for a private investor.[6]

Let us come back to our basic experimental design. Before the subscription process starts the n subjects are informed about the repartitioning scheme which may be a purely proportional, or a random, procedure, or a combination of both. In all repartitioning scheme variants all subscribers are treated equally in the sense that there are no subscribers who are given a preferential treatment of any kind by the issuing consortium.[7] A *random repartitioning scheme* in our experiments means that subscribers are sequentially drawn and get what they have ordered until the volume of issued shares is completely spent. Combinations of the proportional and the random repartitioning scheme mix elements of both, for instance by first choosing randomly a number m with $0 < m \leq n$, and then drawing m subscribers randomly who will receive a proportional repartitioning of the issued volume of shares. Remaining shares may either be allocated proportionally, or randomly, amongst the other $n - m$ subscribers.

Subscribing by the participants proceeds in several rounds, say k rounds, and after each round the participants are informed about the actual rate of oversubscription. The intuition of this is that also in real IPOs subscribers are informed—with a time lag—about the oversubscription rate by the mass

[6] To be precise, however, in real IPOs the issuing price is determined interactively with demand in the so-called bookbuilding procedure, and is not announced as a fixed price, but as a price span.

[7] Admittedly, this contrasts to real IPOs where usually institutional investors, or customers of the going public stock company, implicitly or outspokenly, are given a preferential treatment in the repartitioning procedure.

media. In order to avoid that subjects wait to increase their orders until the last round of the subscription period they are informed that a random process has been implemented by which the whole subscription procedure may be stopped after each round with a predetermined positive probability.

After the last round the repartitioning scheme is exercised and the subjects are informed about the final rate of oversubscription, the number of shares they receive and their individual total payoff.

In further design variants, the totally issued volume of shares may be announced to the subjects, or not, and there is also the possibility of an additional amount of issued shares, the so-called 'greenshoe', if the oversubscription rate exceeds a certain critical threshold value. The decision about whether a greenshoe may come, or not, what its volume will be, and which conditions are sufficient for exercising it may either be discretionary, or following a prescribed rule. For the subjects the discretionary case clearly means that exercising the greenshoe option is random.

Summing up, obviously one may conceive of a myriad of design variants. This may be achieved either by parameter variations, or by structural variations concerning the chosen repartitioning scheme, the greenshoe procedure and, last but not least, the quantity and exactness of information on any item of the experiment given to the subjects. Furthermore, subscribing itself may be costly for the subjects in the experiment in that each subscribed share causes certain costs. The intuition for that is that the necessity to raise enough liquid funds for financing the expected shares raises costs in real life from interests, or collaterals.

The *experimental evidence* shows a clear pattern. In *a proportional repartitioning scheme* the subscribers' readiness to overstate their intrinsic demand was steadily increasing in subsequent rounds when there were no subscription costs. The following Figure 2 shows the observed evidence of subscribers' behaviour for 3 experimental groups a1, b1, d1 à 12 subjects. For every group an experiment consisted of 4 repetitions of a 5-rounds subscription procedure. The subscription procedure could be interrupted after each round with a probability of 0.2.

Even at first sight the evolution of total orders has an exponential functional shape. The reader should note, moreover, that in the fourth repetition of the group a1 experiment the value of the observed variable is far beyond the end of the scale. To be more precise, the observed variable in the diagram is not the absolute number of ordered shares, but the ratio

$$\frac{\text{subscribed shares} - \text{offered shares}}{\text{subscribed shares}}$$

The exponential like evolutions of orders in this experiment may be viewed as somewhat "anarchic", or, at least, uncontrollable. The reader should note that this happened even though more than 100 repartitioned shares were unfavourable for a subscriber. So it is natural to ask whether one can implement suitable designs by which the oversubscription behaviour can be controlled.

Fig. 14.2. Evolutions of subscription orders in a stock issuing experiment with a proportional repartitioning scheme without subscription costs (3 groups a1, b1, d1)

$$\text{observed variable} = \frac{\text{subscribed shares} - \text{offered shares}}{\text{subscribed shares}}$$

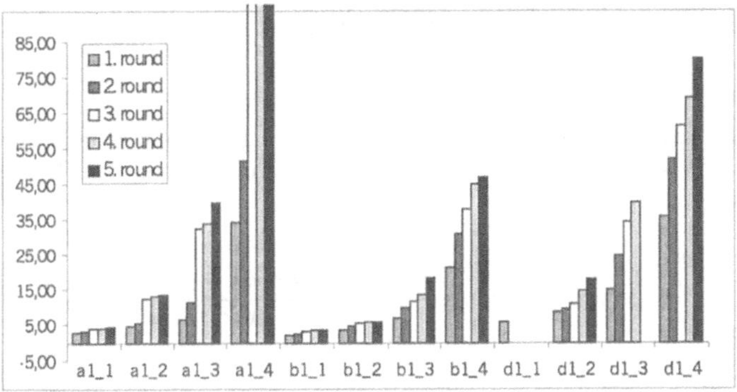

The evidence in our experiments shows further under which circumstances subscriptions are significantly constrained. Besides a pure scientific interest in studying subscribers' behaviour there are, in fact, good reasons for looking for design variants achieving a significant containment of orders. First and foremost, a massive oversubscription causes a strict rationing of the subscribers through the final repartition, i.e. the repartitioning rate is low. This means that the expectations of all those subscribers will be disappointed who did not oversubscribe sufficiently. Thus, a controlled oversubscription would help to reduce the emotional distortions of subscribers and thus would support what is called "Aktienkultur" in Germany. Moreover, high oversubscription rates are costly, as we have seen, and thus cause inefficiencies on the individual level as well as on the aggregate level. To be sure, these arguments equally apply to the "Mengentender subscriber's dilemma" (cf. section 14.2).

Of course, subscription costs per ordered share set an absolute limit to any subscriber to a "rational" overstatement of his intrinsic demand. If the subscription costs are $c > 0$ per share and the reward per allocated share up to 100 shares is r, then the largest break-even point lies at $z * c = 100 * r$, so that $z = \frac{100r}{c}$.[8] In this case, there is an equilibrium in contrast to the first design. There is obviously no equilibrium so that we have observed a behaviour of the participants which could not have been guarded by a theoretical solution. It is our conviction that this type of experimental work where no theoretical reference solution exists is a particularly exciting and promising part of experimental economics. In order not to complicate things

[8] To be sure, this calculation requires the subject finally to receive the intrinsically demanded shares. Thus, this value is an upper bound for a break-even point.

we do not want to go into details here as to the calculation of the equilibrium order values if subscribing is costly. For our purposes it is enough that the empirical evidence shows a significant lowering of orders if constraints caused by subscription costs come into play.

Not only transaction costs, but also the announcement of a possible greenshoe constrains the subscribers' proneness to overstate their intrinsic demand as the typical evidence in Figure 14.3 shows.

Fig. 14.3. Evolutions of subscription orders in a stock issuing experiment with a proportional repartitioning scheme and an announced greenshoe (5 groups a2, b2, e1, g1, h1)

$$\text{observed variable} = \frac{\text{subscribed shares} - \text{offered shares}}{\text{subscribed shares}}$$

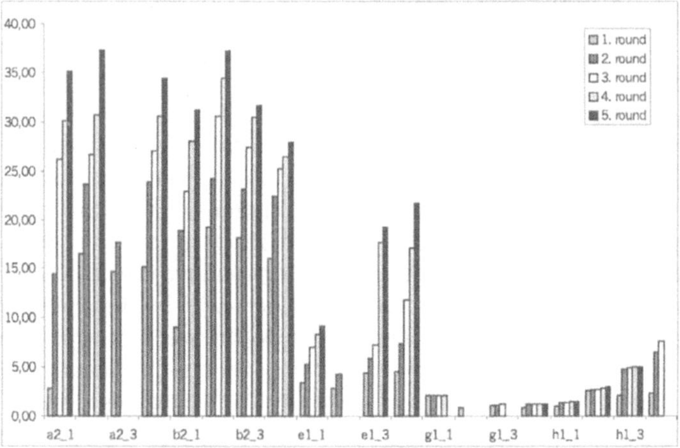

Particularly interesting from the theoretical as well as from the empirical point of view is the case where the total amount of issued shares equals the total amount of intrinsically demanded shares, and this is also common knowledge. In this "*equality case*" one should intuitively expect that the oversubscription rate approximately equals one. From the theoretical viewpoint, however, there is a continuum of "λ-equilibria": If all subjects subscribe the same fixed, but arbitrary number $\lambda \geq 100$ of shares, they realize an equilibrium. Interestingly, the empirical evidence shows a significant slow-down, but not a complete disappearance of oversubscription.

But the strongest disciplinary effect on aggregate oversubscription has the application of a random repartitioning scheme, or a combined repartitioning scheme with random elements, as Figure 14.5 below shows.

Fig. 14.4. Evolutions of subscription orders in a stock issuing experiment with a proportional repartitioning scheme and equality of the issued and the intrinsically demanded number of shares (2 groups e2 and f2)

$$\text{observed variable} = \frac{\text{subscribed shares} - \text{offered shares}}{\text{subscribed shares}}$$

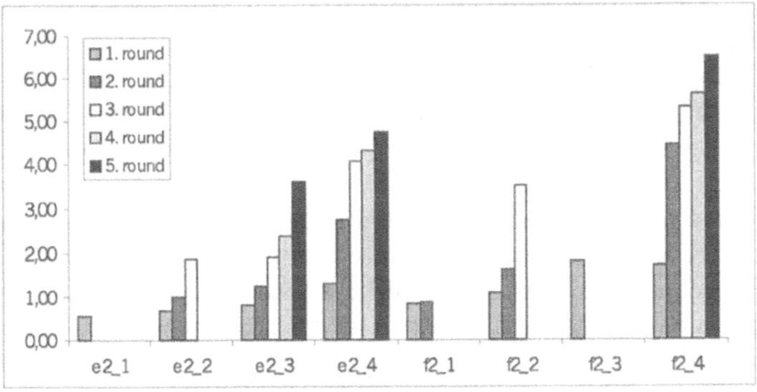

Fig. 14.5. Evolutions of subscription orders in a stock issuing experiment with a random repartitioning scheme (4 groups c2, d2, g1, h1)

$$\text{observed variable} = \frac{\text{subscribed shares} - \text{offered shares}}{\text{subscribed shares}}$$

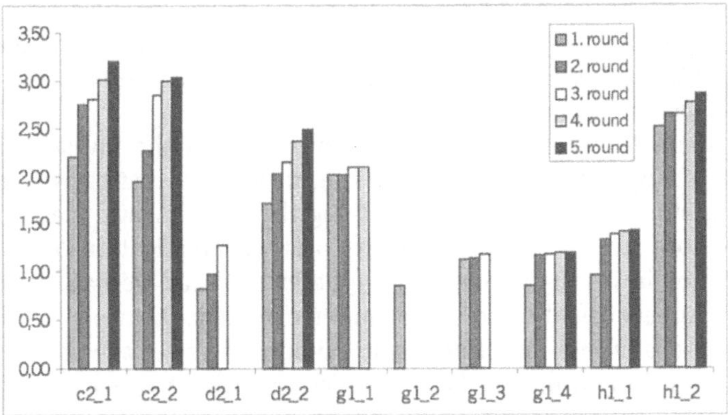

14.6 Summary and Concluding Remarks

It has been the aim of our contribution to show the importance and ubiquity of the phenomenon of high order strategic thinking in economics. For the first time this had systematically been analyzed by O. Morgenstern in the early 20th century and had later been called a beauty contest by J. M. Keynes. In Section 14.4 we have examined high order strategic thinking from the viewpoint of evolutionary biology. It turned out that the ability to form expectations and guesses of higher order about the expectations and guesses of other subjects, called "theory of mind" by R. Dunbar, is not an exclusive achievement of homo sapiens sapiens. Apparently, it is also part of the behavioural repertory of primates, and possibly also of other ape species. The evolutionary advantage of having a "theory of mind", moreover, is obvious from the fact that the ability to manipulate and to cheat creates a valuable degree of freedom for an individual interacting with other subjects.

In the economic context high order strategic thinking unequivocally is pervasive since any decision in a strategic situation with at least two subjects involved naturally requires from rational subjects to form expectations about the expectations of the other side, and to iterate this consideration further and further. We revisited O. Morgenstern's argument (the so-called Morgenstern paradox) that strategic thinking inevitably ends up in an unsolvable dilemma for the subjects involved. Looking more closely, however, we saw that Morgenstern's conclusion in no way is compelling. For instance, there can be a theoretical solution like in the Nagel/Selten number choosing game to which the observed iteration process of re-adapted guesses might converge. Another possibility is given by a pragmatic solution where subjects take into account the other subjects' bounded rationality and, thus, get to a "pragmatic" solution as in the case of the Morgenstern paradox, or in the Selten/Nagel experiment.

The main focus of our paper, however, lies on the investigation of an example of high order strategic thinking in a stock issuing which we have called the subscriber's dilemma. Applying the experimental method we, first and foremost, are interested in an explorative investigation of decision behaviour, not in testing theoretical hypotheses. What we have found out in our experiments corroborates the common experience that people do perform iterative steps of high order strategic thinking if they have the opportunity to do so, but only a few. In fact, in a design without transaction costs subjects increased their aggregate successive orders exponentially in successice rounds. Only when subscription became costly, or got risky by a random repartitioning scheme, orders were reduced by the subscribers.

References

[1] Dunbar, R. (1996). *Groming, Gossip, and the Evolution of Language.* London: Faber and Faber.

[2] Grunberg, E. and F. Modigliani (1954). The Predictability of Social Events. *Journal of Politcal Economy 62*, 465–478.

[3] Grunberg, E. and F. Modigliani (1963). Economic Forecasting when the Subject of the Forecast is Influenced by the Forecast: Comment. *American Economic Review 53*, 734-737.

[4] Lehmann-Waffenschmidt, M. (1985). Prognostizieren mit Rckwirkungen. In: *Aspekte bankwirtschaftlicher Forschung und Praxis*, Hrsg. Pallaschke, D. and H. Guthard, Frankfurt: Knapp. S. 69–83.

[5] Lehmann-Waffenschmidt, M. (1990). Predictability of Economic Processes and the Morgenstern Paradox. *Schweizerische Zeitschrift für Volkswirtschaft und Statistik 2*, 147–161.

[6] Morgenstern, O. (1928). *Wirtschaftsprognose. Eine Untersuchung ihrer Voraussetzungen und Möglichkeiten.* Springer Verlag.

[7] Morgenstern, O. (1935). Vollkommene Voraussicht und wirtschaftliches Gleichgewicht. *Zeitschrift für Nationalökonomie 6*, 337–357.

[8] Nagel, R. (1995). Unraveling in Guessing Games: An Experimental Study. *The American Economic Review 85*(5), 1313–1326.

[9] Nagel, R. (1999). A Survey on Experimental Guessing Games: A Study of Bounded Rationality and Learning. In: *Games and human behaviour*, ed. by D. V. Budescu, I. Erev, R. Zwick; London, Lawrence Erlbaum.

[10] Nagel, R.; Selten, R. (1998). Das Zahlenwahlspiel – Ergebnisse und Hintergrund. *Spektrum der Wissenschaft*, 16–22.

[11] Nagel, R., A. Bosch-Domènech and A. Satorra (1999). *One, Two, (Three), Infinity: Iterated Reasoning in Newspaper Beauty-Contest Experiments.* Universität Pompeu Fabra, Barcelona.

[12] Rothschild, K. W. (1969). *Wirtschaftsprognose, Methoden und Probleme.* Springer Verlag.

[13] Stahl II, D. O. and P. W. Wilson (1994). Experimental Evidence on Players' Models of Other Players. *Journal of Economic Behaviour and Organization 25*, 309–327.

[14] Tietzel, M. (1981). Über die Unmöglichkeit von Wirtschaftsprognosen. *List Forum 11*, 31–44, 194–197.

[15] Tietzel, M. (1985). *Wirtschaftstheorie und Unwissen.* Mohr Verlag.

15 Imitation in a Two–Level Hexapoly

Axel Ostmann, Reinhard Selten, and Reinhard Tietz *

15.1 Introduction

Horst Todt has described in "Pragmatic Decisions on an Experimental Market" 1972[1] and in "Anbieterverhalten bei komplexen Marktstrukturen" 1975[2] an experimental tourist market with two vacation resorts each having three hotels. Each hotel chooses its category in terms of individual quality, its bed capacity, price, and advertising. Each resort also has a neighbourhood standard affected by the total of its three hotels' contributions to "face-lifting" activities. The contribution rules determining this total investment are set by majority vote. Thus two levels of competition are mixed, the individual level and the group level. Both competitive and co-operative relations may be taken into account. The experimental results of Todt indicate that the most prevalent behaviour, apart from capacity-oriented activity, is imitation of the most similar competitor. Todt argues that such imitative behaviour can be thought as governed by what he calls principles of pragmatic decisions. The aim of our paper is to investigate these principles by simulating their impact and to develop out of their core a behavioural theory of imitation and experimentation in the general context of oligopolies.

First Todt's hexapoly is presented, section 15.2, and the principles of pragmatic decision introduced, section 15.3. In section 15.4 a pragmatic decision model is developed with decision rules whose effects can be simulated. Section 15.5 then identifies and defines a most similar competitor. Using this definition of which other actors are most similar we present some simulation results in section 15.6. After a short note on necessary and relevant deviations from the setup discussed so far, section 15.7, we develop a general theory of imitation and experimentation, section 15.8.

---

* We are greatly indepted to Robin Pope who spent much time on looking at the paper and who made many valuable suggestions for improvement.

[1] Horst Todt (1972). Pragmatic Decisions on an Experimental Market. In Heinz Sauermann (ed.): Contributions to Experimental Economics. Vol. 3. pp. 608-634. Tübingen: Mohr.

[2] Horst Todt (1975). Anbieterverhalten bei komplexen Marktstrukturen. In Otwin Becker & Rudolf Richter (eds.): Dynamische Wirtschaftstheorie. Theorie - Experiment - Entscheidung. Heinz Sauermann zum 70. Geburtstag. pp. 232-246. Tübingen: Mohr.

15.2 Todt's Model

The two-level hexapoly is modelled by Todt as dynamic game[3] with discrete time structure. The players of this game are the 6 hotels represented by the numbers 1 to 6. Let $G = \{1, 2, 3\}$ and $H = \{4, 5, 6\}$. G and H represent the two resorts with three hotels each. The state of a resort is conceptualised as infrastructure capital z_G respectively z_H. The state $x(i)$ of the hotel i is the triple of its account $a(i)$, of its capacity $b(i)$ and its category $c(i)$. Whereas capacity is measured in non-negative numbers, category is a binary variable representing a lower category $c = 1$ and an upper standard $c = 0$.

In each period there is a binding cash constraint on each hotel. All outlays, including investments, for making changes $D(i)$ have to be paid for now. There are no loans. In each period changes $D(i)$ in state $x(i)$ will be realised only one period later. Thus each hotel decides now on: its proposal for the running period's group level investment tax rate t which will determine its resorts' infrastructure next period; on its own price for the running period $p(i)$, on its own advertising investment for the running period $q(i)$, its own capacity investment which will determine $b'(i)$, how many beds it will have next period; and on its own category investment which will determine $c'(i)$, its own quality next period. The individual hotel's set of decision in each period can be represented by the following vector[4].

$$y(i) = \big(t(i), p(i), q(i), b'(i), c'(i)\big) \tag{15.1}$$

Correspondingly the set of decisions by the six hotels can be represented by a matrix with rows y(i).

The payoff in a period for an individual hotel i, $u(i)$, i.e. its profit in that period, is determined by its number of visitors $V(i)$, the group face-lifting decision T, and its cost function B_3.

$$u(i) = V(i)\big(p(i) - T\big) - B_0\big(D(i)\big) - B_1\big(V(i), c(i)\big) - B_2\big(b(i), c(i)\big) - B_3\big(q(i)\big) \tag{15.2}$$

The group decision T can be set as the median[5] value of t within the resort R hotel i belongs to. The vector of the numbers of visitors V is a function of

[3] A complete specification and an extense analysis and discussion is found in Todt's habilitation thesis (Todt 1970, pp. 17-110).

[4] All components of the vector are non-negative.

[5] Todt's original version slightly differs in this respect. He assumes that voting power is proportional to a hotel's capacity. This has some consequences with respect to the existence of exceptional equilibria, i.e. such equilibria in which a single player holds the majority of votes. We restrict our attention to the normal situations where the median voter determines the infrastructure investment. A discussion why these exceptional situations are of the minor importance and of some alternative rules of determining the group policy can be found in Todt's habilitation thesis (Todt 1970, pp. 111-118).

the pair z of states of the two resorts, of the states of each of the all hotels, and of all six hotels' decisions on prices and advertising activities. Within the limits of admissible values (non-negativity and not exceeding capacity and the cash flow constraint), this function can be written as product of a vector A representing the attraction potential of the hotels and a matrix K representing the industry's current competitive structure with respect to location and category competition:

$$V = AK \tag{15.3}$$

The attraction vector $A = \big((A(1), ..., A(6)\big)$ is determined by

$$A(i) = \max\{0, F_1(z_R) + F_2(q(i)) + F_3(p(i), c(i))\} \tag{15.4}$$

Thus the individual attraction potential $A(i)$ is non-negative and depends on the state z_R of the resort R to which hotel i belongs (discussed below), on the category of the hotel, and on its own decisions on advertising and price. The attraction potential shows the usual monotonicity and convexity properties.[6]

The elements $k(i,j)$ of matrix K represent the influence of the hotels i and j on each other's potential visitors. We set $k(i,i) = 1$. For $i \neq j$ the influence is negative and it can be assumed that $k(i,j)$ only depends on whether the two hotels are in the same resort and on whether they are of the same category. The absolute value of $k(i,j)$ can also be interpreted as strength of competition. Where two hotels of the same category are located in the same resort, the value of $k(i,j)$ is set at its minimum value, at -0.2. Where hotels either belong to different resorts or to different categories the value of $k(i,j)$ is set higher, at -0.1. Where there is minimal competition, all the other cases, the value of $k(i,j$ is set at -0.05.

Having derived the number of visitors, let us examine the cost functions B_j in (15.2). The cost B_0 of a state change is 5 times the capacity if the category is changed plus 5 times the extent of the capacity change (no change - zero cost). Note that for simplicity in this model it is assumed that the costs for downgrading are the same as for upgrading. The category specific variable (visitor-dependent) cost part is set as

$$B_1\big(V(i), c(i)\big) = V(i)\big(12 - 4c(i)\big) \tag{15.5}$$

Correspondingly the category specific fixed cost part is defined as

$$B_2\big(b(i), c(i)\big) = b(i)\big(13 - 6c(i)\big) \tag{15.6}$$

The cost of advertising B_3 is assumed to be simply the money spent for: $B_3\big(q(i)\big) = q(i)$.

[6] The functions F_j are chosen as $F_1(z_R) = 60 + 2z_R^{0.5}$, $F_2\big(a(i)\big) = \big(12 + 2a(i)\big)^{0.5}$, and $F_3\big(p(i), c(i)\big) = -0.5\big(c(i) + 3\big)p(i)$.

The transition function updates the states of the hotels (account, capacity, category) and state of the resorts. The state of a resort is conceptualised as a capital good resulting in the following transition equation:

$$z_R(t+1) = 0.9 z_R(t) + 0.1 T \sum_{i \in R} V(i) \qquad , R \in \{G, H\} \tag{15.7}$$

Note that for this scaling of the capital and the investment we get a steady state $\underline{z}_R$ for

$$\underline{z}_R = T \sum_{i \in R} V(i) \tag{15.8}$$

In his analysis Todt derives solutions under some additional assumptions. The derived partial solutions refer to a fixed category vector or - as we have called it - a fixed competitive structure. He shows that one-period Nash-equilibria of each of the corresponding games can be characterised by a unique pair of values L_R [7]

$$L_R = T^{-1} \sum_{i \in R} V(i) \qquad , R \in \{G, H\} \tag{15.9}$$

Using the additional requirement of "stationarity" (15.8) we get a unique solution[8] for every competitive structure.

For example (rounded up to integers), in the case of a uniform structure in which there are only lower standard hotels, the (stationary partial) equilibrium $(t(i), p(i), q(i), b'(i)) = (28, 45, 2, 8)$, resulting in individual profits of 9 and in an infrastructure of 684.

In a second step Todt derives a global solution by preference comparison of the partial solutions. It turns out that there is a unique optimal partial solution referring to the competitive structure with two hotels of the upper standard in one resort and two hotels of the lower standard in the other one. The respective equilibrium (rounded up to integers) is represented by the matrix Y_{opt} (cf. table 15.1, note that the last column represents the fixed structure).

The corresponding profit vector is given by (1214,1214,555,603,603,1666), the values for the infrastructure are $z_G = 7336$ and $z_H = 7864$. In comparison to the above mentioned equilibrium of the uniform lower category structure taxes, prices, advertising, payoffs and infrastructure show significantly larger values.

---

[7] In his habiltation thesis Todt (pp. 62ff) examines the equivalent values $\left(\sum_{i \in R} V(i)\right) \left(T \sum_{i \in R} V(i)\right)^{-0.5}$

[8] In most cases these solutions are interiour and admissible solutions. By admissible we mean that profits are non-negative.

Table 15.1. Y_{opt}

49	108	675	55	0
49	108	675	55	0
49	83	186	39	1
49	82	253	46	1
49	82	253	46	1
49	113	1103	71	0

Up to symmetry[9] there are 10 different possible competitive structures. The competitive structure is called locally uniform if at least at one resort all hotels are of the same category. Let us denote the locally uniform structure with r hotels of upper category by $U(r)$ $(r = 0, 1, 2, ..., 6)$. Note that $U(0)$ and $U(6)$ are globally uniform, i.e. all hotels are of the same category. The other three (not locally uniform) structures either have an overall majority of hotels of the upper or of the lower category or have three hotels of either category. We refer to these cases as "upper majority" UM, "lower majority" LM, and "equal numbers" EN respectively. The optimal solution Y_{opt} refers to the structure EN.

15.3 Pragmatic Decisions

Horst Todt introduced the concept of a pragmatic decision to characterise the typical boundedly rational decision behaviour observed in an experiment referring to above analysed hexapoly. This particular experiment consisted in 10 trials with a duration of about 9 hours each. Each hotel was managed by a group of two or three subjects. The exact procedure is described in Todt 1972 and 1975.

At the beginning all hotels were of lower category ($c = 1$) and had a capacity of $b = 12$ units (this means 60 beds times 200 nights; i.e. the unit is a thousand stays overnight; period length is a touristic season or calculatory year). Infrastructure is hidden information; the corresponding initial capital stock is 144 for every resort. There is a preliminary period 0 in which the subjects observe the uniform decisions $y(i) = (4, 25, 12, 12, 1)$ for all hotels. Let us denote the 6×5-matrix in which all rows are (4,25,12,12,1) by Y_{zero}. This policy is stationary but far from the (above mentioned partial) equilibrium. The corresponding payoff of 60 per hotel is significantly above the equilibrium payoff of 9. These 60 units of money constitute each hotel's initial account.

[9] Up to symmetry means that structures which show the same pair of numbers counting the upper category hotels in each resort are essentially the same. So e.g. the structure (0,1,0,1,1,0) and the structure (0,1,1,0,0,1) can be considered as equivalent.

In the following 20 periods the subjects have to make their decisions in the following way:

- firstly, every hotel independently decides on whether (and how) to change states;
- in a second stage the local infrastructure investment is determined in a face-to-face negotiation between the members of the resort;
- finally, the hotels independently chose their price and their advertising policy.

The initial account is exactly the cost of changing the category in the first period.

Todt derives two versions of pragmatic behaviour. In the first version he assumes that a pragmatic decision is governed by two principles of pragmatic decision called the principle of neighbourhood imitation and the principle of decisive impact. In a second version he adds the priority of consolidation. A pragmatic decision is one that conforms to the two respectively to the three principles. The experimental results show 41% (version 1) respectively 47% (version 2) of the decisions conforming to the two respectively to the three principles where these are applicable.[10]

The two principles and the additional third one are (cf. Todt 1972, p.629):

"The principle of neighbourhood": Consider the decisions and success only of actors whose situation is nearest to yours (such actors are called your neighbours). If there are neighbours showing higher success than you, then imitate the most successful. Your neighbours are the hotels of the your category in your resort if there are any; if there are none and if there are others of the same category in the other resort then they are your neighbours. If you are the only one of your category in both resorts then the other hotels of your resort are your neighbours.

"The principle of ordering imitation instruments": Rank your available instruments by their decisiveness. Change of category is considered as the most far-reaching decision. Next to that changing bed capacity can be judged as having a more decisive impact than price changes, and the price changes as having a more decisive impact than advertising investment. Identify the instrument with the lowest impact that you have set differently from your most successful neighbour, and change its setting toward that of this neighbour.[11]

---

[10] In order to avoid biases due to some end effect behaviour Todt only refers to data from period 1 to period 19.

[11] Changes in category are rare events. On average in a trial between three and four changes were observed (Todt 1970, pp. 135-139). In contrast price changes and changes in advertising occured about 60 times on average, capacity changes about 33 times (Todt 1972, p. 624). Expansions of capacity that show no success are rarely revised.

"The priority of consolidation": If the bed occupancy rate is below 90% of capacity you should not apply the first two principles. Instead try to consolidate first by reducing the price or by increasing advertising investment.

The three principles can be seen as defining a family of imitation rules that restrict imitation in two ways. First, only a few candidates for the model have to be evaluated and second, in times of crisis the attention focuses only on oneself. From theoretical grounds it can be argued that imitation alone tends to worsen the outcomes (see below). Since the three principles reduce the information used significantly as compared to other global imitation rules we should expect rather bad results. Calling the respective decision behaviour pragmatic Todt suggests that this is not true. In his articles there is no proof of this conjecture. The experimental results do not straightforwardly support his conjecture. There are 9 out of the 60 experimental hotels which go bankrupt. Bankruptcy occurs in 7 of the 10 trials of the experiment. Since of the decisions only 41% (respectively. 47%) are pragmatic in the sense of following the two respectively the three principles where applicable, one may think that cases of bankruptcy are due to not behaving pragmatically. But it is also true that some mismanagement is compatible with the principles. Take for example a hotel of lower category at the first resort that copies the higher price of its model at the second resort in a situation where the infrastructure at the first resort is rather bad compared with that in the second one. Such a behaviour may be pragmatic in the sense defined but it also can result in heavy losses for the imitator.

15.4 Specification of Decision Rules

Horst Todt's three principles do not specify a specific decision in a given situation but only exclude some possible decisions in some situations. Let us define an agent to be a set of rules that generate in every situation a unique decision. According to this definition the principles of pragmatic decision are compatible with a large family of agents. The aim of the following considerations about designing rules and then running some simulations is to answer the question if it is possible to define a small set of rules in the spirit of Todt's pragmatic decision making that are simple[12] yet successful enough to serve as a guide for a low-cost boundedly rational behaviour in two-level oligopolies. This test is something like a consistency test since all hotels are run by the same set of rules and we do not test how these agents behave in presence of

[12] Since in the experiment, no rules for evaluating past decisions and revising decisions were detected, we restrict our attention to a set of rules that are "simple" in the sense that they are forward looking without an evaluation of the past.

alternative rules of decision making. In particular, our pragmatic agents meet no aggressive competitors, that for example, try to ruin their opponents[13].

Reconsidering the three principles of pragmatic decision and the initial conditions for the experiment (Y_{zero} and the infrastructure), we note that beyond the principles something has to be assumed about changes in the (category) structure and in the tax rate voted for. Whereas changes in category have to be performed if the "presumably more attractive" (and indeed more profitable) non-uniform structure is to be reached, no change in the tax rate is needed for success as long as the other resort keeps to the initial tax rate. Thus our agent model includes no rule for changing the tax rate, but it specifies a simple subagent for handling category change. The rules of the subagent approximate Todt's findings in this regard.

The agent's architecture is given in figure 15.1. The agent can carry out seven possible actions that are given at the seven endpoints of the flow chart. All intermediate elements are binary branches defined by a question that can be answered by yes (1 at the arrow) or no (0 at the arrow)

The central element is whether the consolidation priority has to be acted upon, whether bed occupancy is "above 90% capacity?". This divides the graph into an upper and a lower part. The upper part concerns the rules for changing the category. The lower part concerns Todt's three pragmatic principles.

Rules for Changing the Category

The main goal of category change is to reduce competition (cp. Todt, p. 626). Not all hotels at one resort should be in the same category. On the other hand it may seem risky to change category because the fixed costs, even in the case of a downgrade in category, are substantial. Moreover in the experiment it was risky to be the first to change category because the function was not known. Thus how the market will develop for the new, the upper category was not foreseeable for the subjects.

Rule 1.1 Pioneering (refers to category change type 1). We assume that such adventurous innovation with such unknown consequences occurs only if the hotel is prospering, reducing the chance of bankruptcy if the risky choice proves afterwards bad. A hotel is defined as "prospering" if its account is larger than 150% of the cost of the change. Since other criteria are lacking, the change is modelled as a chance move (in our simulation runs we assume a probability of 1/2 for a change).

Rule 1.2 Category imitation (refers to category change type 2). Once hotels of both categories are present the risk of changing category may seem smaller

[13] Todt reports that in the experiments such aggressive behaviour or coalition forming in order to ruin some opponent were not observed.

Fig. 15.1. The agent shown as flow chart

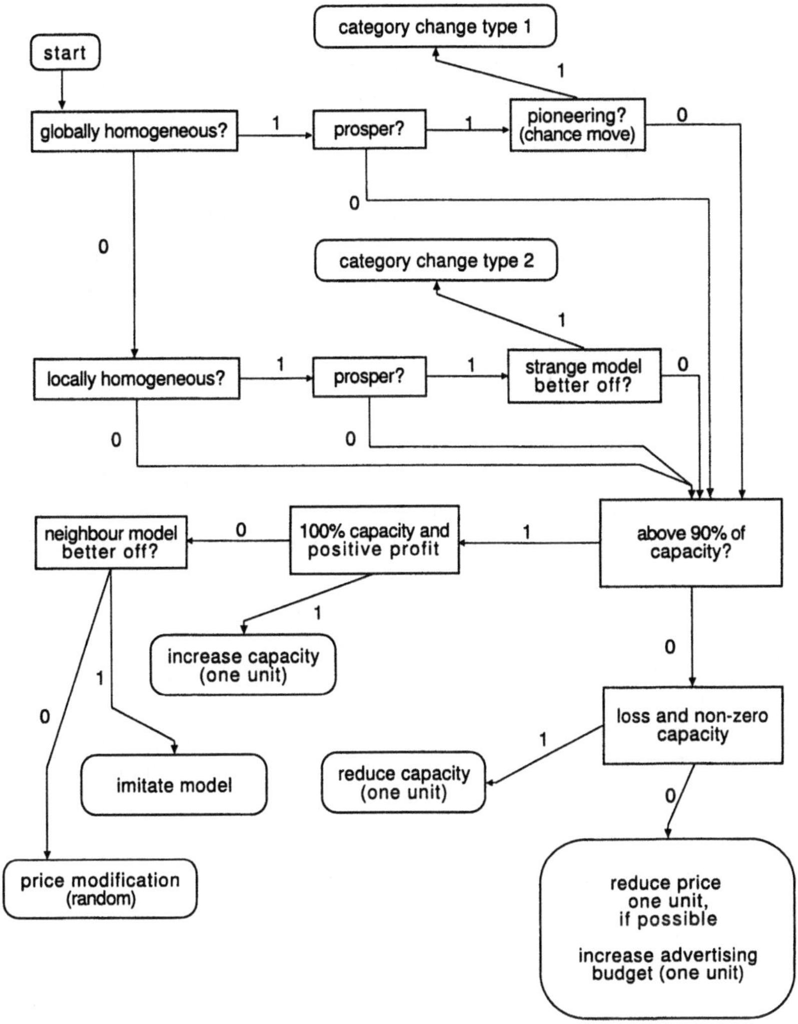

since the success of both categories can be observed and evaluated. In such a situation hotels in a homogeneous resort may be motivated to change category if they observe the success of the strange category at the other resort. We assume that a hotel in the homogeneous resort which is prospering changes the category if there is a hotel of that category at the other resort showing a larger profit than the respective hotel itself.

Consequences of the Rules of Category Change

The most important decision happens in the third period of play. This is the (first[14]) time pioneers may appear (in period 0, agents observe the preset actions, in period 1 the prosperity condition prevents category change, the category change action of period 2 only take effect in the third period). According to the category imitation rule in the five locally but not globally uniform cases $U(r)$, $r = 1, 2, ..., 5$ and after the (last) pioneering a category imitation can take place. In the two globally uniform cases $U(0)$ and $U(6)$ the pioneering rule stays active. With respect of the rules of category change, the seven uniform structures can be called transitory. In the three cases of a structure without local homogeneity (UM, LM, and EN as defined in the last paragraph of the preceding section) the rules for category change become inactive. In Todt's experiment 10 of the reported 34 category changes took place in period 3 (it is the mode and the median) and there were no changes after period 12 (Todt 1972, p.618).

For an individual pioneering probability $p = 0.5$ the probability to get a stable[15] structure is $36/64 = 0.5625$ in period three. For both smaller and larger pioneering probabilities the probability for stable structures decreases[16]. It is rather improbable that no pioneer will appear up to period five[17].

The change from a (not globally uniform) transitory structure to a stable structure needs not happen. In cases of uniform upper standard resorts $U(3)$ and $U(6)$, it is in most cases too expensive for upper standard hotels to change back. In general the financing restriction is the nearly exclusive reason for the fact that the structure remains transitory. In case that a stable structure cannot be attained within a few periods the account of some hotels become negative what refers to the ruin of the respective hotels.

Rules for Adapting the Capacity

The elements "above 90% of capacity" and "100% capacity and positive profit" serve to represent the crucial distinction inherent in Todt's pragmatic principles between times in which there is an opportunity to expand, times of normality, and times of crisis. Whereas in times of full capacity the opportunity to expand is taken, in times of crises, capacity is reduced. The latter rule should help to prevent ruin. But the property of the rules to lead

[14] In the case of uniform decisions on category in the next period the pioneering rule applies a further time.

[15] With respect to the set of rules.

[16] For $p = 1/n$ we get a probability for stable structures of $3(n-1)^2n^{-4}$; for $n = 2, 3, 4, \ldots$ we get 0.56, 0.44, 0.32, 0.23, 0.17, 0.13, 0.11, 0.09, ...

[17] For $p = 1/n$ we get a probability for a globally homogeneous structure after 3 trials of 0.00003, 0.0007, 0.0057, 0.018, 0.038, 0.062, 0.090, 0.120, ... ($n = 2, 3, 4, \ldots$).

the hotel back into normal times is not a guarantee against ruin. In normal times the other two instruments, price and advertising, are used to enhance success.

Rule 2.1 Capacity expansion. If attracted visitors exhaust the capacity and profit is positive, the capacity is expanded by one unit (here: =2, this represents 10 beds).

Rule 2.2 Capacity reduction. If attracted visitors are below 90% of capacity ("crisis") and profit is negative, capacity is reduced by one unit.

Rules for Pricing and Advertising

Rule 3.1 Adaptation to category. This rule refers to the change of category (both endpoints). The set price under the new category is not less than the former price plus the cost added of 10 if the new state is the upper category and minus the cost saved if the new state is the lower category. If possible the price of the model to follow is set.

Rule 3.2 Critical state pricing. In times of crises and under the condition of positive profit the advertising budget is increased by one unit and the price is reduced by one unit.

The above two rules to adapt after a category change or in times of crisis (if possible) are needed to exclude some bad mismanagement.

The **core of the pricing and advertising rules** refers to the first two principles and is specified by the following imitation rule:

Rule 3.3 Imitation. In normal times so-called neighbours are tested if they gain more profit. The best neighbour's success is interpreted as due to its price and advertising policy. Thus the own policy adapts in direction of the model's corrected price and advertising budget. The corrected price is calculated as price minus the model's tax rate plus the own tax rate. We assume that the own decision is the midpoint between the model's corrected price and the former own price and the midpoint between the respective advertising budgets.

The imitation rule deviates from other usual imitation rules in a very important way: not each opponent can serve as model but only a few. The learning is a say local one dependent on the neighbourhood structure. Before we define and characterise the neighbourhood structure, or as we will call it the "imitation structure", let us add the last one of the agent's rules. It refers to the normal-times management and the case that no more successful neighbour can be found.

Rule 3.4 Price experimentation. If in case of normal times no more successful neighbour can be found price experimentation takes place (cp. Todt 1972, p. 625). This means that it is determined by random if the price is increased, is hold constant, or is lowered by one unit. In our standard version we assume equal probabilities for these events. In the price increase version the probability of a lower price is zero and the both other events are equal in probability. There is also the null version that excludes price experimentation by holding the price constant. Note that for price experimentation there is no direct evaluation of the experiment and by lack of memory a revision can only take place if neighbours become more successful.

15.5 The Imitation Structure

As described in the section before imitation only refers to "neighbours". Neighbours of an actor are only such competitors that are in the most comparable market position (Todt 1972, p. 626). With respect to our specific setup Todt defines a corresponding **degree of kinship** for two hotels by counting the doubled difference in category plus the difference in place. Differences in category are assumed as making the market position less comparable than differences in place. The **reference group** $I(i)$ of a hotel i is defined as the set of hotels j that are the most akin to i.

For example the category vector $c = (1,0,1,0,1,0)$ (this is a representation of the structure EN) gives rise to the (symmetric) matrix of kinship degree – cf. table 15.2

Table 15.2. Matrix of kinship degree

1	3	1	4	2	4
3	1	3	2	4	2
1	3	1	4	2	4
4	2	4	1	3	1
2	4	2	3	1	3
4	2	4	1	3	1

We now restrict the reference to the most akin hotels and define the incidence matrix $Z = (z_{ij})$ by setting $z_{ij} = 1$ if and only if $j \in I(i)$. We get the incidence matrix representing the imitation structure (cf. table 15.3).

Note that this imitation structure is not symmetric: 4 is "neighbour" of 2, but 2 is not "neighbour" of 4. In consequence this means that the hotel being single at one place may imitate hotels of the other place, but never will be imitated by other hotels.

Note that also for larger setups such reference groups partition the set of actor into distinct components within those learning can take place. These regions of influence may be driven from smaller sources of influence like in

Table 15.3. Incidence matrix

0	0	1	0	0	0
0	0	0	1	0	1
1	0	0	0	0	0
0	0	0	0	0	1
1	0	1	0	0	0
0	0	0	1	0	0

the structure above. Thus learning of good policies is restricted in two ways: first good policies from outside a component cannot be copied, second it may happen that some actors inside a component cannot be copied. In our example EN the sets $\{1,3,5\}$ and $\{2,4,6\}$ are the regions of influence but only the sets $\{1,3\}$ and $\{4;6\}$ are sources of learning.

In the case the imitation structure is symmetric a region and its source coincide. With the only exceptions of the three structures EN, $U(2)$, and $U(4)$ all other corresponding imitation structures are symmetric.

15.6 Some Simulation Results

By varying rule 3.4 we got three versions of the agent system simulating the behaviour in the hexapoly. In the following the three versions of the agent - standard, price increase, and null - are characterised by the corresponding set of new prices: $\{p-1, p, p+1\}$, $\{p, p+1\}$, and $\{p\}$ respectively (in the following we assume equal probability on each set). Remember that the capacity management of the agent leads the process to normal times. In such times the rules of imitation and experimentation take over. Whereas imitation alone implies convergence within the source sets of the imitation structure, the presence of experimentation generates some variation. Thus only for the version "null" we get converging paths of evolution. This is why we consider the results for this version as a baseline.

In all simulation runs we report on, the initial state of the hexapoly is the same as in Horst Todt's experiment. Since all decisions of the hotels conform to the principles of pragmatic decision we expect less ruins than observed in the experiment. Furthermore the relatively friendly values at the beginning should guarantee a moderate success with less variance than observed in the experiment.

The Version "Null" Without Price Experimentation

In case that the evolving structures are locally uniform it is clear that the corresponding hotels have suffered from ruin – imitation can only copy losses. In case of the appearance of the structures EN, LM, and UM in period 3 we get the following general characteristic of development:

- Up to symmetry (multiple models) the process is deterministic.
- Imitation only occurs if structure EN evolves. In such a case imitation takes place in period 16 and 17.
- After period 3 there is no more change in price (34 respectively 24) and advertising (13).
- There is no crisis. Thus there are no reductions in capacity.
- During the process infrastructure, profits, and capacities are increased.
- The process is expanding capacity much longer than the 20 periods of the experiment; only after 150-187 rounds the are no more changes of the figures for profits and infrastructures up to 3 digits behind the decimal point (capacity being a count variable shows no more changes).
- Imitation leads to equal profits (up to an arbitrary small number) for hotels of the same source of imitation structure. For the structures UM and LM profits are constant within category. For the structure EN the hotel being single at a resort with respect to category gains more than the corresponding hotels at the other place.

Table 15.4 and 15.5 give some global evaluations of the simulation runs.

Table 15.4. Capacity, total profit, and infrastructure in the long run

structure	capacity	total profit	infrastructure 1	infrastructure 2
EN	172	655.67	339.93	315.63
UM	164	585.93	309.19	309.19
LM	164	655.69	314.65	314.65

For EN infrastructure 1 refers to the resort LM with a majority of the hotels of lower category, correspondingly infrastructure 2 refers to the resort UM.

Table 15.5. Capacity, total profit, and infrastructure in the 20th period

structure	capacity	total profit	infrastructure 1	infrastructure 2
EN	154	637.37	262.48	251.17
UM	152	534.44	244.09	244.09
LM	152	597.57	250.13	250.13

For EN infrastructure 1 refers to the resort LM with a majority of the hotels of lower category, correspondingly infrastructure 2 refers to the resort UM.

The Versions "Standard" and "Price Increase"

The following results refer to runs with 20 periods. Compared to the baseline "null" capacity and infrastructure are larger under the "standard" condition, and in most cases profits are smaller. Under the condition "price increase" capacity and infrastructure are smaller if compared with the baseline, and in most cases profits are larger. Under both conditions we observe much imitation. An important observation is that we get less runs ending in a locally homogeneous structure and less runs with ruins as without price experimentation. In some runs the uniform structures $U(x)$ evolved in period 3 can be transformed into EN, UM, or LM. In a set of 20 runs for each condition we observed only 2 ("standard") respectively 3 ("price increase") runs ending in a uniform structure (the expected number of uniform structures evolved in period 3 is 8.75 out of 20). Under the condition "null" EN, UM, and LM evolved only in period 3.

It can be expected that the more probable a price increase is by experimentation the lower the investment in capacity and infrastructure will be. The respective relations are also found in table 15.6 comparing the different versions of the agent for the case that EN evolved.

Table 15.6. Capacity, total profit, and infrastructure by agent version; structure EN, period 20.

version	capacity	total profit	infrastructure 1	infrastructure 2
null	154	637.37	262.48	251.17
price increase	148	768.34	247.71	249.22
standard	158	529.05	272.96	248.72

Infrastructure 1 refers to the resort LM with a majority of the hotels of lower category, correspondingly infrastructure 2 refers to the resort UM.

15.7 Going Beyond the Given Setup

In the hexapoly of Horst Todt a focal feature of the setup is the **dynamic** of the infrastructure. Nevertheless the principles of pragmatic decision do not refer to the respective issues like the determination of an adjusted tax rate. The rules of our agents hold the tax rate constant. Due to the initial settings it is relatively easy to generate a path of expansion. With other initial settings this might be a problem. Since the focus of the principles of pragmatic decision is imitation and experimentation, an improved strategy for the development of a theory has to start with a simpler environment namely by substituting a repeated game environment for the dynamic game environment.

Neglecting the dynamic features of Horst Todt's hexapoly also means, that no changes in the competitive structure occur. Consequently in the following theoretical considerations the imitation structure is fixed. On the other side the imitation structure can be rather general; it may or may not be derived from specific circumstances, we take it as exogeneously given. If we neglect the infrastructure, category changes, and capacity changes in the hexapoly, the competition between the agents reduces to what has been called "normal times" in the previous sections - what remains is the focus on imitation and experimentation.

In the second principle and in the imitation rule 3.3 it was assumed that the previous action of a player should be corrected in direction of the action of the most successful neighbour. For a theoretical analysis it is much more advantageous to specify **imitation** as simply copying the action of the immitated player. One advantage is that finite sequences to stationary states can replace the slow convergence in other specifications of imitation principle – every act of copying tends to reduce the number of strategies involved.

Also with respect to the concept of **experimentation** some deviations from the original concept may improve the validity of the behavioural model. As noted before the former concept of experimentation lacks of some rules of evaluation. Usually an experiment can fail, and some consequences or revisions should take place. Similar as Schumpeter in his view of the interaction of imitation and innovation we assume that experimentation is the exceptional case and that it only takes place if no more change by imitation would occur.

15.8 The Imitation Model

This section presents a new concept of an "imitation equilibrium" and explores it in the context of simple oligopoly models. The concept is inspired by Horst Todt's experimental observations, but it does not claim to be an exact formalisation of his ideas. It is a theoretical approach to the kind of imitation behaviour he describes in the framework of simple standard oligopoly models.

In the following the class of oligopoly models will be described, to which the concept is applicable. Such an **imitation model**

$$M = (G, I, D)$$

has three constituents:

- An n-player **normal form game** $G = (S_1, \ldots, S_n, H)$ where S_i is player i's **strategy set** and H is the **payoff function** which assigns a payoff vector

  $$H(s) = \big(H_1(s), \ldots, H_n(s)\big)$$

  to every **strategy combination** $s = (s_1, \ldots, s_n)$ with $s_i \in S_i$ for $i = 1, \ldots, n$. The sets S_i are non-empty, but no special structure needs to be imposed on them. For $i = 1, \ldots, n$ the $H_i(s)$ are real numbers. $H_i(s)$ is called **player i's payoff** at s.
- An **imitation structure** I which assigns a subset $I(i)$ of the player set $N = \{1, \ldots, n\}$ to every $i \in N$ such that i does not belong to $I(i)$. The players $j \in I(i)$ are called **similar** to i and $I(i)$ is called player i's **reference group**.

- A **deviation restriction** $D = (D_1, \ldots, D_n)$, which for every player $i = 1, \ldots, n$ specifies a **deviation set function** D_i, which assigns a subset $D_i(s_i)$ with $s_i \notin D_i(s_i)$ to every $s_i \in S_i$. This set $D_i(s_i)$ is called i's **deviation set** at s_i.

Interpretation

The normal form G is interpreted as describing an ongoing oligopoly situation, repeated over discrete or continuous time. The strategies are combinations of action parameters and the payoffs are objective functions. We shall look at an example where the strategy sets are closed and convex subsets of Euclidean spaces, e.g. the set of all production quantities x_i, with $x_i \geq 0$, but the framework is kept more general than that. In our example the payoffs will be profits, but other kinds of objectives could be looked at.

Two players may have the same strategy set. Imitation of player j by player i means that player i changes its current strategy s_i and adopts player j's current strategy s_j. Obviously this requires that s_j is in S_i. Imitation of player j by player i is impossible unless their strategy sets overlap.

The imitation structure I must be thought of as exogeneously given. The players in the reference group of i are those whom he can observe and whom he thinks of being sufficiently similar to him to make it reasonable to imitate them if they are more successful than he is. It makes no sense to imitate somebody who is very dissimilar to oneself. This connection of imitation and similarity is an important aspect of Horst Todt's experimental results.

Another feature of Horst Todt's description of the behaviour of his subjects is what he calls "experimentation". A player i who has at least as high profits as every player j in i's reference group may experiment in the sense of deviating to a slightly different strategy. The deviation function D_i describes the set $D_i(s_i)$ of strategies which are suitable as such experimental deviations. In the case of a continuous strategy set, the deviation set $D_i(s_i)$ may be a small neighbourhood of s_i (without s_i itself), but we do not exclude the case $D_i(s_i) = S_i \setminus \{s_i\}$ for every $s_i \in S_i$ and for every $i = 1, \ldots, n$. We call this the case of unrestricted deviations.

Presumably experimentation tries out whether one's payoff can be improved. If the new strategy results in an payoff at least as high as the one obtained before experimentation, then the player will stay at the new strategy, but if it is lower the player will return to the old strategy. The idea of return to the old strategy after unsuccessful experimentation is not explicit in Horst Todt's work but it is natural to connect it with his notion of experimentation.

The interaction of imitation and experimentation raises a conceptual issue which needs to be addressed by a formal theory. What is quicker, imitation or the return from experimentation? We shall come back to this question later.

Some Auxiliary Definitions

All definitions will refer to a fixed but arbitrary imitation model $M = (G, I, D)$. We say that player j is a **success model** of player i at the strategy combination $s = (s_1, \ldots, s_n)$ if the following conditions (a) to (d) are satisfied:

(a) $j \in I(i)$
(b) $s_j \in S_i$
(c) $H_i(s) < H_j(s)$
(d) for no player k with $k \in I(i)$ we have $s_k \in S_i$ and $H_k(s) > H_j(s)$

The set of all success models of player i at s is denoted by $M_i(s)$. If $M_i(s) \neq \emptyset$ we also say that player i is induced to imitate the respective success models.

For two strategy combinations $s = (s_1, \ldots, s_n)$ and $u = (u_1, \ldots, u_n)$, we write $s \to u$ and say s is **linked to u by imitation** if the following conditions (i) and (ii) hold:

(i) $u_i = s_j$ for some $j \in M_i(s)$ if $M_i(s) \neq \emptyset$
(ii) $u_i = s_i$ if $M_i(s) = \emptyset$

It may happen that there are success models j and k – $j, k \in M_i(s)$ – showing different strategies $s_k \neq s_j$. Therefore more than one strategy combination can result from s by an imitation step.

We can distinguish strategy combinations according to if they can be linked to some other strategy combination by imitation. If for the strategy combination s the sets $M_i(s)$ are empty for all players, s is called an **imitation stop**. Other strategy combinations are called **imitation generators**. An imitation generator is not necessarily linked to an imitation stop. Therefore we introduce the notion of an "imitation chain", which describes a possible course of an imitation process starting with an imitation generator and successively linking strategy combinations by imitation if it is possible.

Formally an **imitation chain** is either a finite chain $s(1), \ldots, s(m)$ $(m > 1)$ or an infinite chain $s(1), s(2), \ldots$ for which $s(k) \to s(k+1)$ holds for all k; if the chain is finite $s(m)$ has to be an imitation stop. In the infinite case all members of the chain are imitation generators.

We say that an imitation generator s has **finite reach** if all imitation chains starting at s are finite. An imitation stop u is **reachable** from s if at least one imitation chain starting at s ends with u. The set of all imitation stops reachable from s is denoted by $R(s)$.

Interpretation and Informal Discussion

The "success model conditions" (a) to (d) express Horst Todt's principle of imitating the most successful among the closest relatives, if one's own success is lower. The imitation set is the set of i's closest relatives. Of course, the strategy to be imitated must be available to the imitator. This is expressed by (b). As required by (c) only closest relatives with higher payoffs can be imitated and (d) makes sure that one of the closest relatives with the highest payoffs is imitated in the case of an imitation opportunity.

It is assumed that imitation is a strong motivational force. At an imitation generator each player with an imitation opportunity immediately copies a strategy of one of the respective success models. This idea leads to the notion of linking by imitation. At the resulting strategy combination new opportunities may be available which lead to further links and so on. This is formalised by the notion of an imitation chain.

Experimentation is assumed to be a weaker motivational force. Imitation must rum its course before experimentation comes into play. This means that experimentation occurs at imitation stops only. It is a feature of Horst Todt's account of the behaviour of his subjects that only a player i may experiment who is at least as successful as the most successful ones in his reference group.

It is important how one thinks about the events after an experimental deviation. We take the point of view that imitation is strong and fast and runs its course after a deviation until an imitation stop is reached again. If the deviator is involved in this process and takes an imitation opportunity at some link of the evolving imitation chain, then the experiment is thereby obliterated, in the sense that the deviator draws no conclusions from his experiment. Of course, this is not more than a plausible behavioural assumption.

Now suppose that along the imitation chain the deviator never meets an imitation opportunity and that the imitation chain is finite. Then at the imitation stop reached at the end the success or failure of the experiment is evaluated by the deviator. If the deviator's payoff is now lower than immediately before the deviation, a return to the old strategy is indicated. Otherwise the deviator sticks to the new strategy.

In case of a return to the old strategy, again an imitation chain is started which may or may not lead back to the original imitation stop. The concept of "imitation stability" of an imitation stop s will require that s is finally reached again after every deviation within the deviation set $D_i(s_i)$ of any potential deviator, regardless of whether the experiment is obliterated or evaluated, and regardless of how imitation sequences are chosen in cases of non-uniqueness of continuation.

Admittedly the imitation stability concept sketched above is quite complex, but it seems to provide a natural picture of the interaction of imitation and experimentation. Of course, it cannot be more than a hypothesis to be examined by experimental research. It is an empirical question to what extend the concept is behaviourally relevant.

Further Auxiliary Definitions

Consider a strategy combination s. We say that an imitation stop u is **reachable** from s with **involvement of player** i, if there exists an imitation chain

$(s(1), \ldots, s(m))$, $s(1) = s$, $s(m) = u$, such that for some k, $0 < k < m$, the success model set $M_i(s(k))$ of player i is not empty. The set of all imitation stops reachable from s with involvement of player i is denoted by $R_i(s)$. The symbol $R_{-i}(s)$ will be used for the complement $R(s) \setminus R_i(S)$ with respect to the set $R(s)$ off all imitation stops reachable from s.

A player i is called a **potential deviator** from an imitation stop s, if

$$H_i(s) \geq H_j(s)$$

holds for every $j \in I(i)$ with $s_j \in S_i$. The set of potential deviators from s is denoted by $P(s)$.

Let $s = (s_1, \ldots, s_n)$ be an imitation stop and let u_i be a strategy of player i different from s_i. We shall use the notation $s \setminus u_i$ for the strategy combination which results from s by replacing s_i by u_i and changing nothing else.

Imitation Stability

An imitation stop $s = (s_1, \ldots, s_n)$ is **imitation stable** if for $i \in P(s)$ and $u_i \in D_i(s_i)$ the following conditions (1) to (4) are satisfied:

(1) $s \setminus u_i$ has finite reach (i.e. every imitation chain starting with $s \setminus u_i$ is finite)
(2) $R_i(s \setminus u_i) = \{s\}$ or $R_i(s \setminus u_i) = \emptyset$
(3) for every $v \in R_{-i}(s \setminus u_i)$ we have $H_i(v) < H_i(s)$
(4) for every $v \in R_{-i}(s \setminus u_i)$ the strategy combination $v \setminus s_i$ has finite reach and satisfies $R_i(v \setminus s_i) = \{s\}$.

Interpretation

The experimental deviation must be evaluated after finite time. Therefore condition (1) needs to be imposed. Condition (2) concerns the case in which player i's strategy s_i is changed to another one by taking an imitation opportunity. If this happens the experiment is discontinued and will not be evaluated at the new imitation stop. In this case stability requires that this new imitation stop is the old one, which means that nothing else can be reached with involvement of player i.

Condition (3) concerns the case that a new imitation stop v is reached without the involvement of the deviator and that there the deviator's payoff is lower than at the original imitation stop s. In this case the experiment speaks against the deviation u_i and the deviator returns to s_i. Thereby $v \setminus s_i$ becomes the point of departure of a new imitation sequence. Stability requires that the new imitation sequence reaches s.

If after the deviation u_i a new imitation stop v is reached without the involvement of i, then at v the deviator's strategy is u_i and not s_i which means v is different from s. If the deviator's payoff at v is at least as high as s then the deviator sticks to v and a return to s is excluded. Therefore stability requires that no such v can be reached without the involvement of the deviator.

The definition of imitation stability is based on a very specific picture of the interaction of imitation and experimentation in a process set in motion by an experimental deviation. It is important that in this process imitation is faster than evaluation, in the sense that the deviator does not evaluate success or failure before imitation has run its course. This seems to be appropriate for a theory which emphasises imitation rather than experimentation. However, other assumptions could be made, e.g. one could think of the evaluation immediately following a deviation before any imitative response takes place. In this way one obtains a very different theory.

Application to the Symmetric Linear Cournot Oligopoly

The symmetric Cournot oligopoly can be looked upon as n-person game with the oligopolists $i = 1, \ldots, n$ as players and profits as payoffs. We shall make use of the following symbols:

x_i	supply of oligopolist i
s	total supply
p	price
c	constant unit cost
K_i	costs of oligopolist i
H_i	profits of oligopolist i

The usual relations are assumed:

Quantities: $x_i \geq 0 \quad ,(i = 1, \ldots, n)$

$$s = x_1 + \cdots + x_n$$

Demand: $$p = \begin{cases} b - as & , \text{ for } s \leq b/a \\ 0 & , \text{ else} \end{cases}$$

– the constants a and b being positive

Costs: $K_i = cx_i \quad ,(i = 1, \ldots, n)$, where c is a positive constant

Profits: $H_i = (p - c)x_i \quad ,(i = 1, \ldots, n)$

For the following we assume that the profitability condition $b > c$ is fulfilled (otherwise profits are negative for all positive x).

Cournot Equilibrium In Cournot equilibrium quantities, prices and profits are as follows:

$$x_i = \frac{b-c}{a(n+1)}$$

$$p = c + \frac{b-c}{n+1}$$

$$H_i = \frac{(b-c)^2}{a(n+1)^2}$$

There is no need for a detailed derivation of these formulas since the theory of Cournot equilibrium is elementary. Due to the profitability condition the Cournot price is above unit costs and Cournot profits are positive.

The Imitation Model The Cournot model is a normal form game whose strategy sets are all equal to the set of non-negative numbers and whose payoffs are the profits H_i. Application of the imitation equilibrium concept requires the specification of an imitation structure I and a deviation restriction D. We shall look at the simple case that for $i = 1, \ldots, n$ the reference group $I(i)$ is the set of all players j with $j \neq i$ and that $D_i(x_i)$ fills the whole strategy set with the exception of x_i.

Imitation Equilibrium As we shall see the imitation model has a uniquely determined imitation equilibrium, namely

$$x_i = \frac{b-c}{an}$$

This equilibrium is connected to the price $p = c$ and to the profits $H_i = 0$ (for $i = 1, \ldots, n$).

We first show that this strategy combination $x = (x_1, \ldots, x_n)$ is an imitation equilibrium. Obviously it is an imitation stop and each player is a potential deviator. Assume that player i deviates to a quantity y_i. Consider the case $y_i > x_i$. In this case all players have a negative profit at $x \setminus y_i$ and player i has the lowest profit since her quantity is highest. A single imitation step involving i leads back to x. Now consider the case $y_i < x_i$. In this case all players have a positive profit at $x \setminus y_i$ and player i again has the lowest one since her quantity is lowest. Here, too, a single imitation step involving i leads back to x.

It remains to show that the model has no other imitation equilibria. In an imitation equilibrium all oligopolists must have the same profits. We distinguish here three possible cases concerning the relationship of the price p to the unit cost c:

1) $p > c$

2) $p < c$
3) $p = c$

In the cases 1) and 2) the profits of the oligopolists cannot be equal unless all of them have the same supply x_0. This is different in case 3) where it is sufficient that all supplies sum up to $(b-c)/a$.

Consider first case 1). Here the common supply x_0 satisfies the condition

$$p = b - anx_0 > c.$$

Suppose that one of the players, say player j, deviates to a supply x_+ with $x_+ > x_0$ and

$$b - anx_+ > c.$$

Obviously such an x_+ can be found. Immediately after the deviation player j has a greater profit than the others and all of them are induced to imitate him. This leads to a new imitation stop $(x_+, \ldots, x_+)$.

It may happen, that here player j's profit is at least as great as at $(x_0, \ldots, x_0)$. In this case player j is not induced to return to x_+. However this leads to a strategy combination where player j earns less than the others and therefore is induced to imitate them.

Thereby $(x_+, \ldots, x_+)$ is reached and the process ends there. We can conclude that no imitation stop with $p > c$ is imitation stable.

Now consider case 2). Here the common supply x_0 satisfies the condition

$$p = \max\{0, b - anx_0\} < c$$

Suppose that player j deviates to a supply x_- with $x_- < x_0$ and

$$0 < b - anx_- < c$$

Obviously such an x_- can be found. Immediately after the deviation player j has the highest profit (the lowest loss), since unit profits are negative and j supplies less than the others. Therefore all others imitate j and the imitation stop $(x_-, \ldots, x_-)$ is reached. There player j has a higher profit (a lower loss) than at $(x_0, \ldots, x_0)$. Consequently j has no reason to return to x_0. Therefore $(x_0, \ldots, x_0)$ is not imitation stable.

Now consider case 3). It is necessary to exclude the possibility that an imitation stop $(x_1, \ldots, x_n)$ with unequal quantities for at least two oligopolists is imitation stable. Consider an imitation stop of this kind. Let j be one of the players with the greatest supply in $(x_1, \ldots, x_n)$ and let k be one of the players with the smallest supply in $(x_1, \ldots, x_n)$. We have $x_k < x_j$. Suppose that j deviates to a quantity $x_{j+} > x_j$. After the deviation k has the highest profit (the lowest loss) and all players with greater supplies including j imitate him. Thereby a new imitation stop is reached at which the process ends. We can conclude that no imitation stop with $p = c$ and uneven supplies is imitation stable.

This completes the proof.

Comment

The unique imitation equilibrium of the symmetric linear Cournot oligopoly is nothing else than the competitive equilibrium at which price equals marginal costs. Imitation works like a competitive force which pushes profits down to zero. This is known in the literature on evolutionary process involving imitation.

With the imitation equilibrium concept we take a somewhat different approach. Instead at looking at a full-fledged dynamic process we investigate stability against imitation and experimentation. Of course, this also involves assumptions about an underlying dynamic process, but to some extent less detailed ones.

The analysis of symmetric linear Cournot oligopoly does not change if the model is modified by the presence of fixed costs, the same ones for every oligopolist. However in this case profits at the imitation equilibrium are negative. A situation with persistent losses may evoke other behavioural tendencies besides imitation and experimentation. The oligopolists may try hard to avoid losses by co-operation. It is doubtful whether the concept of imitation equilibrium will be behaviourally relevant under such conditions.

References

[1] Todt, H. (1970). Ein Markt mit komplexen Interessensstrukturen: Eine theoretische und experimentelle Untersuchung. Unpublished Habilitation Thesis. Frankfurt.

[2] Todt, H. (1972). Pragmatic Decisions on an Experimental Market. In Heinz Sauermann (ed.): *Contributions to Experimental Economics*. Vol. 3. pp. 608-634. Tübingen: Mohr.

[3] Todt, H. (1975). Anbieterverhalten bei Komplexen Marktstrukturen. In Otwin Becker & Rudolf Richter (eds.): *Dynamische Wirtschaftstheorie. Theorie - Experiment - Entscheidung. Heinz Sauermann zum 70. Geburtstag.* pp. 232-246. Tübingen: Mohr.

[4] Weibull, J. W. (1995). *Evolutionary Game Theory.*

List of Contributors

Friedel Bolle and
Alexander Kritikos
Lehrstuhl für
Volkswirtschaftstheorie, insb.
Mikroökonomie
Europa-Universität Viadrina
Große Scharrnstr. 59
D–15230 Frankfurt (Oder)
Germany

Johannes Bröcker
University of Technology
Faculty of
Traffic Sciences
Department of Business Management and
Economics
D–01062 Dresden
Germany

Walter Buhr and
Thomas Christiaans
FB 5 –
Wirtschaftswissenschaften
Volkswirtschaftslehre II
Universität – GH Siegen
D–57068 Siegen
Germany

Michael Carlberg
Universität der Bundeswehr
Hamburg
Institut für Theoretische Volkswirtschaftslehre
Postfach 700822
D–22008 Hamburg
Germany

John-ren Chen
Institut für Wirtschaftstheorie und
Wirtschaftspolitik
University of Innsbruck
Universitätsstr. 15
A–6020 Innsbruck
Austria

Werner Güth
Humboldt-University of Berlin
Department of Economics
Institute for Economic Theory III
Spandauer Str. 1
D–10178 Berlin
Germany

Manfred J. Holler
Institute of SocioEconomics
University of Hamburg
Von-Melle-Park 5
D–20146 Hamburg
Germany

Alexander Karmann and
Marco Lehmann–
Waffenschmidt
Managerial Economics
Fakultät Wirtschaftswissenschaften
Technische Universität Dresden
Mommsenstraße 13
D–01062 Dresden
Germany

Axel Ostmann, Reinhard Selten
and Reinhard Tietz
Universität Karlsruhe
FZU
D–76128 Karlsruhe
Germany

Karin Peschel
Christian–Albrechts–Universität
Institut für Regionalforschung
Olshausenstr. 40
D–24098
Kiel
Germany

Klaus Schöler
Universität Potsdam
Wirtschafts- und
Sozialwissenschaftliche Fakultät
Lehrstuhl für
Volkswirtschaftslehre,
insbesondere
Wirtschaftstheorie
Postfach 900327
D–14439 Potsdam
Germany

Jochen Schumann
Westfälische Wilhelms-Universität
Lehrstuhl für Volkswirtschaftslehre
Universitätsstraße 14–16
D–48143 Münster
Germany

Arnis Vilks
Handelshochschule Leipzig
Jahnallee 59
D–04109 Leipzig
Germany

Hans Wiesmeth
Technische Universität Dresden
Fakultät Wirtschaftswissenschaften
Mommsenstraße 13
D–01062 Dresden
Germany

Contributions to Economics

Giuseppe Gaburro (Ed.)
Ethics and Economics
1997. ISBN 3-7908-0986-1

Frank Hoster/Heinz Welsch/
Christoph Böhringer
CO_2 Abatement and Economic Structural Change in the European Internal Market
1997. ISBN 3-7908-1020-7

Christian M. Hafner
Nonlinear Time Series Analysis with Applications to Foreign Exchange Rate Volatility
1997. ISBN 3-7908-1041-X

Sardar M.N. Islam
Mathematical Economics of Multi-Level Optimisation
1998. ISBN 3-7908-1050-9

Sven-Morten Mentzel
Real Exchange Rate Movements
1998. ISBN 3-7908-1081-9

Lei Delsen/Eelke de Jong (Eds.)
The German and Dutch Economies
1998. ISBN 3-7908-1064-9

Mark Weder
Business Cycle Models with Indeterminacy
1998. ISBN 3-7908-1078-9

Tor Rødseth (Ed.)
Models for Multispecies Management
1998. ISBN 3-7908-1001-0

Michael Carlberg
Intertemporal Macroeconomics
1998. ISBN 3-7908-1096-7

Sabine Spangenberg
The Institutionalised Transformation of the East German Economy
1998. ISBN 3-7908-1103-3

Hagen Bobzin
Indivisibilities
1998. ISBN 3-7908-1123-8

Helmut Wagner (Ed.)
Current Issues in Monetary Economics
1998. ISBN 3-7908-1127-0

Peter Michaelis/Frank Stähler
(Eds.)
Recent Policy Issues in Environmental and Resource Economics
1998. ISBN 3-7908-1137-8

Jessica de Wolff
The Political Economy of Fiscal Decisions
1998. ISBN 3-7908-1130-0

Georg Bol/Gholamreza Nakhaeizadeh/Karl-Heinz Vollmer (Eds.)
Risk Measurements, Econometrics and Neural Networks
1998. ISBN 3-7908-1152-1

Joachim Winter
Investment and Exit Decisions at the Plant Level
1998. ISBN 3-7908-1154-8

Bernd Meyer
Intertemporal Asset Pricing
1999. ISBN 3-7908-1159-9

Uwe Walz
Dynamics of Regional Integration
1999. ISBN 3-7908-1185-8

Michael Carlberg
European Monetary Union
1999. ISBN 3-7908-1191-2

Giovanni Galizzi/
Luciano Venturini (Eds.)
Vertical Relationships and Coordination in the Food System
1999. ISBN 3-7908-1192-0

Gustav A. Horn/
Wolfgang Scheremet/
Rudolf Zwiener
Wages and the Euro
1999. ISBN 3-7908-1199-8

Dirk Willer
The Development of Equity Capital Markets in Transition Economies
1999. ISBN 3-7908-1198-X

Karl Matthias Weber
Innovation Diffusion and Political Control of Energy Technologies
1999. ISBN 3-7908-1205-6

Heike Link et al.
The Costs of Road Infrastructure and Congestion in Europe
1999. ISBN 3-7908-1201-3

Contributions to Economics

Simon Duindam
Military Conscription
1999. ISBN 3-7908-1203-X

Bruno Jeitziner
Political Economy of the Swiss National Bank
1999. ISBN 3-7908-1209-9

Irene Ring et al. (Eds.)
Regional Sustainability
1999. ISBN 3-7908-1233-1

Katharina Müller/Andreas Ryll/
Hans-Jürgen Wagener (Eds.)
Transformation of Social Security:
Pensions in Central-Eastern Europe
1999. ISBN 3-7908-1210-2

Stefan Traub
Framing Effects in Taxation
1999. ISBN 3-7908-1240-4

Pablo Coto-Millán
Utility and Production
1999. ISBN 3-7908-1153-X

Frank Riedel
Imperfect Information and Investor Heterogeneity in the Bond Market
2000. ISBN 3-7908-1247-1

Kirsten Ralf
Business Cycles
2000. ISBN 3-7908-1245-5

Michele Bagella/
Leonardo Becchetti (Eds.)
The Competitive Advantage of Industrial Districts
2000. ISBN 3-7908-1254-4

Frank Bohn
Monetary Union and Fiscal Stability
2000. ISBN 3-7908-1266-8

Michael Malakellis
Integrated Macro-Micro-Modelling Under Rational Expectations
2000. ISBN 3-7908-1266-8

Stefan Baumgärtner
Ambivalent Joint Production and the Natural Environment
2000. ISBN 3-7908-1290-0

Henri Capron, Wim Meeusen (Eds.)
The National Innovation System of Belgium
2000. ISBN 3-7908-1308-7

Tobias Miarka
Financial Intermediation and Deregulation
2000. ISBN 3-7908-1307-9

Chisato Yoshida
Illegal Immigration and Economic Welfare
2000. ISBN 3-7908-1315-X

Nikolaus Thumm
Intellectual Property Rights
2001. ISBN 3-7908-1329-X

Johannes Bröcker/Hayo Herrmann (Eds.)
Spatial Change and Interregional Flows in the Integrating Europe
2001. ISBN 3-7908-1352-4

Kirstin Hubrich
Cointegrated Analysis in a German Monetary System
2001. ISBN 3-7908-1352-4

Nico Heerink et al. (Eds.)
Economic Policy and Sustainable Land Use
2001. ISBN 3-7908-1351-6